KEVIN O'ROURKE

A Short History of Brexit
From Brentry to Backstop

A PELICAN BOOK

PELICAN
an imprint of
PENGUIN BOOKS

PELICAN BOOKS

UK | USA | Canada | Ireland | Australia
India | New Zealand | South Africa

Penguin Books is part of the Penguin Random
House group of companies whose addresses can
be found at global.penguinrandomhouse.com.

Penguin
Random House
UK

First published in France as *Une brève histoire du
Brexit* 2018
First published with additional material in
Great Britain as *A Short History of Brexit* 2019
Published in paperback with additional material 2019
001

Copyright © ODILE JACOB, 2018

The present edition is published with
additional material in agreement with the
French publisher, Odile Jacob

The moral right of the author has been asserted

Book design by Matthew Young
Set in 10/14.664 pt FreightText Pro
Typeset by Jouve (UK), Milton Keynes
Printed and bound in Great Britain by
Clays Ltd, Elcograf S.p.A.

A CIP catalogue record for this book is available
from the British Library

ISBN: 978–0–241–39823–4

To the fellows and staff of All Souls College

Contents

Preface to the Paperback Edition

I have taken the opportunity to bring the story forward to 7 August 2019, and to make a small number of minor changes to the previous edition. My thanks go once again to Stuart Proffitt, as well as to Ruth Pietroni, Corina Romonti, Ben Sinyor, and everyone else at Penguin.

Saint Pierre d'Entremont
7 August 2019

Preface to the English Language Edition

This book was originally written for a French audience, unfamiliar with the details of recent British political history but interested nonetheless in making sense of what was happening on the other side of the English Channel. I have therefore included more material on recent British events than some readers in the UK may find strictly necessary. As I worked on the manuscript, however, it became clear to me that to tell the story properly, and to explain why the negotiations between the UK and EU have proved so difficult, a recital of British history alone was not enough. The book is therefore just as much about Ireland and the European Union as it is about the turbulent relationship between the UK and Europe: it's about why the EU developed in the way that it did, and is reacting to Brexit in the way that it is. It's about the ways in which the intertwined histories of Britain, Ireland and the rest of Europe are shaping the Brexit negotiations of today, and about the impossibility of predicting what will happen tomorrow.

My hope is thus that British readers, many of whom are already familiar with the work of Hugo Young, Tim Shipman and others, will find a fresh perspective in these pages, and that the book will help other English-speaking readers to understand where Brexit came from, and why the process of extricating the UK from the European Union has proved so fraught.

I am extremely grateful to Stuart Proffitt for helping me to improve the English-language manuscript in numerous ways. The usual disclaimer applies more than it usually does. I also thank Rebecca Lee, Claire Péligry, Ruth Pietroni, Corina Romonti, Ben Sinyor and everyone at Penguin who helped get this book published so quickly.

Dublin
19 December 2018

Acknowledgements

I have incurred many debts while writing this book. I am especially grateful to Odile Jacob, who has been tremendously supportive, and to my editor Gaëlle Jullien, whose idea it was in the first place and who provided me with many insightful comments on the manuscript. Gaëlle and I met because of my participation in the 2017 Journées de l'économie in Lyon, France, and I thank those responsible for organizing the event, in particular Pascal Le Merrer and Éric Monnet, as well as Éric Albert who moderated a stimulating panel discussion on Brexit in which I participated.* I have also greatly enjoyed working with Christophe Jaquet, who was an excellent, responsive and flexible translator.

In addition to Gaëlle, I particularly want to thank those who read the manuscript in whole or in part, and provided me with encouragement and invaluable feedback: Graham Brownlow, Rosemary Byrne, Ian Crawford, Zoé Fachan, Henrik Iversen, Declan Kelleher, Dennis Novy, Andrew O'Rourke and Alan Taylor. I am also very grateful to Alex Barker, Steve Broadberry, Fred Calvaire, Gilles Cloître, Tony Connelly, Chris Cook, Nicholas Crafts, Éric Delépine, Peter

---

* The event can be viewed at https://www.youtube.com/watch?v=rsgB-8RPDec.

Foster, Chris Giles, David Allen Green, Mark Harrison, Katy Hayward, Morgan Kelly, Philip Lane, Sam Lowe, Philippe Martin, Jacques Mollard, Ollie Molloy, Simon Nixon, Cormac Ó Gráda, Régine Rigaud, Jan Södersten, Jean-Jacques Tardy, Alan Taylor, Karl Whelan and Fred Wilmot-Smith, all of whom answered questions, provided references, discussed Brexit with me, or helped me in various other ways to write this book. I couldn't have written the book without Rosemary's help and as ever I owe her a tremendous debt of gratitude. She and our four children, Ciara, Joseph, Gabriel and Sophie, have had lively discussions with me about many of the issues discussed in this book, and provided me with constant encouragement and emotional and practical support. All five have my love and thanks. I have learned an enormous amount from almost daily exchanges with Alan and Dennis ever since June 2016, and not only about Brexit, while in addition to reading the manuscript closely Zoé very helpfully summarized the history of the border in the Vallée des Entremonts for me.

A *Short History of Brexit* was written during a sabbatical year in Dublin and Saint Pierre d'Entremont, a small village in the Chartreuse that the reader will encounter in the text. My time in Dublin was spent visiting the School of Economics in University College Dublin, whose staff have been magnificently generous to me. I am very grateful indeed to Paul Devereux and Karl Whelan for making it happen. A lot of the arguments in this book have been rehearsed in the UCD Common Room: Morgan Kelly, Dave Madden, Cormac Ó Gráda, Oana Peia and Stijn van Weezel bore the brunt of my opining, although few of my colleagues were entirely spared. It's a real tragedy that the Common Room is being closed by the University administration this winter: a casual act of vandalism that will make UCD duller and less distinctive. It's a lot easier to destroy the social fabric of a community than to build it up from scratch.

I have had the good fortune of being able learn extensively from current and former Irish Permanent Representatives to the EU. It has been a great pleasure to get to know Declan Kelleher, who has taught me a lot, and who along with his colleagues has been doing sterling work for Ireland in Brussels. But my most important intellectual debt is to my father, Andrew O'Rourke, who was Ireland's Permanent Representative in the early 1980s and also served as Secretary General of the Department of Foreign Affairs and Irish Ambassador to Denmark, France and the United Kingdom. He's a modest man and probably won't like me mentioning any of this, but there you are. I have learned a huge amount from him during our walks in Dalkey and Wicklow and look forward to continuing to do so.

Finally, I have benefited greatly from the fact that I am an Irishman who has worked in Oxford since 2011 and also spends a lot of time in France. Being constantly exposed to very different opinions on Brexit has been immensely stimulating, and I am grateful in particular to have had the opportunity to learn about Brexit, and Britain, and British identity, from my British colleagues. When I got the job I presumed that All Souls would be full of accomplished academics, and indeed it is, but I did not anticipate how warm and welcoming a community it would prove to be, or how many friends I would make there. Being a fellow of the College has been an extraordinary privilege and it has also been tremendous fun. So I dedicate this book to the fellows and staff of All Souls College, British and foreign, Leavers and Remainers alike.

Saint Pierre d'Entremont
14 September 2018

Author's Note

In writing this book I have reproduced certain passages from 'Why the EU Won' in *Integrating Regions: Asia in Comparative Context*, edited by Miles Kahler and Andrew MacIntyre, 142–69 (Stanford, California: Stanford University Press, 2013); 'The Davos Lie', *Critical Quarterly* 58, no. 1 (2016): 114–18; '1916', *Critical Quarterly* 58, no. 2 (2016): 118–22; 'Brentry', *Critical Quarterly* 58, no. 3 (2016): 118–122; '2016', *Critical Quarterly* 58, no. 4 (2017): 150–55; 'Independent Ireland in Comparative Perspective', *Irish Economic and Social History* 44, no. 1 (2017): 19–45; 'Not So Very Different', *Dublin Review of Books*, January 2017, available at http://www.drb.ie/essays/not-so-verydifferent; and 'Brexit: This Backlash Has Been a Long Time Coming', Vox.EU (7 August 2016), available at https://voxeu.org/article/brexit-backlash-has-been-long-time-coming. I am very grateful to Miles Kahler, the editors of *Critical Quarterly*, *Irish Economic and Social History* and the *Dublin Review of Books* (Colin MacCabe, Graham Brownlow and Maurice Earls), Stanford University Press, John Wiley and Sons and SAGE Journals, for permission to draw upon my previous work in this manner.

In the later chapters I have wherever possible provided references to sources that are freely available online, so that the interested reader can if he or she wishes learn more about the EU, Brexit and the Brexit negotiations. To make this easier I have reproduced the endnotes online on the Irish Economy blog, where most of what I have previously written about Brexit first appeared.*

---

* http://www.irisheconomy.ie/index.php/2018/12/22/a-short-history-of-brexit.

List of Acronyms

AIFTA: Anglo-Irish Free Trade Agreement

CAP: Common Agricultural Policy

DUP: Democratic Unionist Party

EAEC or **EURATOM**: European Atomic Energy Community

EC: European Communities (ECSC, EEC and EURATOM)

ECSC: European Coal and Steel Community

EDC: European Defence Community

EDF: European Development Fund

EEA: European Economic Area

EEC: European Economic Community

EFTA: European Free Trade Association

EMS: European Monetary System

EMU: European Monetary Union

EPC: European Political Community

EPP: European People's Party

ERDF: European Regional Development Fund

ERG: European Research Group

ERM: Exchange Rate Mechanism

EU: European Union

FDI: Foreign direct investment

GATT: General Agreement on Tariffs and Trade

GDP: Gross Domestic Product

GNP: Gross National Product

IDA: Industrial Development Authority (Ireland)

IMF: International Monetary Fund

IRA: Irish Republican Army. Can refer either to the IRA of the Irish War of Independence or to the IRA of the Troubles.

MFN: Most favoured nation

NAFTA: North American Free Trade Area

OEEC: Organization for European Economic Co-operation

OECD: Organization for Economic Co-operation and Development

OPEC: Organization of the Petroleum Exporting Countries

NATO: North Atlantic Treaty Organization

UKIP: UK Independence Party

VAT: Value Added Tax

VIES: VAT Information Exchange System

WEU: Western European Union

WTO: World Trade Organization

Introduction

On 2 July 2018 the British Prime Minister Theresa May was preparing for a crucial Cabinet meeting to be held four days later at Chequers, her official country residence. Her hope was that she could persuade the warring factions within her Conservative Party to unite behind a common vision regarding what sort of a future relationship the United Kingdom should have with the European Union. In order to negotiate with others you first have to decide what you want yourself, but this was proving extremely difficult: Brexiteers accused her of betrayal. A backbench MP named Jacob Rees-Mogg warned her in a newspaper article published that morning that unless she stood firm to her promises to leave the EU's Single Market and customs union she risked suffering the fate of the Conservative Prime Minister in 1846, Sir Robert Peel: by adopting free trade in that year Peel had split his party and lost office, and the Conservatives found themselves excluded from power for a generation.

What on earth did that have to do with Brexit? And many commentators immediately explained why Rees-Mogg's historical analogy was deeply flawed. But there was a tradition within the British Conservative Party of reaching for just that analogy. In early 1961, as debate raged about whether or not the

UK should apply to join the European Economic Community, several Conservative MPs fretted that this would undermine Britain's historic links with the countries of the former Empire. The Conservative Prime Minister Harold Macmillan noted in his diary on 19 May that things were 'getting terribly like 1846'.[1]

What is going on here?

Brexit did not emerge out of nowhere: it is the culmination of events that have been under way for decades and have historical roots stretching back well beyond that. As we will see, even the history of the nineteenth century has something to tell us about why British attitudes towards Europe evolved in the way they did. But the European Union also has a past that explains why it operates in the way that it does today, and this past naturally shapes the ways in which the Union has responded to the challenges posed by Brexit. And finally there is Ireland, the member state (other than the UK itself) most affected by Brexit and a country where history continues to matter politically. The issue of the Irish border is at the very heart of the current Brexit negotiations. If the UK leaves the EU without a deal because of Ireland, which at the time of writing (August 2019) seems entirely possible, then citizens all over Europe will be affected.

My aim is thus to give readers the historical background they need to understand Brexit. I cannot predict what will happen next, but hopefully this book will provide some understanding of how we got to where we are today, as well as of whatever it is that will happen in the future.

I do not make any great claims to originality: the individual parts of the story are well known. For readers who want to know more I can give no better advice than to read Hugo

Young's *This Blessed Plot* for the backstory; Tim Shipman's *All Out War* on the decision to leave the EU; and Tony Connelly's *Brexit and Ireland* on the negotiations that followed. I have drawn on all three, and on many other authors, in writing the account that follows. But I hope there is some merit in bringing the different parts of the British story together, and even more in telling the story not only of the UK, but of the EU and of Ireland as well. For it is the way in which these three different histories are interacting that is shaping the negotiations currently under way.

It is impossible to write about Brexit completely dispassionately and so it is important to be open about one's potential biases. I was born in Switzerland to an Irish father and a Danish mother and grew up in London, Dublin and Brussels; I live in Ireland, work in England, and am a municipal councillor in Saint Pierre d'Entremont, a small village in France. In other words, I am what you might call a European, and my background inclines me to sympathy with the European project.

At the same time, as an economic historian of globalization and deglobalization I am deeply conscious that international economic integration doesn't benefit everyone, and that I am precisely the sort of person who has tended to do well out of it. As an economist and middle-of-the-road Keynesian, I have been a frequent critic of European Monetary Union in general, and its crisis management since 2008 in particular.* As a citizen I share the concerns about Europe's democratic deficit that were so brilliantly expressed by my late compatriot Peter

---

* EMU is not particularly relevant to Brexit since the UK was never a member, although it does make a brief appearance in Chapters 8 and 9.

Mair, and I have said so in print.[2] Perhaps these personal and professional considerations cancel each other out to some extent. But it is the fact that I am Irish that makes it most difficult for me to be dispassionate, since the implications of Brexit for my country are truly alarming. And so I have tried to strike a balance between trying to be objective and saying what I think: how successfully I have done so you will have to judge for yourself.

After a chapter on why it was that Europe developed supranational institutions after the Second World War, and why the UK has traditionally been so hostile to these, successive chapters deal with the ways in which the globalization and imperialism of the nineteenth century continued to influence twentieth-century Britain, and how the UK reacted to post-1945 European integration. The narrative ends with the formation of the Single Market in the 1980s and early 1990s, a largely British achievement that continues to define the European Union today. There is then an Irish interlude, telling the story of how EU membership transformed the Irish economy and played a major role in bringing peace to Northern Ireland: this will hopefully help to clarify why it is that the Irish border has become such a central issue in the Brexit negotiations. I then describe and analyse the British decision in 2016 to leave the EU, and provide an account of the negotiations that followed. The book ends with a brief discussion of the possible futures towards which Brexit may be headed as of today (7 August 2019).

Before examining British attitudes towards Europe it is important to understand why European integration took the form that it did, so that is where I will begin.

CHAPTER 1
The Origins of Supranational Europe

One of the things that Britain has traditionally most disliked about the European Union is its supranational nature. As Theresa May put it in September 2017,

> The profound pooling of sovereignty that is a crucial feature of the European Union permits unprecedentedly deep cooperation, which brings benefits. But it also means that when countries are in the minority they must sometimes accept decisions they do not want, even affecting domestic matters with no market implications beyond their borders. And when such decisions are taken, they can be very hard to change. So the British electorate made a choice. They chose the power of domestic democratic control over pooling that control.[1]

Ever since the foundation of the European Coal and Steel Community in 1951, European integration has not just involved independent governments cooperating voluntarily. Rather, it has been defined by the creation of supranational political, bureaucratic and judicial institutions such as the European Commission in Brussels, the European Parliament in Brussels and Strasbourg, and the European Court of Justice in Luxembourg. This makes it unusual: other organizations designed to promote regional cooperation have much less in the way of institutional infrastructure. For example, the North American Free Trade Area (NAFTA) has a Secretariat which is responsible for resolving disputes, with national offices in each of the three countries involved (Canada, Mexico and the United States); a Free Trade Commission which brings together government representatives from the three countries; and a variety of committees and working groups.[2] That's it. There is no suggestion that the three countries involved are doing anything more than cooperating in a mutually beneficial manner.[3] The European Union is very different.

The EU is not a supranational state, but its 28 member states have agreed to pool some (but not all) of their sovereignty in a uniquely structured and institutionalized manner. This has always led to criticism from Eurosceptics, and not only in Britain. Why did European regional integration involve the creation of so many supranational institutions? Why did it not just involve looser intergovernmental structures, as the British traditionally wanted? During the 1950s only a minority of European countries – just six – were willing to go down the supranational route. Most countries, like Britain, favoured intergovernmental cooperation. And yet it was the minority vision that eventually won out: the overwhelming majority of European countries are today members of the EU.

The question of why nearly all European countries eventually decided to join the EU is intimately connected with the creation of the Single Market in the 1980s and early 1990s, and will be considered later in this book. This chapter will discuss some of the reasons why the original six founding member states – the three Benelux countries, France, Germany and Italy – decided to go down a supranational route in the first place. There are several deep structural factors, relating to European geography, history and economics, which increased the demand for European integration in the aftermath of the Second World War, and which help to explain why the original six founding members thought that this should be expressed in supranational institutions.

The Legacy of War

The first and most obvious reason for European integration is that by the 1950s it was clear that political fragmentation in the continent had become increasingly and unacceptably costly. There are many natural barriers within Europe, such as the Alps, the Pyrenees and the English Channel, which is one of the reasons why would-be conquerors of Europe, since the fall of the Roman Empire, have found it impossible to unify the continent by military means. Many economic historians have argued that this fragmentation was traditionally a source of competitive advantage for the continent.[4] It made it more difficult for absolutist rulers to suppress dangerous ideas, for a Voltaire could always escape to Geneva. Once there, his ideas were free to circulate elsewhere thanks to a common elite European culture. Even more importantly, perhaps, the political and military competition that fragmentation implied gave Europe an undisputed 'comparative advantage in violence'. This helps to explain such bizarre episodes in world history as tiny Portugal seizing Brazil and dominating much of Asia's maritime trade during the sixteenth century – a time when Portugal's population was not much more than 1.25 million.[5]

By the twentieth century, however, the costs of political fragmentation were becoming unbearable because of the arrival of modern industrial warfare. During the First World War deaths of military personnel amounted to 1.6 per cent of the total population in Britain, 3.4 per cent in France and 3 per cent in Germany. The Second World War was even more destructive since it was no longer concentrated along a more or less static front, and involved very heavy aerial bombardment across the continent. In addition the Nazis directly targeted civilian populations. Total deaths, both military and civilian, were equivalent to 0.7 per cent of the pre-war population in the UK, 1.5 per cent in France and 9 per cent in Germany.[6]

The timing of moves towards greater European unity, and American support for that aim, are thus hardly surprising.[7] This history also explains the importance of the Franco-German relationship as a driver of European integration. The importance of that relationship can be seen indirectly by comparing Europe with Asia: to a European, the extent to which memories of the Second World War still poison relationships between China, Japan and Korea is disturbing. One could speculate that a *rapprochement* between China and Japan might one day play a catalysing role in the context of East Asian integration, but the contrasts between the post-war Franco-German and Sino-Japanese relationships remain striking.

The contrast between the ways in which the two world wars are remembered in Britain and the continent is also striking. Armistice Day celebrations are an occasion for patriotism everywhere, in France as in Britain, but the day feels very different on the two sides of the English Channel. Sometimes the French complain when Monsieur or Madame le

Maire has to read the speech written for the occasion by some Secretary of State or Minister up in Paris. The eleventh of November is a day for villages to come together and remember their dead: who needs politicians? But on the rare occasions when I've been able to get to Saint Pierre d'Entremont and attend the Armistice ceremonies, the speeches have struck me as being generally pretty good, especially since 2014: pedagogical is the word that immediately comes to mind. Last year, for example, we learned that

> The French army was not the only one to sacrifice itself. At the cost of heavy losses the Canadians led the attack at Vimy and the British at Passchendaele, while the Italians were defeated at Caporetto. The United States abandoned isolationism and took the side of the Entente. The arrival of American soldiers changed the balance of power and would contribute to forging the eventual victory . . . Profoundly shaken by two revolutions, Russia signed an armistice with Germany on 15 December.[8]

There is no pretence that France fought alone, even though her losses were particularly heavy.

Yes, the French are rightly proud of their country and its armed forces. But all those names – those familiar names – and all those crosses, in such a small village, leave no one in any doubt about how dreadful war is. And if there is a political message it tends to be pro-European. French Prime Minister Édouard Philippe's words at Compiègne in 2017 are typical:

> When you live in Compiègne, or further away, in Belgium, the Netherlands or Germany, to love peace is to love

Europe. Her peoples and cultures, and her diversity
of course. It's to love wandering there, studying there,
discovering her beauty and history. But it's also to love
the political Europe: her freedoms and shared citizenship.
It's to love her with her imperfections and failings.
Despite her complexity and delays. Yes, if you're European,
to love peace is to love Europe: a Europe that reminds us
of the eternal values that unite us, and the disasters that
we mourn.[9]

The eleventh of November in France is deeply patriotic, but
doesn't strike this foreigner as being excessively nationalistic. I am not entirely sure that the same can be said of Britain,
and Armistice Day is certainly not seen as an occasion for reminding the British of the need for European integration. As
a schoolboy in 1953, William Wallace sang at Queen's Elizabeth's coronation. Now a Baron and member of the House of
Lords, he served for the Europhile Liberal Democrats in the
2010–15 coalition government in London. He recalls a memo
written for David Cameron, the Prime Minister of the time,
warning that 'we must ensure that our commemoration [of
the First World War] does not give any support to the myth
that European integration was the result of the two World
Wars.'[10] If words fail you then I'm afraid I can't help, for they
fail me too.

You will hear no mention, and see no sign, of the sacrifices
of the French, the Italians, the Russians or the Americans at
the Remembrance Sunday ceremony held at the London Ceno-
taph on the second Sunday of November. This is a strictly
British affair, although the High Commissioners of the countries

of the British Commonwealth (the former British Empire) lay wreaths.* Poppies commemorating British soldiers who died in the First World War and subsequent conflicts are ubiquitous in Britain in the week or two leading up to the ceremony. British soldiers, it should be noted, not soldiers or civilians more generally.

Since 2014 the ambassador of Ireland, once a part of the United Kingdom but independent since 1922 and not a member of the Commonwealth, has also laid a wreath. Since the peace process of the 1990s Ireland has increasingly recognized the role played in the Great War by Irishmen like my grandfather. In November 2017 the Irish Taoiseach (Prime Minister), Leo Varadkar, even wore a poppy – embedded within an Irish shamrock – in the Dáil, Ireland's parliament. In an Irish context his gesture was a rejection of nationalism – Irish nationalism. In Britain, while the dominant tone may be one of traditional patriotism, it would be difficult to describe the symbols and ceremonies associated with 11 November as anti nationalistic. The legacy of war in most of Europe has been support for European integration. This has not been the case in the United Kingdom.

The Aftermath of the Industrial Revolution: Relative Decline

Europe was the first continent to experience the Industrial Revolution. As such it enjoyed an enormous increase in its relative economic, military and political power, symbolized by the European empires of the nineteenth century.

---

* The Dutch King and German President participated in 2015 and 2018 respectively.

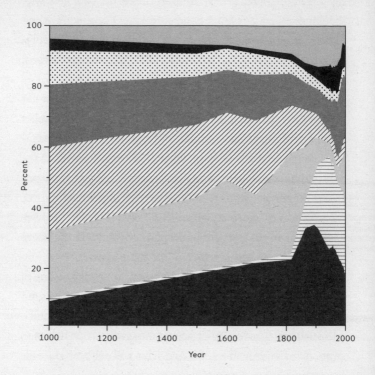

Figure 1.1
Shares of world GDP, 1000–2008

Rest of World
Latin America
Africa
Rest of Asia

India
China
British offshoots
Western Europe

Source: Maddison (2010)

Figure 1.1 tells the story in graphical form. At the start of the second millennium people around the world were (roughly speaking) all equally poor, and so the sizes of different economies depended more than anything else on their populations. China and India had the world's largest populations, then as now, and so they had the largest economies. China accounted for 23 per cent of the world's GDP (or output) in 1000, while India accounted for 28 per cent. Western Europe, in contrast, accounted for just 9 per cent. There followed eight centuries during which Western Europe's share of world output slowly rose: it was slightly more than 20 per cent 800 years later, at the start of the nineteenth century. But then European incomes exploded. Western Europe's share of world output peaked at 34 per cent in 1900, with four 'British offshoots' (Australia, Canada, New Zealand and the United States) accounting for a further 18 per cent. With plenty came power: industrial military technology overwhelmed local resistance across the globe. The share of the Earth's surface controlled by Europeans rose from 37 per cent in 1800 to 84 per cent in 1914.[11] And Europe's rise corresponded to the relative decline of the rest of the world: by 1950 India and China both accounted for less than 5 per cent of world output.

In the long run, however, modern industry spread across the globe, and the relative decline of Europe was the inevitable consequence.[12] Europe's primacy was already ending at the beginning of the twentieth century, as the US emerged as the world's largest industrial power. The two world wars hastened the transition from a Western European-dominated world, and by 1945 the two leading military powers were clearly the US and USSR. Not everyone wanted to admit this: the European colonial powers, in particular, were reluctant to accept their diminished status. In 1942 Winston Churchill famously proclaimed that he had 'not become the King's First Minister in order to preside over the liquidation of the British Empire';[13] in 1945 a politician from French Guiana, Gaston Monnerville, declared to the Provisional Consultative Assembly in Paris that 'Without her empire France would only be a liberated country. Thanks to her empire, France is a victorious country.'[14]

The years that followed quickly revealed such statements to be delusional. First the Dutch were expelled from Indonesia, while the British left India and Palestine. Then it was the turn of the French in Indochina. Ghana gained its independence from Britain in 1957; by the 1960s the European empires had all but vanished. A key question for European statesmen was then how to avoid being overwhelmed by the Soviet Union and condescended to by the US. Greater unity seemed an obvious solution. Europe's diminished status was perhaps more obvious, earlier, on the continent than in Britain. France, Germany, Italy and the Benelux countries had all been defeated in one way or another during the war. By contrast the UK had remained undefeated throughout the conflict, and it retained much of its empire during the crucial decade from 1945 to 1955. Perhaps it is not surprising that the need for small and medium-sized European powers to band together in an increasingly dangerous world was not obvious to everyone in London.[15] But in Paris, on 5 July 1957, Maurice Faure, the Minister of State for Foreign Affairs, was clear on the issue when defending the Treaties of Rome* in the Assemblée Nationale: 'You see, my dear friends, we still maintain the fiction that there are four Great Powers in the world. Well, there are not four Great Powers, there are only two: America and Russia. There will be a third at the end of the century: China. And it is up to you as to whether or not there will be a fourth: Europe.'[16]

The Aftermath of the Industrial Revolution: The Role of the State

Industrialization created a large class of workers that eventually started to demand higher wages, safer working conditions and state-provided social insurance programmes. Meanwhile industrial warfare required the mobilization of large conscript armies, and this gave governments an incentive to supply such demands for reform. If citizens were expected to fight for their countries then the state had to provide them with educational and other public services that would increase their identification with the state and ensure their loyalty.

Late nineteenth-century globalization also led to a demand for state regulation and social insurance policies that could protect workers against the insecurities, real or perceived, associated with open international markets. The late nineteenth and early twentieth centuries thus saw the introduction of a wide range of labour market regulations across Western

---

* There were two treaties signed in Rome in 1957, one establishing the European Economic Community (EEC) and the other establishing the European Atomic Energy Community (EAEC or EURATOM). These are collectively referred to as the Treaties of Rome. The Treaty of Rome, in the singular, generally refers to the treaty establishing the EEC, and that is how I will use the term later in this book.

Europe, as well as old-age pensions, and sickness and unemployment insurance. Interestingly, these reforms were most
widespread in those countries most exposed to the globalization of the period.[17]

The two world wars gave a further impetus to the growing involvement of the state in domestic economies and to
the development of social welfare systems. The aftermath of
the First World War saw a significant extension of the electoral franchise, as well as an increase in the influence of trade
unions and socialist parties. In 1942 the British Beveridge Report
proposed the creation of a National Health Service, as well
as better public housing and social welfare policies.[18] French
women were granted the right to vote in 1944. The defeat
of Churchill in 1945 and the election of a British Labour government reflected the desire of ordinary workers who had suffered so much during the war to see their lives improve in its
wake. Given the experience of the Great Depression, they were
hardly going to be willing to 'leave it to the market': a push
for greater government intervention in the economy was a logical consequence.

These heightened expectations on the part of ordinary
people coincided in most of Europe with the widespread feeling that traditional nation states had failed their people – they
had failed in providing economic security during the interwar
period, and in providing physical security after 1939.[19] The
three crucial constituencies that had to be placated were agricultural voters, whose disillusionment had led them to support extremist parties during the interwar period in many
countries; workers; and those dependent on the welfare
state. The solution was to ensure rising living standards for

the agricultural sector; to provide workers with rising wages and full employment; and to establish modern welfare states.

Accomplishing all three goals required an extension of government intervention in the economy. So did the economic growth strategies pursued by governments after 1945. These relied on high investment facilitated by complex corporatist bargains between capital and labour: the extension of the welfare state was a key part of these bargains.[20] As the economic historian Alan Milward says,

> in the long run of history there has surely never been a period when national government in Europe has exercised more effective power and more extensive control over its citizens than that since the Second World War, nor one in which its ambitions expanded so rapidly. Its laws, officials, policemen, spies, statisticians, revenue collectors, and social workers have penetrated into a far wider range of human activities than they were earlier able or encouraged to do.[21]

What does all this have to do with the need for supranational European integration?[22] On the one hand, the lesson of the interwar period was that European countries needed mixed economies, with governments that were more proactive in ensuring economic security for their citizens. But on the other hand, the interwar period also showed the dangers of protectionism, and the need for Europe-wide free trade if prosperity was to be achieved. The challenge was how to reap the benefits of trade, without undermining the ability of governments to provide that security. During the negotiations that eventually led to the Treaties of Rome, for example, French officials worried that laxer regulations in Germany and other countries would place French car manufacturers at an unfair disadvantage. The working week had already been lowered to 40 hours in France, while it was still 48 hours in Belgium and Germany. Since workers in France in fact worked as many hours as their colleagues elsewhere, this meant that French employers had to pay more overtime. Similarly, French women enjoyed (in theory) equal pay with men, while women could legally be paid less than men in other countries. The French therefore sought a level playing field, demanding that the new common market should have a standardized working week, standardized rules regarding overtime payments, equal pay for men and women, and similar rules regarding paid holidays.

The Germans resisted standardizing the working week and overtime rules, and in the end there was a compromise: the treaty establishing the European Economic Community (EEC) included a protocol stating that unless overtime hours and rates in other member states had converged to levels similar to those in France, France would be allowed to impose safeguard measures to protect its industries. The treaty also established the principle of equal pay for equal work for men and women, and committed member states to maintaining 'the existing equivalence between paid holiday schemes'.[23] In the event, the *Trente Glorieuses* and the German *Wirtschaftswunder* intervened:* living standards and social protections increased so rapidly everywhere, and especially in Germany, that the issue was defused. But this did not mean that the

---

* The *Trente Glorieuses* is how the French refer to the period between 1945 and 1973, which saw Europe's golden age of economic growth. The German term is *Wirtschaftswunder* or 'economic miracle'.

issue was unimportant: on the contrary, it was essential that the domestic social welfare systems which underpinned governments' political legitimacy as well as their economic growth strategies not be undermined by the development of Europe-wide free trade. 'The problem genuinely was how to construct a commercial framework which would not endanger the levels of social welfare which had been reached . . . The Treaties of Rome had to be also an external buttress to the welfare state.'[24]

In short, economic prosperity required trade, but political stability required welfare states. In order to achieve both prosperity and stability a free trade area was not enough: you needed European integration to set a common regulatory framework so as to prevent destructive races to the bottom. In this way Europe would come to the rescue of the European nation state.[25] But it did so by establishing the sorts of supranational institutions that many on the other side of the English Channel were allergic to.

Agriculture

A further consequence of Western Europe's precocious industrialization was that it became a large net importer of agricultural goods, something to which European farmers naturally objected. From the mid-nineteenth century onwards steamships and railways lowered the cost of shipping food from the prairies of the New World to the markets of the Old, reducing European prices and agricultural incomes. This 'grain invasion' sparked agricultural protection across much of the continent that would become a permanent feature of the European landscape.[26] What the grain invasion failed to achieve, the Great Depression of the 1930s finally accomplished in such traditionally free-trading countries as the UK and the Netherlands.

After the Second World War all European governments wished to achieve food self-sufficiency for strategic reasons, and widespread agricultural intervention became the norm across the continent.[27] Governments promoted agricultural production by a variety of means: guaranteeing farm incomes, and encouraging agricultural investment and better farming practices. They also guaranteed prices for farmers. This meant raising domestic prices above world levels, and insulating domestic agricultural markets from world markets by means of strict import controls. By the early to mid-1950s food shortages were becoming less of a problem, and food surpluses started to emerge as a result of the guaranteed prices. At the same time low farm incomes remained a problem, with rising productivity and migration from the countryside to cities being insufficient to bridge the gap between agricultural and non-agricultural living standards. Faced with the inherent contradictions of the situation, agricultural policy in Europe became 'increasingly complicated' and more intrusive.[28]

No European government of the 1950s could have contemplated a liberalization of agricultural production. There were therefore two logical choices facing politicians wishing to liberalize European trade. The first was to liberalize trade in industrial products alone, maintaining existing national agricultural policies. German industries would have gained from this, but such a bargain could never have been acceptable to France, Italy or the Netherlands, with their large agricultural sectors: in the early 1950s agriculture accounted for 13 per cent of GDP in France and the Netherlands, and no less than 22 per cent in Italy. Even more importantly from a political point of view, it accounted for 26 per cent of male employment in France in 1954, 20 per cent in the Netherlands in 1947, and 42 per cent in Italy in 1951.[29]

This left the second alternative, which was to liberalize intra-European trade in agricultural products as well, but to replicate national agricultural policies at the European level – in other words, to develop some sort of Common Agricultural Policy. Such a policy would require a lot more intergovernmental cooperation than a mere free trade area: for example, decision-making rules on setting minimum agricultural prices, and rules for financing the consequences of surplus production. Liberalizing trade between the six founding member states thus required supranational institutions, and as we have seen many other considerations pointed in the same direction. The next chapter will discuss how Britain's historical experience and political requirements were very different.

Nineteenth-century Legacies

British exceptionalism can be exaggerated. Today's United Kingdom may bear the imprint of Mrs Thatcher, and seem to other Europeans a bastion of market liberalism. But when compared to the United States, the UK, with its National Health Service and welfare state, appears thoroughly European. UK history can also seem exceptional and in many respects it is – but so is every country's. Her island status and overseas empire have often been seen as setting Britain apart from the rest of Europe, but as the Irish historian Brendan Simms argues, British history is 'primarily a continental story . . . her destiny was mainly determined by relations with the rest of Europe rather than with the wider world.'[1]

As in any other country, security was the major concern for British leaders in the past. That meant engaging with Europe, for that is where the threats came from. Like other European states, Britain participated in an interminable series of wars throughout the eighteenth century, culminating in the struggles against Napoleon, in which Britain was the ally of Austria, Prussia, Russia and others. Britain was a participant in the Concert of Europe that followed, fought in Crimea, and did not stand aside in 1914. In behaving in this manner she was a typical and far from isolated European state.

And yet, Britain's distinctive history left its mark on British attitudes and interests – on the country's idea of itself – and this mattered in the aftermath of the Second World War when the future of Europe was being determined. The century that followed Waterloo saw the first great globalization, with Britain and her Empire playing a key role in the process. The debates and concerns of that era continued to echo well into the twentieth century.

The First Industrial Nation in a Globalized World

The Industrial Revolution, which began in Britain in the late eighteenth and early nineteenth centuries, is the central event in modern economic history. The spread of modern industry across the globe is today transforming the world, bringing prosperity to hundreds of millions in Asia and elsewhere. The initial impact of the Industrial Revolution was very different, however. As noted in the previous chapter it created an asymmetric world, which Europeans in general, and the British in particular, were able to dominate not only militarily but also economically. Local producers across what we now call the developing world were unable to compete with the new technologies, as their markets were subjected to an invasion of European manufactured goods.[2] Like the grain invasion encountered in the previous chapter this was made possible by the transport revolutions of the nineteenth century. Steamships and railways greatly reduced the protection previously afforded by distance to such producers: the gains of textile manufacturers in Lancashire were the losses of traditional producers in India and elsewhere.

But the process of economic growth gave rise to asymmetries and imbalances *within* the newly industrializing countries as well. As the first industrial nation, the process was particularly advanced in Britain. Labour and capital were pulled into those sectors of the economy where technological progress was fastest: industry in general, and cotton textiles, metallurgy and engineering in particular. The result was a large increase in the share of the labour force employed in industry, and a corresponding drop in the importance of agriculture. By 1871 only 22.6 per cent of the British labour force was employed in agriculture, as opposed to slightly more than half in France – where the Industrial Revolution had already been spreading for quite some time – and more than two-thirds in Sweden.[3]

Not only were people living and working in towns and cities rather than the countryside, but there were many more of them than before. England's population rose from 5.2 million in 1700, to 8.6 million a century later, to no less than 30.3 million in 1900.[4] These extra millions had to be fed, but Britain (and Ireland, an important source of food) were no larger in territorial extent at the start of the twentieth century than they had been 200 years previously. Agriculture was more productive, it is true, but the reality was that this much larger and less agricultural population increasingly had to be fed with imported food. In addition, the factories in which more and more people worked also had to be fed, in large part with imported raw materials such as cotton from the United States, Egypt and elsewhere. In other words, Britain was becoming increasingly dependent on imported food and raw materials grown on land in other continents. It paid for these imports by exporting manufactured goods, and by earning interest and profits on the capital that it had invested overseas.

Rapid industrialization and structural change thus went hand-in-hand with increasing dependence on the international economy.[5] This had a variety of political implications, both international and domestic. Internationally, Britain now had a vital strategic need to maintain the naval hegemony that had been secured at Trafalgar – allowing a foreign power to threaten British supplies of food and raw materials was too dangerous to contemplate. Blockade was something that the United Kingdom did to others at times of war, not something that others could be allowed to do to it. In the late nineteenth century, when Germany underwent a similar process of structural change, and became increasingly dependent on international markets for its economic survival also, the predictable result was a naval arms race, and war plans involving blockades and counter-blockades. Questions of national security would become inextricably linked with international trade.[6]

Domestically, political divisions opened up between traditional agricultural interests and the rising manufacturing and commercial classes. Food was expensive to produce on a small, crowded island, and both farmers and the aristocratic landlords from whom they often rented their land were understandably reluctant to see Britain's agricultural markets opened up to competition from abroad. The party that defended these agricultural interests, in Britain as in other European countries, was the Conservative Party, while the Liberals, who represented the new bourgeoisie, favoured free trade.

In one of history's great unexpected twists, it was a Conservative Prime Minister, Robert Peel, who made the decisive move towards free trade in 1846 by abolishing the Corn Laws. The wars with France had kept British grain prices high by limiting imports, and landlords were determined to protect their incomes after 1815. The Corn Law of 1815 thus prohibited imported grain from being sold domestically unless British domestic prices rose above a certain threshold: this effectively blocked imports for several years. In 1828 such prohibitions were replaced by a tariff (import tax) on grain imports, to be administered on a sliding scale: as domestic prices fell, import duties were increased. The aim and effect of these policies was to make grain more expensive in the UK, thus protecting the interests of UK grain producers, and not surprisingly many Conservative landowners objected strongly to their removal.[7] The reasons for Peel's change of heart on the matter, and his success in getting the measure passed by Parliament, are varied and complex, and have given rise to an enormous scholarly literature. The Reform Act of 1832 had expanded the electoral franchise in cities, more favourable to the liberalization of trade than the countryside. Some landlords had by this stage diversified their wealth, owning industrial shares as well as agricultural land. And Sir Robert found it increasingly difficult to justify making workers pay more for their bread: a theme that would continue to resonate in British politics for many decades.[8]

Whatever the reason for the Prime Minister's conversion, the Conservative Party split on the issue, Peel lost his job, and a free market Liberal administration came to power – with disastrous consequences for the millions of Irish who were suffering during the potato famine, and for whom the market alone could provide no solutions. A belief in the virtues of free trade eventually became a cornerstone of British political orthodoxy. There were however some Conservatives who remained doubtful. In 1881 a Fair Trade League was founded, advocating an end to commercial treaties with other countries 'unless terminable at a year's notice', so as to avoid 'entanglements' impeding the adoption of whatever trade policy might be required at the time. The League also advocated moderate tariffs on imports of food from outside the Empire, and tariffs on manufactured goods from countries refusing to accept British manufactured exports 'in fair exchange'. It received the support of Tories such as Sampson Lloyd and the Earl of Dunraven, but the Conservative Party was divided on the issue of fair trade in the 1885 general election: 'Many found it wiser to declare themselves free-traders and opposed to any reversal of the fiscal legislation of 1846. Others attempted to gain fair-trade support in the constituencies by a frank espousal of that cause. Still others attempted to straddle the issue.'[9]

Tariff Reform

Conservatives were, on the other hand, very keen on another aspect of nineteenth-century globalization, the British Empire. They were proud of Britain's many possessions in Africa and Asia, but of special emotional importance were Australia, Canada and New Zealand. All three had large British populations and were seen as being part of the British family. All three had seen large inflows not only of British workers, but of British capital, which had helped to develop their frontiers, expand their agricultural output, and provide the infrastructure with which food and raw materials could be cheaply transported back to Britain. All three would eventually fight by Britain's side in the two world wars, and were crucial in providing manpower and economic supplies during those conflicts. But all three were also on their way to becoming effectively independent, and there were some who feared that this might in the long run deprive Britain of a vital strategic asset and undermine her greatness – at a time when this was already under threat from the rapidly industrializing Germany and United States.

Conservatives were not alone in caring about the future of the British Empire, or indeed of the United Kingdom. In 1886 a group of politicians split from the Liberal Party on the issue of whether or not Home Rule (a form of limited self-government) should be granted to Ireland. Chief among these were Lord Hartington, whose brother had been murdered by Irish nationalists in Dublin in 1882, and Joseph Chamberlain, a Birmingham-based self-made businessman and promoter of radical causes within the party. In 1885 Chamberlain had called for, among other things, universal male suffrage, the disestablishment of the Church of England, land reform and free public education;[10] but his radicalism had its limits, and he objected violently to Prime Minister Gladstone's Home Rule proposals. He denied that 'it is sufficient to find out what the majority of the Irish people desire in order at once to grant their demands. I can never consent to regard Ireland as a separate people with the inherent rights of an absolutely independent community. Accordingly, if Irish nationalism means separation I for one am prepared to resist it.'[11]

Granting Home Rule to Ireland would not only show weakness to foreign enemies and other subject peoples, it would be a betrayal of the Protestants of Ulster, who were connected by 'race and religion and sympathy' with the Anglo-Saxon Protestants of Britain.[12] Chamberlain, Hartington and other Liberals opposed to Home Rule thus formed the Liberal Unionist Party. The Liberal Unionists went on to serve in government alongside the Conservatives and eventually merged with the latter in 1912, becoming the Conservative and Unionist Party of our own day. The coalition was a slightly awkward one: defined by attitudes towards Ireland, in an era when the 'Irish Question' largely dominated British politics, it contained both traditional Conservatives, suspicious of social change, and radical ex-Liberals who welcomed it, at a time when the working classes were growing in political influence.

Chamberlain was Colonial Secretary from 1895 to 1903: a convinced imperialist, he believed in 'this race, the greatest governing race the world has ever seen; in this Anglo-Saxon race, so proud, tenacious, self-confident and determined, this race which neither climate nor change can degenerate, which will infallibly be the predominant force of future history and universal civilization'.[13] Like many others at the time, and not only in Britain, he believed that 'our rule does, and has, brought security and peace and comparative prosperity to countries that never knew these blessings before. In carrying out this work of civilisation we are fulfilling what I believe to be our national mission.'[14]

On 15 May 1903 Chamberlain delivered a speech in Birmingham in which he asked his audience if they would rather that the self-governing colonies of the Empire remain closely united with the UK, or each go off 'in his own direction under a separate flag'.[15] In order that the former and more desirable option prevail, it was essential that Britain and her colonies adopt a system of preferential tariffs, imposing lower taxes on imports from each other than they did on imports from the rest of the world. Such a scheme would help to keep alive the hope of a Federal Union, and ensure that the British Empire be 'self-sustaining and self-sufficient'.[16] Imperial preferences would help to secure 'a commercial union which, in some shape or another, must precede or accompany closer political relations, and without which, as all history shows, no permanent co-operation is possible'.[17] A Jean Monnet for a jingoistic world, Chamberlain wished to use trade policy as a tool to promote political union, with important strategic benefits: as Avner Offer put it, he 'sought to create a Zollverein, a customs union, to underpin a Kriegsverein, a military union'.[18]

There was a big problem with the proposal, however. How could the UK offer lower tariffs to her Empire than to the rest of the world, when she was unilaterally offering zero tariffs to everyone?[19] In George Dangerfield's words, it was necessary 'to build a tariff wall around England for the single purpose of knocking holes in it, through which Imperial goods might pass'.[20] In other words, there had to be tariffs on French, German and American goods, if Australian or Canadian goods were to receive preferential treatment. And there was an even bigger problem: the goods which Australia, Canada and New Zealand exported to the UK, and which would have to be given special treatment, were largely foodstuffs: wheat, meat and butter. So imperial preference required imposing tariffs on food from the US or continental Europe, and that in turn inevitably meant increasing the price of food. Protection of any kind was anathema to many Conservatives and Liberal Unionists, but taxes on food imports were especially toxic, since food represented a large share of working-class expenditure.

With the Conservatives once again split on the issue of trade policy, the Prime Minister, Arthur Balfour, manoeuvred frantically to keep his government together: if it were to fall, he argued in a letter to Hartington, by now the Duke of Devonshire, 'I, and I suspect many others of our colleagues, would be in the embarrassing, and indeed, somewhat ludicrous position, of having to say that on the point which divided us, we had not made up our *own* minds, and could not, therefore, pretend to give a decided lead to anyone else.'[21] There followed a period of intense negotiation within the British government, with Balfour suggesting compromise language that the two warring factions could live with: the British government should have 'fiscal freedom', that is the freedom to negotiate commercial treaties with other countries while disregarding free trade doctrine; any tariffs that it imposed should nonetheless not have protection as their 'primary object'; and tariffs should not increase the average cost of living of the working man. What all that meant in practical terms was far from clear. As a historian of the controversy comments, Balfour was a great believer in 'verbal formulas as a means of resolving genuine conflicts of belief.'[22] The tactic sometimes worked: Balfour's 'success in isolating the Duke of Devonshire from the doctrinaire free traders in the Cabinet rested in part on the Duke's inability to understand the precise differences between Balfour's position and Chamberlain's. In this, the Duke was in distinguished company, which included many other leading politicians, members of the public, and even the Monarch himself.'[23]

In the long run, however, it was all to no avail: the Duke of Devonshire ended up resigning from government anyway, and the Conservatives remained hopelessly divided: they were trounced by the free-trading Liberals in the 1906 general election, and remained out of power until the war.[24] 'By 1913 tariff reformers were a small minority even within the Unionist party . . . Even so, their influence within the party was disproportionate to their numbers . . . all the leaders of the Conservative party between Balfour's resignation and the Second World War came originally from the tariff reform wing of the party, and moreover from the extreme end of that wing.'[25]

Chamberlain's Revenge

The 1906 general election ensured that Britain would remain a free-trading nation until the outbreak of war in 1914. And the war proved that even in the absence of an imperial trade bloc, Britain's overseas possessions could still play a crucial role in ensuring her security. Even better, countries no longer part of the Empire, notably the United States, could also play such a role. The economic resources of the New World were essential in enabling Britain and her allies to defeat their enemies, while the Allied blockade of Germany undermined morale there, and was maintained until the peace treaties of 1919 had been signed.[26]

Total war meant pervasive government intervention in the economy, and the abandonment of Britain's traditional free trade policy. It also meant the international coordination of the Allies' economic efforts, a task in which the young Jean Monnet was intimately involved along with his British, Italian and American colleagues. After the war the British government introduced protection for industries regarded as being important for national security. Nonetheless, the UK reverted to a broadly free-trading policy: the descendants of the tariff reformers would have to wait a little longer.

The post-war United Kingdom also recognized that both it and its Dominions (Australia, Canada, the newly independent Irish Free State, Newfoundland, New Zealand and South Africa) were 'autonomous Communities within the British Empire, equal in status, in no way subordinate one to another in any aspect of their domestic or external affairs, though united by a common allegiance to the Crown, and freely associated as members of the British Commonwealth of Nations'.[27] It even acknowledged that India – not a settler colony – should eventually become self-governing within the Empire. Imperial conferences were held at regular intervals, at which delegates from the UK, the Dominions and India discussed matters of mutual interest, including economic policy. These conferences were not just talking shops: they promoted cooperation on scientific research, forestry, transport and communications, intra-imperial migration, and a wide range of other subjects. The 1926 conference, for example, not only adopted the declaration regarding the status of the Dominions cited above; it also agreed *inter alia* that workers who had been incapacitated following work-related accidents, and their dependants if they had been killed, should continue to receive compensation after moving to another part of the Empire.[28] But there was no formal constitution defining the Commonwealth, setting out its purposes, or specifying decision-making rules. This sat well with the British political system, which famously functions without a written constitution, and the fact that the Commonwealth worked effectively during both the interwar period and the war that followed helped to shape British attitudes towards international cooperation more generally.

In 1929 the Great Depression struck the world economy, and with it came demands for protection everywhere. Britain was no exception. In October 1931 a general election returned a 'National Government' to power, dominated by protectionist Conservatives. Joseph Chamberlain's son Neville was appointed Chancellor of the Exchequer, and wasted no time in pursuing his father's trade agenda. Within weeks tariffs had already been introduced on some manufactured and horticultural goods, and the following February a decisive move was made towards imperial preference: a general tariff on imports (subject to some exceptions) was introduced, with imports from the Empire still being admitted duty-free. As Chamberlain said to the House of Commons, with his mother in the visitors' gallery, and his half-brother Austen sitting on the Conservative benches,

> There can have been few occasions in all our long political
> history when to the son of a man who counted for
> something in his day and generation has been vouchsafed
> the privilege of setting the seal on the work which the

father began but had perforce to leave unfinished. Nearly
29 years have passed since Joseph Chamberlain entered
upon his great campaign in favour of Imperial Preference
and Tariff Reform. More than 17 years have gone by
since he died . . . His work was not in vain. I believe he
would have found consolation for the bitterness of his
disappointment if he could have foreseen that these
proposals, which are the direct and legitimate descendants
of his own conception, would be laid before the House of
Commons, which he loved, in the presence of one and by
the lips of the other of the two immediate successors to his
name and blood.[29]

The commitment to imperial preference was further strengthened at the Imperial Economic Conference held in Ottawa
later that year. A series of bilateral treaties was signed between
the participants according each other preferential tariff treatment, while Britain and her Dominions continued to raise
trade barriers against the rest of the world (although not by
as much, in general, as other countries). If the aim was to increase trade within the Empire at the expense of trade with
the rest of the world, it seems to have been effective. Between
1930 and 1933 the proportion of British imports coming from
the Empire rose from 27 to 38 per cent. Recent research suggests that the switch to imperial preference can account for as
much as 77 per cent of this dramatic increase in the share of
the Empire.[30]

The Principle of Non-discrimination: General Most-Favoured-Nation Treatment

The British Empire was not the only trade bloc during this period, and the 1930s saw a general tendency towards increased trade within blocs, at the expense of trade between them. This was true of other European countries, such as France, who already had empires and who, like the British, traded more with them during the decade; and it was also true of countries who did not yet have empires but who aspired to have them in the future, such as Germany. In other words, international trade became less multilateral during the 1930s: rather than buying from some countries and paying for these imports by selling to others, states increasingly bought from the same countries or groups of countries to whom they sold their exports, in bilateral fashion. Observers at the time and subsequently believed that this decline in multilateral trade not only reflected, but exacerbated, the international tensions of the period: during the war, the well-known New Zealand economist John Condliffe wrote that it is now 'so obvious as to hardly need statement that bilateral trade took on aggressive and destructive aspects as international rivalries were sharpened in the era of what is now known as pre-belligerency'.[31] The rise of imperial trade blocs strengthened the hand of nationalists in countries such as Japan who argued that it was safer to seize territory and become economically self-sufficient than to rely on international markets for one's survival.

On 14 August 1941, some four months before the United States entered the war, Winston Churchill and Franklin

Roosevelt met secretly in Placentia Bay, off the coast of Newfoundland. They issued an eight-point document known to history as the Atlantic Charter, the fifth point of which reads, 'They will endeavour, with due respect for their existing obligations, to further the enjoyment by all States, great or small, victor or vanquished, of access on equal terms, to the trade and to the raw materials of the world which are needed for their economic prosperity.'[32] In the light of the 1930s the consequences of unequal access to trade and raw materials seemed too dangerous for it to be permissible any longer.

It is therefore hardly surprising that the very first Article of the General Agreement on Tariffs and Trade (GATT), signed in 1947, prohibited trade policies which discriminated in favour of some countries and against others. In the jargon of trade policy, all signatories to the GATT became each other's most-favoured-nation, implying that no one else could be more favoured than them. This commitment to general non-discrimination remains at the heart of international trade law today, with consequences for Brexit that we will encounter later.

There were two major exceptions to the principle of non-discrimination permitted by the treaty. First, Article XXIV recognized

the desirability of increasing freedom of trade by the development, through voluntary agreements, of closer integration between the economies of the countries parties to such agreements . . . Accordingly, the provisions of this Agreement shall not prevent, as between the territories of contracting parties, the formation of a customs union or of a free-trade area.[33]

The definitions of customs unions and free trade agreements permitted by Article XXIV are spelled out in the text, and since they matter a lot for current debates about Brexit it is worth reproducing them (almost) in full:

> 8 (a) A customs union shall be understood to mean the substitution of a single customs territory for two or more customs territories, so that
>
> i) duties and other restrictive regulations of commerce . . . are eliminated with respect to substantially all the trade between the constituent territories of the union or at least with respect to substantially all the trade in products originating in such territories, and,
>
> ii) . . . substantially the same duties and other regulations of commerce are applied by each of the members of the union to the trade of territories not included in the union;
>
> (b) A free-trade area shall be understood to mean a group of two or more customs territories in which the duties and other restrictive regulations of commerce . . . are eliminated on substantially all the trade between the constituent territories in products originating in such territories.

The question of what 'substantially all the trade' actually means is an important one that we will return to later in this book, since it limits what is and is not legally possible for Britain after Brexit.

The second major exception to the principle of non-discrimination permitted by the GATT was a series of exemptions allowing Britain, France, Belgium, the Netherlands and the United States to continue their preferential trading relationships with current or former colonies.[34]

Britain thus entered the post-war world with her imperial preferences intact. While this was a source of considerable irritation to the United States, there was no reason to think that these preferences could not continue into the future. And in the Commonwealth Britain had a model for successful international cooperation, relying not on formal supranational institutions but on voluntary agreement between independent countries. Even better, the Commonwealth was a group of countries in which the United Kingdom quite naturally played a leading role, and enjoyed an unusual degree of influence. Perhaps this was a model that might serve as a useful template elsewhere?

CHAPTER 3
The Path to Rome

As the American diplomat and historian Benjamin Grob-Fitzgibbon emphasizes in a stimulating recent book, many British political leaders in 1945 thought of their country as being both European and imperial. As he also points out, there was nothing particularly unusual about this, since 'From the seventeenth century onwards, European-ness and imperialism became synonymous. To be European *was* to be imperial.'[1] European states had in the past fought each other for control of territory in other continents, but their shared colonial experience now gave them a common identity which might, perhaps, help in forging a shared future. Even better, the resources of the British, French, Dutch, Belgian and Portuguese empires might, if combined, enable Europe to maintain its geopolitical status in a world that would otherwise be dominated by the two rising superpowers, the United States and the USSR. In the minds of many Britons there was no need to choose between Europe and the British Empire, and several reasons to think that greater European unity was essential in the aftermath of a devastating conflict.

As early as 1940 there had been proposals in Britain for sharing sovereignty with another European country, namely France. Jean Monnet was yet again working to coordinate the economic efforts of the two allies, and convinced the British government to seek political union with his native country. On 16 June de Gaulle transmitted the offer to Paul Reynaud's French government in Bordeaux, but Reynaud lost power to Marshal Pétain on the same day. Pétain, who favoured an armistice with the Germans, asked why France would wish to 'fuse with a corpse'.[2] And so it is perhaps not so surprising that Winston Churchill emerged after the war as one of the leading champions of a united Europe. Out of power since July 1945, in September of the following year he gave a speech in Zurich in which he called for the construction of 'a kind of United States of Europe'. 'The first step in the recreation of the European Family must be a partnership between France and Germany. In this way only can France recover the moral and cultural leadership of Europe . . . In all this urgent work, France and Germany must take the lead together.' (At this stage, it must be said, the French doubted the wisdom of giving the Germans such a role.) Over the next two years Churchill tirelessly advocated for a united Europe, which he regarded as being fully compatible with Britain's imperial commitments. Indeed, Britain's claim to continuing great-power status lay precisely in the fact that the country, uniquely, lay at the centre of 'three interlinked circles': the first and most important was the British Commonwealth and Empire, the second was the English-speaking world, and the third was a united Europe.[3]

How closely did Churchill want the UK to become involved with such a united Europe, and how united did he think Europe should become? On the one hand, the Zurich speech talked of Britain and her Commonwealth becoming 'friends and sponsors of the new Europe' alongside the United States and (hopefully) the Soviet Union, suggesting that the UK would be keeping a certain distance from it; on the other, at a meeting to launch his United Europe Movement in May 1947 he argued that 'If Europe united is to be a living force, Britain will have to play her full part as a member of the European family.'[4] On the one hand, Churchill advocated the creation of a Council of Europe and a 'uniform currency': 'Luckily coins have two sides, so that one can bear the national and the other the European superscription.'[5] On the other, he wanted 'a European assembly without executive power . . . The structure of constitutions, the settlement of economic problems, the military aspects – these belong to governments.' He argued in favour of a European Army, but felt that 'a Parliament of Europe [was] quite impracticable'. Not surprisingly, historians have disagreed about his true feelings on the subject: a contemporary complained that on Europe 'Churchill decided to have it both ways.'[6]

The Labour government in London was certainly not in favour of a system in which a European Parliament – which would inevitably contain many German and Italian members, at least in the long run – would be able to take decisions that would be binding on the United Kingdom. The British Foreign Secretary, Ernest Bevin, eventually came to accept that there was a need for 'some sort of federation in Western Europe whether of a formal or informal character', given the challenges posed by an aggressive Soviet Union, but he 'hoped it would not be necessary to have formal constitutions' – the British Commonwealth provided a more flexible and desirable model.[7] As already noted in Chapter 1, a resistance to supranational political institutions that would have the ability to impose policies that Britain did not want soon became a defining characteristic of British attitudes towards European integration. Others elsewhere took a different view.

Britain at the Heart of Europe

Despite such differences in opinion, the late 1940s saw a burst of institutional innovation in Western Europe. By the end of the decade three major international organizations had been created, in the economic, security and political spheres. All three included the UK as a leading founder member, and all three operated on essentially intergovernmental lines: they involved cooperation between governments rather than the creation of supranational institutions. At the same time, future battle lines were already being drawn between federalists and 'intergovernmentalists'.

The origins of post-war European economic cooperation are largely American.[8] When the US decided in 1947 to provide Marshall Aid to Europe, one of the things that it insisted on was that the aid programme be administered by the Europeans themselves. A Committee for European Economic Co-operation was set up for this purpose in 1947, and was made permanent and re-baptized the Organization for European Economic Co-operation (OEEC) in April of the following year.[9] The OEEC involved seventeen European countries which would be the key players in the manoeuvres and counter-manoeuvres of the succeeding decade.[10] It is helpful to classify these countries into three groups. First, there were 'the Six': the three Benelux countries, France, Germany and Italy. Second, there were the 'Other Six': the three Scandinavians

(Denmark, Norway and Sweden), the two neutral alpine states (Austria and Switzerland), and the UK. Third, there were five peripheral and less industrial countries: Greece, Iceland, Ireland, Portugal and Turkey. In accordance with the wishes not just of Britain, but of the Scandinavians and the Low Countries as well, the OEEC was strictly intergovernmental in nature – contrary to the wishes of France.[11] Decisions were taken by the Council of Ministers and required unanimity (meaning that no country could ever be made to accept a decision that it did not agree with).

In addition to organizing the distribution of Marshall Aid, the OEEC had a remit to advance European economic integration: it was supposed not only to lower trade barriers, but also to study the feasibility of creating a European customs union. The British Foreign Secretary was keen on the idea, and the UK participated in the study group set up to examine the issue. Early on, however, it became clear that membership of a customs union would be difficult for Britain, given its policy of imperial preferences and commitment to the Empire. A customs union, as the name suggests and as we saw in the previous chapter, implies by definition a common external tariff policy for all member states. If Britain joined a European customs union it would be unable to set its own, preferential, tariffs on goods arriving from the Commonwealth. Unless the customs union as a whole did the same, or some means were found of merging a Commonwealth customs union with a European one, imperial preference would have to go – and there was absolutely no sign that the Dominions were willing to become involved in a customs union with each other, let alone in one involving European countries also. On the other hand, if the rest of Europe were to form such a customs union, and Britain remained outside it, its industries would find themselves being discriminated against in continental markets. A British expert committee appointed in 1947 to study the issue concluded that 'a continental customs union had little economically in its favour other than the damage which would be caused by being excluded from it'.[12] A more succinct statement of a certain British view of Europe would be hard to find. Once a customs union was on the table, it would become difficult if not impossible to avoid choosing between Europe and the Empire, and neither option was appealing.

The OEEC did not make much headway on the question of a customs union, but it was otherwise largely successful in pursuing its objectives. One of its main achievements was to restore multilateral trade within Europe, which in turn required the re-establishment of convertible currencies (that is to say, currencies which could be freely exchanged with each other on international currency markets). Absent convertible currencies, it was difficult for a country (let us say France) to run a trade deficit with a second country (let us say Germany), and to pay for these excess imports by running a trade surplus with a third country (let us say Britain): for this would require being able to convert the surplus British pounds that had been gained from the trade with the UK into German marks, to enable French importers to buy goods from across the Rhine.

Without convertible currencies there was thus a tendency to seek balanced trade, not with the world as a whole, but with individual trading partners. This was needless to say extremely inefficient, in much the same way as barter is inefficient (since as generations of economics undergraduates have learned, barter relies on a mutual coincidence of wants); and just as barter is what inevitably happens when you do not have an acceptable domestic currency, so the tendency to bilateral rather than multilateral trade arose from the lack of internationally convertible currencies that could serve as an international means of payment.[13] Under the auspices of the OEEC, and with the active assistance of the United States, the European Payments Union was therefore established in 1950. This was extremely successful in facilitating the re-establishment of a multilateral European trading system and the resumption of convertible currencies. Without these achievements the adoption of more ambitious free trade proposals in Europe would have been strictly impossible.[14] The OEEC also made considerable progress in removing non-tariff barriers to trade among its members such as quotas (quantitative restrictions on the amount of goods that can be legally imported).

NATO was another organization where American input was crucial by definition. In 1948 the three Benelux countries joined France and Britain in signing the Treaty of Brussels, a 50-year collective security agreement that also called for 'collaboration in economic, social and cultural matters'.[15] The Brussels Treaty soon became redundant, due to Western European weakness and growing fears about the Soviet Union. The Berlin blockade, which began just three months later, highlighted both the gravity of the Soviet threat, and the reliance of Western Europe on American military support. The result was the signature of the Atlantic Pact, establishing

NATO in 1949, by twelve countries: the five Brussels Treaty countries, three Nordics (Denmark, Iceland and Norway), Italy and Portugal, and Canada and the US. Greece and Turkey were admitted three years later.

Finally, in 1949 the Council of Europe was established as a two-tier structure, involving both a European assembly, meeting in public, which is what the federalists wanted, and a ministerial committee meeting in private, and making decisions on the basis of unanimity, which is what the British wanted. The Consultative Assembly, as it was called, and which met in Strasbourg, became a focal point for pro-federalist politics during the 1950s. However, the structure of the Committee of Ministers ensured that the Council of Europe would become an organization based on intergovernmental cooperation. Its major contribution was in the area of human rights, with the European Convention for the Protection of Human Rights and Fundamental Freedoms being opened for signature in 1950, and the European Court of Human Rights established in 1959.

A British politician surveying the European scene at the start of 1950 would probably have felt quite pleased. Western Europe was being stabilized, economically and politically, with the active support of the US. A web of interlocking institutions had been created in order to facilitate this, in particular the OEEC and NATO, with Britain a leading member of both. And while the federalists had obtained a European assembly, the organizational framework that had been erected to date was intergovernmental rather than supranational.

The Path to Rome[16]

Events were soon to take a new and very different turn. In May 1950 the French foreign minister Robert Schuman announced a proposal to pool Western Europe's coal and steel industries, and have them administered by a new supranational authority. His declaration stated that 'this proposal will lead to the first concrete foundations of a European federation indispensable to the preservation of peace.'[17] The plan had been devised by Jean Monnet, who had collaborated with British economic planners during two world wars, advocated an Anglo-French union, and was certainly no Anglophobe. Indeed, after the war he retained the hope that Anglo-French cooperation could be the basis for a new Europe. The British general election of February 1950 was however a disappointment to him – it focused on purely British themes, notably the future of the Empire, at a time when European integration was the major issue elsewhere. Monnet concluded that France needed to take the lead in pushing for greater European integration, and that a Franco-German alliance, rather than an Anglo-French one, needed to be at the heart of this.[18]

News of the Schuman Plan came as a complete shock in London. The Foreign Secretary was informed of its existence only hours before it was publicly announced, in contrast to the Americans, whose approval for the proposal had already been sought and received (for the American Secretary of State Dean Acheson it was 'manna from heaven').[19] All European countries, including Britain, were invited to participate in the venture, but had to first agree to the establishment of the supranational High Authority and to the pooling of coal and steel production. The British protested that they could not reasonably be expected to agree to all of this before entering talks: these were matters that needed to be decided during negotiations, not before them. To no avail. In addition, the Labour government had just nationalized the British coal industry, and party members were reluctant to commit to pursuing the same economic policies as right-wing continental governments. Finally, a coal and steel community would require common tariffs, which would interfere with Britain's imperial preferences. Guy Mollet (then the French Minister of State with responsibility for the Council of Europe, in effect the Minister for European Affairs) suggested to the British Foreign Secretary that Schuman had devised both the plan and the preconditions attaching to talks regarding it with the specific intention of making it impossible for the British to become involved.[20] Whether or not that is true, they did not feel able to do so.

The British were not alone in taking this attitude, and only 'the Six' were willing to negotiate on the basis of the French preconditions. The result was the Treaty of Paris, establishing the European Coal and Steel Community (ECSC), signed in 1951. Ratification was completed the following year. The ECSC was committed to establishing a common market in coal and steel, without tariffs, quotas, restrictive practices, discriminatory subsidies or other measures, and with a common tariff on imports from the rest of the world. It also took on functions in areas not directly related to trade, such as investment, research, health and safety, and the housing and resettlement of workers.

The ECSC established an ambitious supranational institutional framework. Four institutions were created: the High
Authority, the Council of Ministers, the Court of Justice and
the Common Assembly. The High Authority administered the
Community and had decision-making power. In addition, it
had the power to fine firms in breach of the treaty, and to collect production levies. The Authority had nine members, and
decisions were made by simple majority voting. It was thus a
clearly supranational institution. The purpose of the Council was to coordinate the actions of the High Authority and
of member states. It was composed of one minister representing each state. In some matters its consent was needed,
and it made decisions on the basis of either unanimity or
weighted majority voting. The Court of Justice was charged
with making sure that the treaty was respected, and had the
power to annul the actions of the other institutions. Finally,
the Common Assembly was a purely advisory body, which
did however have the power to dismiss the High Authority.

Recent historical scholarship has not been particularly
kind to the ECSC.[21] One of Monnet's major aims was the
decartelization of German heavy industry, and the High Authority was given widespread powers to bring this about.
The attempt proved a failure, partly because the needs of the
Korean War implied that a costly reorganization of German
industry could not be contemplated. Nor did the ECSC succeed in creating a single market for coal and steel. Domestic
coal subsidies and price controls remained, given the importance of coal prices for ordinary families as well as industry,
while steel tariffs were not eliminated. German exports to

European countries outside the ECSC grew more rapidly than those to the ECSC.[22]

The ECSC did provide the institutional blueprint for future European institutional development, at least superficially. The four institutions it established – the High Authority, Council of Ministers, Court of Justice and Common Assembly – correspond well to the Commission, Council, Court of Justice and European Parliament of our own day. Indeed, the Court of Justice and Assembly became institutions of all three Communities (the ECSC; the European Economic Community, or EEC; and the European Atomic Energy Community, or EURATOM) in 1958. The Court of Justice in particular has played a crucial role, ensuring that the Communities developed on the basis of the rule of law. It was thus essential in maintaining the supranational character of the Communities, although obviously it would not have had the influence that it did had member states not agreed to be bound by its rulings. (The fact that they did was crucial for subsequent developments, but *ex ante* they might not have.) Similarly, the High Authority and Council were merged with the corresponding bodies of the EEC and EURATOM in 1967, becoming the Commission and Council of what henceforth became known as the European Communities (EC). (You may be more used to the term 'European Community', but the EEC, ECSC and EURATOM in fact jointly constituted the 'European Communities' and I am going to be pedantic and use the phrase from now on.) However, as we will see, the EC would become a much less supranational, and much more intergovernmental, organization than the ECSC.

Nevertheless, the ECSC was an important development.

For the historian John Gillingham its crucial contributions were: first, to permit the reintegration of Germany into Europe as a state which could sign treaties with others on the basis of equality; and second, to provide politicians and negotiators with valuable lessons on the process of negotiating and implementing experiments in integration.[23] It also provided the political framework within which German heavy industry could be allowed to revive without threatening Germany's neighbours. Of even greater importance to our story, however, is the impact that it had on Britain's relationship with the process of European integration. Until May 1950 Britain had been at the heart of the process; after May 1950 it would become increasingly peripheral.

The second major development during this period had Asian and American origins. The outbreak of war in Korea in June 1950 prompted an increasingly overstretched US to call for West German rearmament within NATO. This prospect horrified the French and other victims of Nazi aggression. The solution, proposed by the French government in October, and known as the Pleven Plan, was to set up a common European army, so that Germany could contribute to NATO without doing so under a separate German command. This was to be done within a European Defence Community (EDC) that was to involve similar supranational institutional structures as the ECSC. The Americans were supportive. The UK did not wish to join the EDC because of the organization's supranational nature, but was also supportive of the initiative in both words and deeds. In particular, when the Dutch government stated that it would not be willing to enter such a system of collective defence without the UK being involved, the British government agreed that it would enter into a mutual defence agreement with the new body. On this basis the European Defence Community Treaty was signed in May 1952, with the new Anglo-EDC treaty coming into force on the same day.[24] Britain was still capable of playing a constructive and even decisive – if semi-detached – role in the process of European integration.

In turn, the EDC sparked negotiations on an overarching European Political Community (EPC) to which both the EDC and ECSC were to be subordinate. However, the French had always viewed the Pleven Plan as the lesser of several evils, and remained opposed to German rearmament. Eventually, in August 1954, the French National Assembly rejected the EDC treaty, and with it the EPC fell as well. The problem of how to handle German rearmament was therefore solved by expanding the 1948 Brussels Treaty to include Germany and Italy, while removing the anti-German language of the original. The treaty establishing the resultant organization, the Western European Union (WEU), was signed in October 1954. The WEU came into being, and Germany joined NATO, in May of the following year.

For federalists this sequence of events must have seemed a debacle. However, the debates surrounding the EDC led ultimately to the Messina process and the creation of the EEC.[25] As a low-tariff country, the Netherlands was not particularly happy with the trade liberalization programme of the OEEC, which emphasized the removal of quotas but left tariffs unaffected. This meant that a country like the Netherlands was obliged to scrap its quotas, retaining only low tariffs to protect its domestic industry. Larger, high-tariff countries like Britain and France also abolished their non-tariff barriers to trade, but since their tariffs were much higher than those of the Netherlands, the net impact was to liberalize their trade by much less. As a result, it was difficult for the Dutch to expand their manufactured exports, while agricultural exports, which were very important to the country, were excluded from the OEEC's liberalization efforts.

The solution was to engineer a reduction in tariffs in the Netherlands' major export markets, but it seemed difficult to envisage progress being made within the context of either the OEEC or GATT. On the other hand, the Dutch had found that their interests had been well protected in the negotiations leading to the formation of the ECSC. By a happy coincidence, two of the ECSC's members (Belgium and Germany) were the Netherlands' biggest export markets, and a further two were large high-tariff countries (France and Italy). It was therefore logical for the Netherlands to propose, in 1952, that the European Defence and Political Communities should form a customs union. Discussion of the Beyen Plan, named after the Dutch foreign minister who proposed it, was wide-ranging and covered many of the issues that would eventually be tackled in later negotiations. One notable feature of the Plan, on which the Dutch insisted, is that there would be no scope for national governments to determine the pace of trade liberalization – rather, a precisely defined schedule would be written into the treaty. This would become a central part of the Treaty of Rome* bargain. Dutch doubts regarding

---

* As we saw earlier there were in fact two Treaties of Rome. As noted then, when people refer to 'the' Treaty of Rome they generally mean the treaty establishing the EEC, and that is how I use the term here and henceforth.

whether their partners could be relied upon to deliver on their promises led to the development of supranational institutions designed to lock in the concessions that countries had made to each other. In turn, those supranational institutions were valued by other participants in the negotiating process for their own sake.

As soon as the Mendès-France government that had been responsible for the defeat of the EDC fell from power in France, in February 1955, Beyen revived his customs union proposal. In June 1955 the foreign ministers of the Six met at Messina and agreed to set up a committee, headed by the Belgian Paul-Henri Spaak, to study the establishment of a common market and a nuclear energy community. The Spaak Committee became a treaty-drafting committee in May 1956.

The OEEC was still the basic building block of Western European economic integration – even though it had become much less important after the ending of the Marshall Plan in 1952, and was becoming a victim of its own success in dismantling quantitative restrictions on trade and moving European currencies towards convertibility. Moreover, Britain remained a leading European power, and several members of the ECSC hoped that Britain might join with them in moving towards a customs union and common nuclear community. Indeed, Britain had signed an association agreement with the ECSC in 1954. The Six therefore invited Britain to participate in the work of the Spaak Committee, and the British accepted the invitation. They were present at the first meeting of the Committee in July 1955, and participated for the next five months.

There were two main differences between the British

position and that of the Six.[26] The first, and most important, was the British preference for a free trade area rather than a customs union. Since this is a crucial distinction that matters hugely in the current Brexit negotiations, but whose implications are often ignored, it is worthwhile emphasizing the key differences between the two arrangements, already encountered in Chapter 2. In a free trade area member states agree not to impose tariffs on goods originating in other member states. They are however free to pursue whatever trade policies they like with third countries. In other words, the fact that Canada, Mexico and the United States are all members of the North American Free Trade Area does not prevent Canada from signing free trade agreements with other countries, or indeed with the European Union as happened in 2016.

There is an obvious problem with such arrangements, however. Let us hypothetically imagine that two countries, call them Britain and France, agree to form a free trade area. France will therefore not impose tariffs on British goods. Let us also imagine that Britain has a free trade arrangement not only with France but with New Zealand. Under the terms of the hypothetical Anglo-French free-trade agreement France has agreed not to impose tariffs on imports of British lamb. It has not, on the other hand, agreed to treat New Zealand lamb in the same way. Imagine that France imposes 10 per cent tariffs on imports of New Zealand lamb to protect its farmers. France will obviously not accept that New Zealand lamb be imported duty-free into Britain, under the terms of the Anglo-New Zealand free trade arrangement, and from there be exported duty-free to France. It will therefore have to check all imports of lamb coming from Britain to ensure that only British lamb is admitted duty-free into France, and that New Zealand lamb pays the tariffs that are due. If the good in question is not lamb, but a complex industrial product such as cars, it is less easy to define the good as being British or non-British – since the car may be assembled in Britain, but be made of components largely produced elsewhere. Modern trade agreements therefore specify 'rules of origin' that define whether goods are (in this example) British or not, and are therefore exempt or not from tariffs under the free trade arrangement concerned.

All of this obviously requires customs inspections at frontiers, which cost time and money. An alternative solution is therefore for the countries concerned to form a customs union, which not only prohibits tariffs between member states, but also requires them to impose a common external tariff vis-à-vis the rest of the world (i.e. it requires them to run a unified trade policy). If in our example both Britain and France impose the same tariffs on New Zealand lamb (say 5 per cent), then border controls are no longer needed to verify the origin of lamb traded between the two countries. If British lamb is imported into France, this can be done duty-free, just as in a free trade area. If New Zealand lamb is imported from Britain into France, this is perfectly fine, since the lamb has paid the common 5 per cent tariff anyway. In other words, customs unions do away with the need for customs inspections at internal frontiers, but imply that member states can no longer run their own independent trade policies.

In 1955 the Six opposed a free trade area precisely on the grounds that it would require the maintenance of internal border controls to monitor compliance with the rules of origin, something that they wished to avoid 'for psychological and political as well as for practical and economic reasons'. The common external tariff would also have a 'unifying effect', and 'be useful in GATT negotiations'.[27] For the British, on the other hand, a customs union was problematic precisely because of the common external tariff, with the difficulties that this implied for maintaining Britain's traditional preferences vis-à-vis the Commonwealth.

The second key difference between Britain and the Six had to do, predictably enough, with institutions. Following the collapse of the EDC, there was scepticism among several continental countries regarding the desirability of new supranational institutions, and indeed the word 'supranational' was scrupulously avoided by Spaak in the course of the negotiations.[28] On the other hand, the Six agreed that some new institutional structure was required, whereas the British favoured continuing to work within the framework of the OEEC.

Eventually, in November 1955, the British withdrew from the Spaak Committee, and for the next two or three months displayed a hostile attitude towards the work of the Six. The British Foreign Secretary, Harold Macmillan, sent letters to both Germany and the US, attempting to dissuade them from supporting the common market project on the grounds that it would be both economically and politically divisive. Similar arguments were made at an informal meeting of OEEC delegates that had been convened by the British for the purpose – angering the governments of the Six.[29] The US, as always strongly in favour of European integration, made it clear to Britain that it did not approve of this attitude, and supported the creation of both EURATOM and a European common market. By January or February 1956 initial hostility was being replaced by a realization that the Six might well succeed in forming a customs union, and that Britain needed to find a way to work with it. However, British attempts to sabotage the customs union project, and the fact that these had been abandoned largely because of US pressure, helped to create a climate of suspicion among the Six regarding British intentions, which made it much more difficult for Britain to achieve her subsequent objectives.[30]

On 25 March 1957 the Treaty of Rome was signed, establishing the European Economic Community. The economic ambitions of the treaty were considerable: the EEC was supposed to be not only a customs union, but a common market. The term is not precisely defined, but Articles 2 and 3 of the treaty allow us to infer what is meant by it:[31]

Article 2
The Community shall have as its task, by establishing a common market and progressively approximating the economic policies of Member States, to promote throughout the Community a harmonious development of economic activities, a continuous and balanced expansion, an increase in stability, an accelerated raising of the standard of living and closer relations between the States belonging to it.

Article 3
For the purposes set out in Article 2, the activities of the Community shall include, as provided in this Treaty and in accordance with the timetable set out therein

(a) the elimination, as between Member States, of customs duties and of quantitative restrictions on the import and export of goods, and of all other measures having equivalent effect;

(b) the establishment of a common customs tariff and of a common commercial policy towards third countries;

(c) the abolition, as between Member States, of obstacles to freedom of movement for persons, services and capital;

(d) the adoption of a common policy in the sphere of agriculture;

(e) the adoption of a common policy in the sphere of transport;

(f) the institution of a system ensuring that competition in the common market is not distorted;

(g) the application of procedures by which the economic policies of Member States can be co-ordinated and disequilibria in their balances of payments remedied;

(h) the approximation of the laws of Member States to the extent required for the proper functioning of the common market;

(i) the creation of a European Social Fund in order to improve employment opportunities for workers and to contribute to the raising of their standard of living;

(j) the establishment of a European Investment Bank to facilitate the economic expansion of the Community by opening up fresh resources;

(k) the association of the overseas countries and territories in order to increase trade and to promote jointly economic and social development.

As Chapter 1 suggested, dismantling trade barriers, instituting common agricultural and competition policies, and harmonizing social policies, logically went together. It was not enough to build a common market: that market had to take account of the political needs of the day. These included improving agricultural productivity and living standards, and preventing destructive regulatory races to the bottom. Achieving all of this required supranational institutions to make collective decisions and put them into effect.

Furthermore, not only was the free movement of goods to be promoted, but so was the free movement of 'persons, services and capital'. Given the importance of migration for the Brexit debate it is important to underline this fact, although what the treaty later guaranteed was in fact the free movement, not of all persons, but of workers. Article 48 states that

> Freedom of movement for workers shall be secured within the Community by the end of the transitional period at the latest . . . Such freedom of movement shall entail the abolition of any discrimination based on nationality between workers of the Member States as regards employment, remuneration and other conditions of work and employment . . . It shall entail the right, subject to limitations justified on grounds of public policy, public security or public health:
>
> (a) to accept offers of employment actually made;
> (b) to move freely within the territory of Member States for this purpose;
> (c) to stay in a Member State for the purpose of employment in accordance with the provisions

governing the employment of nationals of that
State laid down by law, regulation or administrative
action;

(d) to remain in the territory of a Member State after
having been employed in that State, subject to
conditions . . .

Contrary to what is sometimes suggested, free movement
of workers is not a recent invention of the European Union:
the principle (if not always the practice) was there right from
the beginning.

The institutional structure of the EEC differed in one crucial respect from that of the ECSC. In the ECSC the supranational High Authority made the decisions, although it had
to consult with the Council on certain issues. In the EEC, it
was the Council – that is, the intergovernmental body representing the member states – which had the power to make
decisions, while the Commission could formulate proposals
that the Council of Ministers then discussed. The Treaty of
Rome thus established a new Community that was far less
supranational than the ECSC, although it retained the Court
of Justice. On the other hand, the treaty also envisaged a gradual transition from unanimity or weighted majority voting
to simple majority voting by 1966. No sooner did that date
arrive, however, than de Gaulle effectively reinstated unanimity as the basic decision rule of the European Communities: the so-called Luxembourg Compromise accepted that
member states could veto policies when 'vital national interests' were at stake. The treaty was seen at the time as a victory
for those governments who believed in an intergovernmental,

rather than a supranational, Europe, and de Gaulle's subsequent actions further strengthened that intergovernmental reality.

That was not how British politicians saw the Treaty of Rome at the time, however. As a result, they had excluded themselves from a customs union that included the three largest continental European economies. Britain was no longer at the heart of Europe, or at the forefront of European integration, as she had been in the late 1940s. How would the British political system react?

Brentry

By the spring of 1956 concerns about the customs union project were becoming more widespread within the OEEC. By abolishing tariffs and quotas among themselves but not vis-à-vis the rest of Europe, the Six would be discriminating against other European countries. It is true that Article XXIV of the GATT, which as we have seen authorized the formation of customs unions, specified that any new customs union should not raise the general tariff level facing outsiders wishing to export to the Six. But nevertheless, a Danish farmer (say) would now find himself at a severe disadvantage relative to his Dutch counterparts in the German market, and this was obviously damaging to his interests.

Meanwhile, the success of the OEEC in dismantling quantitative restrictions on trade left low-tariff countries such as Denmark, Sweden and Switzerland feeling that they were now at a competitive disadvantage vis-à-vis those countries that retained higher tariffs. (You will recall that the Netherlands had also faced the same problem.) This meant that they had an interest in securing lower tariffs in their export markets, regardless of whatever the Six might agree among themselves. A Europe-wide free trade area was appealing to such countries.

Britain, meanwhile, had excluded itself from the customs union project and was therefore facing potential discrimination in the markets of the Six. As a result of its decision, it had also excluded itself from the position of leadership within the new Europe that it had always sought for itself. Or had it? It was still a leading member, and perhaps even the leading member, of the OEEC, which brought together no fewer than seventeen European countries, including all of the Six. Perhaps the OEEC could provide the basis for a wider and shallower Europe that would be more consistent with Britain's preference for intergovernmental cooperation and its Commonwealth commitments?

One important potential obstacle to economic cooperation with the Six involved agriculture, and here the legacy of the nineteenth century loomed large. As was the case elsewhere in Europe, the British government intervened to maintain agricultural incomes and provide incentives to farmers to increase production. However, the UK's historical commitment to cheap food meant that the government did not wish to raise the market prices facing consumers, while its commitment to the Dominions meant that low-cost agricultural producers in Australia, Canada and New Zealand had to be given easy access to the British market. For both of these reasons agricultural tariffs in the UK were generally low, especially on imports from the Commonwealth. British farmers therefore obtained their guaranteed prices by means of a subsidy, known as a deficiency payment, equal to the difference between the average market price and the guaranteed price. These deficiency payments cost money, but since Britain's agricultural sector was relatively small the policy was affordable. Elsewhere in Europe, on the other hand, such a policy would have been ruinously expensive.[1] Farmers in continental Europe were thus protected by raising market prices above world prices, and this required strictly limiting agricultural imports from the rest of the world. In Britain it was the taxpayer who supported the farmer; elsewhere in Europe it was the consumer. It was hard to see how two such different systems could coexist within a unified market.

Plan G

In 1956 Harold Macmillan, by now Chancellor of the Exchequer, asked civil servants to provide a memorandum listing alternative mechanisms for integrating the United Kingdom economically with the rest of Europe. The civil servants provided six of these, and the document was forwarded to Peter Thorneycroft, President of the Board of Trade. He suggested that the best option for Britain was a free trade area that would be OEEC-wide, and involve industrial goods only. The new EEC, when it eventually emerged, could become a member of this wider free trade arrangement. Since this was the seventh option to be suggested, it became known as 'Plan G', and was soon adopted as official British government policy.[2] The hope was that the new free trade area could come into effect at the same time as the EEC so that Britain (and the rest of the OEEC) would at no stage face discrimination in the EEC market.

Plan G had a lot going for it from a British point of view – indeed, perhaps too much. It would be based on intergovernmental cooperation, and would thus require no surrender of national sovereignty. Because it was a free trade area rather than a customs union it would enable Britain to maintain its existing system of imperial preferences. And finally, because it only involved industrial products, and excluded agriculture, it would allow the UK to maintain its existing system of agricultural support. 'Under its terms, the British government could have its cake and eat it, too, aligning itself with its European neighbours without in any way distracting from its Commonwealth relations.'[3] Achieving this desirable outcome would be feasible, since as the Board of Trade put it, 'the possibility of U.K. co-operation would be so welcome that we should be able to enter the plan more or less on our own terms'.[4]

Some British officials seem to also have hoped that Plan G might undermine the customs union project. There were some in Germany, such as the Minister for Economic Affairs Ludwig Erhard, who were suspicious of supranational institutions and whose liberal instincts led them to favour as wide a free trade arrangement as possible. If Plan G provided an alternative way of expanding German industrial exports, perhaps this might lessen Bonn's support for the customs union. Whether this was the main motivation for Plan G, or whether the scheme was a reactive attempt to deal with the consequences of the customs union project in a way that minimized the negative consequences for British industry, and her relationship with the Commonwealth, is a matter of scholarly controversy.[5] The truth may have varied over time, but what mattered politically were European perceptions of British motivations. Here Macmillan's original hostility to the Messina process meant that key actors such as Spaak were deeply suspicious of Plan G.

The British initially hoped that the European free trade area negotiations would take place simultaneously with those establishing the Common Market. However, it soon became clear that the Six would push ahead with the negotiation and ratification of the Treaty of Rome, leaving serious discussion of a free trade area to later. Indeed, the mere possibility that a European free trade area might undermine support for the Common Market, particularly in France and Germany, was a very good reason to get the Treaty of Rome negotiated first.[6] The Treaty of Rome was the priority, not the industrial free trade area proposed by the British, and nothing could be allowed to distract from the main task at hand. It was not until February 1957 that the OEEC Council of Ministers decided to enter into negotiations regarding the establishment of a European Free Trade Area. The following month the Treaty of Rome was signed, and it was ratified by the French Assembly in July. Trade liberalization within the EEC was now due to begin on 1 January 1959, which added a sense of urgency to the free trade area negotiations.

The negotiations placed France in a dilemma.[7] France was not particularly keen on trade liberalization, but supported the EEC project because of its political benefits. In addition, EEC trade liberalization would be gradual; steps would be taken to ensure that French industries would not face unfair competition; and there were important financial compensations, notably the Common Agricultural Policy (CAP) and the European Development Fund (EDF), that would provide money for French overseas territories. The free trade area, on the other hand, involved all of the costs associated with trade liberalization and none of the benefits. The French were therefore hostile to the proposal from the beginning, but initially could not afford to torpedo it for fear of the international opprobrium, inside and outside the EEC, which this would entail.

Two factors came to their rescue. From January 1958 onwards the new EEC Commission, which had strong federalist sympathies, and wanted to avoid the EEC becoming a mere free trade area, emerged as another force strongly opposed to the free trade area proposals. Even more importantly, British diplomatic ineptness meant that France was not as isolated as it would otherwise have been.[8] Not only had Macmillan's ham-fisted attempts to undermine the Messina process damaged trust; when designing Plan G, UK policymakers had been focused on what was required in order to achieve a domestic consensus on the issue in Britain. Not surprisingly, they had produced a blueprint that was indeed a very good deal for Britain – but in so doing they had paid insufficient attention to other countries' interests. For example, the proposal to exclude agriculture left Britain completely isolated, not just among the Six, but among other OEEC members as well: a free trade area involving industrial goods only was unattractive to those European countries for whom agricultural exports were important. Britain also underestimated the determination among the Six to preserve their political unity. Even so, it still required some adroit French diplomatic manoeuvring, combined with a direct challenge by de Gaulle – who had returned to power in June 1958 – to Adenauer to demonstrate his commitment to the EEC by rejecting the free trade area, before the French were able to effectively veto it.

EFTA and the First Enlargement of the European Communities[9]

Almost immediately, discussions began in Geneva to see if it would be possible to negotiate a smaller free trade area. The countries concerned were the 'Other Six', including the UK, plus Portugal.[10] Formal negotiations began in June 1959, and the Stockholm Convention establishing the European Free Trade Association (EFTA) was signed in January 1960.

The Stockholm Convention committed member states to establish an industrial free trade area by 1970. It contained no commitments regarding trade barriers erected against third parties. It was and remains a purely intergovernmental organization, whose sole institution was a Council of Ministers that met only rarely, supported by a small secretariat. It thus reflected British preferences. The result was that the OEEC was now divided into three groups: the EEC, EFTA and the rest (Greece, Iceland, Ireland and Turkey). Greece and Turkey would soon negotiate association agreements with the EEC that offered the prospect of future membership, while Ireland would establish a bilateral free trade agreement with the UK in 1965. Iceland joined EFTA in 1970.

The purpose of EFTA in the eyes of the British was not to serve as a permanent alternative to the EEC, but as a temporary bridge to it.[11] On the one hand, the British hoped that by presenting a united front, the 'Other Six' might maintain some cohesion, and avoid being 'eaten up, one by one, by the Six', as Macmillan put it.[12] Denmark in particular, with its heavy reliance on German as well as British markets, was seen as being potentially vulnerable to falling within the EEC orbit. Less defensively, the hope was also that the continuing importance of EFTA markets for German industry would lead that country to put pressure on its partners (that is, France) to agree to a trade agreement between the two blocs. EFTA was thus conceived as a new tactic to achieve the British objective of a Europe-wide free trade area.

In the first year of its existence, therefore, EFTA was largely concerned with trying to re-launch Europe-wide discussions on free trade. These efforts came to naught, however. There followed one of the most startling reversals of policy in postwar European diplomatic history: Harold Macmillan's decision in 1961 to apply for EEC membership. There were several reasons for this, and there is considerable debate as to which were most important. At least three economic considerations mattered.[13] First, the UK traded more with the EEC than with EFTA, and in the absence of a wider free trade agreement EEC membership might be required in order to protect Britain's export trade there. Second, Commonwealth trade was becoming less important for the UK, as colonies achieved independence and opted to pursue inward-looking trade and development policies. Third, the EEC was at this stage experiencing a golden age of economic growth, which heightened the importance of its markets to Britain, and strengthened worries about British economic performance. The hope was that industrial competition with Germany would serve to improve productivity at home.

There were also important political considerations. A 1960 report produced for the Prime Minister was blunt when it came to describing the decline in Britain's relative international standing since the mid-1950s:

We thought that, even if the Common Market did come off, we should be able to make our own terms for associating with it. The Free Trade Area negotiations proved us wrong . . . In so far as our previous attitude was influenced by our desire to do nothing which might prejudice the Commonwealth relationship, this consideration is now matched by the fear that the growing power and influence of the Six will seriously affect our position in the world – if we remain outside – and this itself will be damaging to our relationship with the Commonwealth.[14]

Particularly important was the attitude of the US.[15] The EEC imposed a direct economic cost on the US by discriminating against its exporters. The US was willing to accept this since the EEC also promoted European political integration. EFTA also discriminated against US exporters, but did not offer any corresponding political benefits. The US was therefore hostile to EFTA, while remaining strongly supportive of the EEC. Gradually British policymakers began to realize that if they wished to retain a special relationship with the US they would need to join the Common Market, rather than remaining aloof from it. For Miriam Camps, an American State Department official and author, this was 'a very important – perhaps the controlling – element in Mr Macmillan's own decision that the right course for the United Kingdom was to apply for membership'.[16] On 9 July 1960 Macmillan noted in his diary that he had

Walked a bit – pondered a lot . . . Shall we be caught between a hostile (or at least less and less friendly)

America and a boastful, powerful 'Empire of Charlemagne' – now under French but later bound to come under German control. Is this the real reason for 'joining the Common Market' (if we are acceptable) and for abandoning a) the Seven b) British agriculture c) the Commonwealth. It's a grim choice . . .[17]

While the British may have been motivated by a mixture of economic and political considerations, Macmillan's decision to apply for EEC membership triggered three other applications that were clearly economically motivated. The British market was sufficiently important to Denmark, Ireland and Norway that all three lodged membership applications to Brussels: if the UK entered the EEC, they would have to enter it also, or face discrimination in a key market.

Macmillan's decision was not risk-free. From the beginning, there were Conservatives who worried about the impact of EEC membership on Britain's relationships with the Dominions, and the supranational nature of the organization the UK might be about to enter. The press was divided on the issue: the *Daily Telegraph*, *Daily Mail*, *Daily Mirror* and *The Times* were on board but the *Daily Express* was fiercely opposed to British membership of what its proprietor regarded as 'an American device to put us alongside Germany'. Politicians were dispatched to explain the new policy to the Dominions, who were however unenthusiastic. On 14 August 1961 the ageing Winston Churchill wrote that if Britain ever had to choose between its historical role as leader of the British Commonwealth and Europe, he would 'choose the Empire and Commonwealth over Europe every time'.[18]

Conservatives had been at the forefront of the united Europe movement of the 1940s, and many were still strongly pro-European. It was the Labour Party that was the more Eurosceptic of the two parties. But as Grob-Fitzgibbon puts it, many

> pro-European Conservatives . . . were now sceptical of British engagement with the Common Market. They had hoped to see Britain leading a united Europe founded on the model of the British Commonwealth, a Europe that was intimately connected to Britain's imperial mission in the world. British entry into an already-existing European organization with a federal structure was not what their vision of 'Europe' had been, a vision that they now struggled to articulate following the collapse of the British Empire.[19]

In the event, those opposed to EEC membership need not have worried – at least, not immediately. As had been the case during the discussions about a European free trade area, there was a division of opinion between France and the other five EEC member states regarding the merits of the UK application, and once again de Gaulle eventually vetoed it, in January 1963. The result was a sharp deterioration in relationships between France and her partners, and an equally sharp improvement in the functioning of EFTA, which decided to speed up the abolition of internal tariffs by three years.

Why did de Gaulle veto British entry? Scholars disagree.[20] On the face of it, the French decision seems surprising, since the General shared Britain's scepticism regarding supranational institutions: the British would have been useful allies in that regard. Indeed, one factor which suggested to the British that 1961 was a good time to try to enter the EEC was precisely the fact that they might be able to work with de Gaulle, and shape the evolution of the Community in a manner that would be to their liking.

Politically, the General was not anxious to see French influence within the EEC diminished in favour of Britain. He also shared Macmillan's view that the UK might serve as a Trojan horse representing US interests within the Community. Needless to say he was as negative about this prospect as Macmillan and, interestingly, Jean Monnet, were positive. British entry would imply a 'different Common Market . . . one that we would build with eleven members. And then thirteen. And then perhaps eighteen . . . The cohesion of its members, who would be very numerous and diverse, would not last long . . . We would end up with a colossal Atlantic community dependent upon and directed by America.'[21]

Alternatively, the American political scientist Andrew Moravcsik argues that economic motives are key to understanding de Gaulle's veto.[22] Crucial for French acceptance of the Treaty of Rome was the assurance that a Common Agricultural Policy would be set up providing French farmers with markets in Germany, as well as high prices. However, the precise details of this policy had not yet been settled, in particular the question of how it would be financed. De Gaulle's fear was that if the British entered the EEC before the final details of the CAP had been negotiated, France would not succeed in obtaining the favourable terms that she required. De Gaulle vetoed a second British application in 1967; if France later relaxed her views on British entry, according to

Moravcsik, this was not just because the General was forced to resign in 1969, but also because the CAP as we know it today had already been 'locked in'.

For whatever reason, the European Communities (EC) opened membership negotiations with Denmark, Ireland, Norway and the UK in 1970.[23] The Labour Prime Minister Harold Wilson, who had long been hostile to EEC membership, had eventually come around to accepting that it was in Britain's best interests to join; but it was the ardently Europhile Conservative Ted Heath, who succeeded Wilson in June 1970, who actually opened negotiations. New Zealand turned out to be a particularly difficult issue to deal with: in 1970 the UK took 90 per cent of its butter exports, 75 per cent of its cheese exports and 86 per cent of its lamb exports.[24] Not surprisingly, the New Zealand government wanted a special deal so that it could continue to sell its dairy products and lamb to Britain. In the event it finally secured the right to sell a reduced amount of dairy products to the EEC as a whole. Nonetheless, there was a widespread perception in Britain that the country was turning its back on its most loyal friends. No fewer than 244 Members of Parliament, including one fifth of the Conservative government's own MPs, and the majority of the Labour Party, voted against EC membership in 1971.

Nevertheless, the negotiations were successfully concluded in January 1972, and the first enlargement of the EC took place a year later. Ireland and Denmark also joined but Norway did not, its voters having rejected EC membership in a referendum.[25] Strikingly, the initial hopes that EFTA would facilitate the negotiation of a free trade area between the Six and the rest of Europe were realized at precisely the same time that Denmark and the UK quit the organization. By this stage EFTA was a fully functioning industrial free trade area, and it was generally accepted that the UK's former partners could not find themselves facing tariff barriers in Britain as a result of Britain joining the EC. The EC therefore negotiated separate free trade agreements, involving most industrial goods, with the remaining EFTA countries (Austria, Iceland, Norway, Portugal, Sweden and Switzerland), as well as with Finland. In this manner EFTA fulfilled the historical purpose that the UK had designed it for.

The 1975 Referendum

The UK joined the European Communities on 1 January 1973. Many of its politicians were unhappy about this state of affairs with the long-run consequences that we know. Indeed, as early as 1975 a referendum was held on whether the country should leave the EC. Harold Wilson had returned to government in the previous year. As has already been mentioned, the British Labour Party that he led was traditionally Eurosceptic. There were a variety of reasons for this. The EEC, and before it the ECSC, were seen as capitalist institutions, membership of which would make it difficult or impossible to pursue socialist policies in Britain. There were impeccably internationalist grounds for preferring the British Commonwealth to Europe, since unlike Europe the Commonwealth was a multiracial organization that 'by its very nature' had to 'think of global not regional problems; of the interest of all races, not just of one'.[26] The protectionist policies of the EEC were damaging to the interests of developing countries. And there were

Labour politicians such as Anthony Wedgwood (as he was then) Benn who were worried about losing sovereignty. As early as 1962 the Labour leader, Hugh Gaitskell, had famously argued that a federal Europe would mean 'the end of Britain as an independent European state . . . the end of a thousand years of history'.[27]

But there were also passionate Europhiles on the Labour benches, notably Roy Jenkins, who resigned the Deputy Leadership of the party in 1972 because of its anti-European stance. Sixty-nine members of the Labour Party had voted to join the EC in 1971: without their support the UK would not have entered, given that a minority of Tories opposed this. How was Harold Wilson to hold his party together? The fact that entry, while planned by him, had actually been negotiated by the Conservatives, gave him a political solution to a political problem: the deal obtained by Ted Heath had clearly not been satisfactory. It was on this basis that he voted against joining the EC in 1971 and 1972, even though as we have seen he had actually become convinced of the pragmatic case for joining. In its 1974 election manifestos (for there were two elections, in February and October), the Labour Party promised that it would renegotiate the terms of British entry, and 'consult the people through the ballot box' once new terms had been obtained.

Wilson returned to office in February 1974 and set about fulfilling his renegotiation pledge. Britain's European partners were happy to help him save face, especially since he was not looking for much by way of renegotiation. The New Zealanders were given a little more, while a new European Regional Development Fund (ERDF) was created to channel money to poorer regions, of which the UK had several. In June 1975 the people were indeed 'consulted by the ballot box': a referendum was held in which they were asked whether or not the UK should stay in the EC. Wilson campaigned in favour of remaining, but his ministers were free to do as they pleased. Tony Benn, then Secretary of State for Industry, argued in favour of withdrawal, as did the Secretary of State for Employment Michael Foot. Foot objected to the loss of sovereignty implied by EC membership in terms that seem strident even today: 'The British parliamentary system has been made farcical and unworkable by the superimposition of the EEC apparatus . . . It is as if we had set fire to the place as Hitler did with the Reichstag.'[28]

The most prominent Conservative 'No' campaigner was Enoch Powell, famous for his 1968 'Rivers of Blood' speech denouncing black immigration into Britain. Even at the time the speech was widely condemned for its racism, and Powell was sacked from the Shadow Cabinet by Heath. Powell was a leading proponent of the view that EC membership undermined British sovereignty, and later became what Hugo Young calls 'the godfather of the successor tribe, to whom nation was not merely something but everything'.[29] By the time of the referendum he was no longer a member of the Conservative Party: he had urged the electorate to vote Labour in 1974 because of that party's hostility to Europe. In the October election he was returned to Parliament not as a Conservative, but as an Ulster Unionist representing the South Down constituency in Northern Ireland. Northern Ireland was fertile ground for an anti-European politician such as Powell, although the religious sectarianism driving many Protestant

Ulstermen to vote No was not to his liking. The fervently anti-Catholic clergyman and politician Ian Paisley was a prominent No campaigner in the province, and made no secret of why he was hostile to the 'Papist Super State': posters informed voters that a 'Yes' vote was a vote for '1. Rome 2. Ecumenism 3. Dictatorship 4. Anti-Christ'.[30]

In a country that still valued moderation, the support of a Paisley or a Powell was not yet an electoral advantage. It was easy for the Yes campaign to portray those opposed to Europe as extremists, and indeed for the most part they were. Ironically, or perhaps not, the terrorist Irish Republican Army (IRA) – Paisley's greatest enemy – also advocated a No vote, as did the Soviet Union. 'Yes' posters made the point simply. On their side were 'The Labour Government. The Conservative Party. The Liberal Party. The National Farmers Union. Australia. Canada. New Zealand'. Against were 'The IRA. The Communist Party. The National Front. International Marxists. The Rev. Ian Paisley'.[31]

The result was an overwhelming rejection of what we now call Brexit, by two to one. The people had conclusively spoken, and the matter was settled.

The Single Market Programme

As we saw in the last chapter, it took a mere two years after entry for the United Kingdom to organize a referendum on its possible exit from the European Communities. Although the result was a decisive affirmation of British membership it was hardly an auspicious start to the new relationship. To make matters worse, the 1970s were a difficult decade economically, and not just in the United Kingdom. The new economic context would have immediate and longer-run political implications in both Britain and the rest of the EC.

The End of the Golden Age

Economic historians commonly refer to the period between 1945 (or 1950) and 1973 as the Golden Age of economic growth, fondly remembered in France as the *Trente Glorieuses*, and in Germany as the *Wirtschaftswunder* (see Chapter 1). The five years after the end of the war saw exceptionally fast growth based on reconstruction, but the economic miracle continued after 1950, by which time reconstruction was essentially complete. There were several reasons for this. Chief among them was Europe's technological backwardness vis-à-vis the United States, which implied that the continent could grow rapidly simply by importing new technologies that had already been developed elsewhere. As already noted in Chapter 1, this required high levels of investment so that the factories embodying the new technologies could be built. Growth was highest in those countries where investment was highest; investment was highest where savings were highest (since savings were needed in order to finance the investment); and savings were highest where companies made large profits, and saved and invested these profits rather than paying them out as dividends. This in turn was facilitated by the corporatist bargains of the period: management and workers cooperated in order to ensure not only high profits, but the reinvestment of these profits so that everyone gained in the long run.[1] Furthermore, investment was more profitable if companies were free to sell beyond their national frontiers, which is why European economic integration was so important to the national growth strategies of the period.

The United Kingdom's economic performance was very disappointing during the Golden Age. Figure 5.1 plots the UK's output (GDP) per capita as a percentage of output per capita in France and Germany. As can be seen, the UK had started the post-war era significantly richer than either country, but higher growth on the continent steadily eroded its relative economic position. By the late 1960s GDP per capita was lower than in either France or Germany. There are several reasons for this poor performance: for example, labour relations were much less consensual in Britain than on the continent, and British industry operated in a relatively uncompetitive environment. The dismal economic context was important in the 1960s in shifting British political opinion in a pro-European direction. The hope was that by eliminating

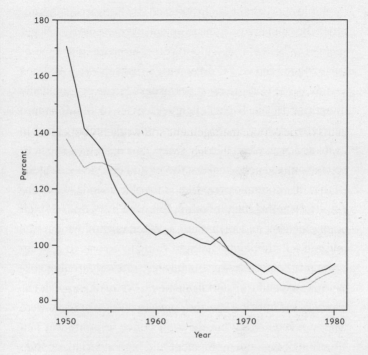

Figure 5.1
British GDP per capita as a percentage of GDP per capita
in France and Germany

— Relative to France

— Relative to Germany

Source: Bolt et al. (2018a, 2018b)

trade barriers, and forcing British industry to compete with Germany in particular, productivity would eventually increase, and with it living standards.

But just as Britain finally entered the European Communities the Golden Age came to an end. At the time the trigger seemed to be the Yom Kippur War that broke out in October 1973, and the OPEC oil embargo that followed. And it is certainly true that the oil shock ushered in an economically disastrous decade. Higher energy prices led to inflation more generally, but they also led to more unemployment as higher costs and prices led to lower sales. This came as a shock to economists and policymakers: theory and experience suggested that the economic cycle should involve periods of low unemployment and high inflation, followed by periods of high unemployment and low inflation. When unemployment was low and inflation high, the right thing to do was to restrain economic demand by raising interest rates, tightening government expenditure, or raising taxes. When unemployment was high and inflation low, the opposite policy responses were what was required. What the right policy response was in a situation of high unemployment and high inflation, or stagflation as it became known, was far less clear. And the decade that followed was very difficult everywhere.[2]

In retrospect, however, even deeper forces were at work. Economic growth in Europe slowed not just temporarily, but permanently. The long-run forces that had promoted rapid growth during the three decades following the war were no longer present. In part Europe was a victim of its own success: you can no longer enjoy rapid catch-up growth when you have already caught up. Nor was it possible to grow rapidly by transferring workers from low-productivity agricultural occupations to higher-productivity jobs in the manufacturing and services sectors, once agricultural employment had declined beyond a certain point. It became more difficult to sustain growth strategies involving the active cooperation of management and unions in the difficult macroeconomic environment of the 1970s, and globalization would eventually make it even more difficult: for what good was it to workers to help sustain profits and investment if the investment happened not domestically, but in other countries? And finally, the institutions that had facilitated catch-up growth might no longer have been appropriate for economies closer to the technological frontier, in which future growth would have to be based, not on importing technologies that had already been invented elsewhere, but on doing the inventing themselves.[3]

Figure 5.2 plots average growth rates in five economies (France, Germany, Japan, the United Kingdom and the United States) during three periods: the Golden Age (1950–73), the remainder of the 1970s and the 1980s. As can be seen, growth slowed everywhere after 1973. It approximately halved in the three European countries charted here, but since the initial growth rate had been much higher in France and Germany (of the order of 4 or 5 per cent) than in the UK (just 2.4 per cent) this implied 1970s growth rates that were still respectable on the continent, but barely more than 1 per cent per annum in Britain. Inflation was also particularly high in Britain: it averaged 15.4 per cent per annum between 1973 and 1980, as opposed to 10.5 per cent in France, and only 4.9 per cent in Germany.[4] In 1976 the British government was forced

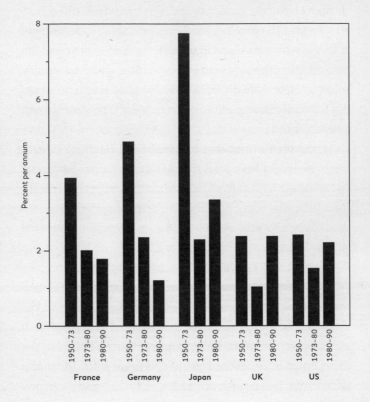

Figure 5.2
Economic growth per capita, 1950–90 (per cent per annum)
Source: Bolt et al. (2018a, 2018b)

to seek an emergency loan from the International Monetary Fund (IMF). It was thus hardly surprising that in 1979 the Conservative Party under Margaret Thatcher swept to power. Nor was it surprising that some in Britain blamed the economic difficulties of the decade on the UK's entry into the EC, which had coincided with the 1973 downturn. The Labour Party remained largely hostile to Europe, and became more so after losing office. In 1980 Michael Foot became party leader, and his party adopted an official policy of seeking British withdrawal.

Margaret Thatcher had succeeded Ted Heath as Conservative Party leader in 1975, and campaigned for a 'Yes' in the referendum. The Tories were still a pro-European party, but Mrs Thatcher had none of the emotional commitment to Europe of her predecessor. On the contrary, she mistrusted the Germans in particular, was suspicious of Catholicism, and detested the continental political tradition of bargaining and compromise.[5] Compromise is indeed not what we first think of when we think of Margaret Thatcher, so it is on the face of it surprising that under her the British government became an enthusiastic supporter of the greatest deepening of European integration experienced since the 1950s. But that is what in fact happened, and the Single Market programme that was constructed on her watch continues to be the major achievement of the European Communities, and the European Union (EU) that succeeded them. Since the Single Market is fundamental to both the EU and Brexit, and since its nature and implications remain surprisingly poorly understood in Britain, it is important to spend some time examining it.

The 1992 Programme

'I want my money back!' When the French think of Mrs Thatcher and Europe, this may be the phrase that immediately comes to mind. The occasion was the European Council (that is to say, the meeting of European heads of state or government) held in Dublin in November 1979, shortly after she had come to power. Britain's dismal economic performance during the 1970s, and earlier, was part of the problem for Mrs Thatcher: since Britain was the seventh poorest of the nine member states, why should she also be one of the largest net contributors to the European budget? The problem was that the Common Agricultural Policy, on which around 70 per cent of the European budget was spent in those days, was of much less benefit to the United Kingdom than it was to more agricultural economies such as France, the Netherlands or Italy.[6] Nevertheless, the abrasiveness with which Mrs Thatcher put forward her demands was shocking to those present, and neither Valéry Giscard d'Estaing nor Helmut Schmidt felt obliged to respond politely.[7]

The battle over Britain's budget contributions continued for the next five years, and in the end Mrs Thatcher did get her money back. However, the summit at which the Europeans finally conceded, held in Fontainebleau in June 1984, was notable for much more than a famous British victory. Europe was in those days undergoing a period of self-doubt, driven in large part by the economic stagnation of the period documented earlier. Unemployment in France, which had been just 2.7 per cent in 1973, and stood at 6.4 per cent in 1980, had risen to 9.5 per cent in 1984. Politically, integration seemed to have stalled, despite the accession of Greece to the European Communities in 1981, and the ongoing accession negotiations with Portugal and Spain. The 1970s recession had led governments across the EC to protect national industries by various means, using their own national health or safety regulations to make it difficult for foreign companies to sell into their markets, or refusing to spend public money on foreign goods. 'Eurosclerosis', both economic and political, was the order of the day.

By this stage, Giscard d'Estaing and Schmidt had been replaced by François Mitterrand and Helmut Kohl. Both men agreed that European integration needed a shot in the arm, and eliminating economic barriers between member states was one way of doing this. As a supporter of the free market, Mrs Thatcher was also very keen on getting rid of protectionist devices across the EC. The Fontainebleau summit agreed 'to put in hand without delay a study of the measures which could be taken to bring about in the near future . . . the abolition of all police and customs formalities for people crossing intra-Community frontiers'. Jacques Delors, who became President of the European Commission in 1985 with the support of Mrs Thatcher, would waste no time in responding to the appeal made at Fontainebleau.

Delors's right-hand man in accomplishing this task was Arthur Cockfield, a member of the British government whose main function at that time was to act as Mrs Thatcher's confidant. At Thatcher's prompting he was sent to Brussels with the specific purpose of drawing up a plan to create a unified single European market: in January 1985 he became Commissioner for the Internal Market, Tax Law and Customs. The result was a White Paper published in June 1985 identifying 297 specific intra-European economic barriers that were to be eliminated by 1992 – hence the common use of the term '1992 programme' to describe the process of creating what became known, not as the 'Common Market', but the 'Single Market'.[8]

The White Paper identified three major types of barriers that needed to be eliminated. The first was physical barriers to trade, notably customs posts at frontiers requiring transporters to submit their cargoes for inspection when driving, flying or sailing between countries. Such barriers were condemned on unsentimental, pragmatic, Anglo-Saxon grounds: 'The reason for getting rid entirely of physical and other controls between Member States is not one of theology or appearance, but the hard practical fact that the maintenance of any internal frontier controls will perpetuate the costs and disadvantages of a divided market.' Time is money, and border delays cost money. At the same time, however, the White Paper recognized that there would be political benefits to eliminating border controls: 'It is the physical barriers at the customs posts, the immigration controls, the passports, the occasional search of personal baggage, which to the ordinary citizen are the obvious manifestation of the continued division of the Community.' Crucially, eliminating this first category of barriers required eliminating the other two, namely technical and fiscal barriers, since physical barriers existed 'mainly because of the technical and fiscal divisions between Member States'. As we will see, this simple logic, spelled out by a Briton more than thirty years ago, is neglected by many in the UK today.

The second category of barriers to be eliminated was thus technical barriers, for example those technical barriers to trade in both goods and services resulting from different national health, safety, consumer or environmental regulations. According to a Commission study, industrialists rated these as the most important and costly barriers facing them at the time.[9] Countries could tailor their regulations in such a manner as to discourage imports from other member states, but different regulations had a more systematic impact on the European economy as a whole. If a company wanted to sell children's car seats across the EC, for example, and if each of the then ten member states had different technical standards that had to be met for the good to be legally sold in their markets, then the company would have to manufacture not one car seat, but ten different car seats, and sell each one not in a single European market of more than 300 million consumers, but in one specific national market, some of which were very small indeed.[10] This was costly for several reasons. The first had to do with what economists call 'economies of scale'. In many industries it is much cheaper per unit to produce larger quantities of goods than smaller quantities, for example because of high fixed costs of investment that can be spread out over a greater number of units. In a fragmented European market European companies tended to be excessively small, and hence inefficient and uncompetitive, especially when compared with their American and Japanese rivals. (It was Japan, rather than China, that scared onlookers in those days.) Second, fragmented national markets implied a lack of competition: instead of large pan-European companies competing against each other across the EC as a whole, you had small national companies enjoying a monopoly position in their own national market. The result was higher prices for consumers, and an even less competitive European economy.

The obvious solution was to ensure that products made in one country could be legally sold in all. This was done in a number of ways. First of all, the Commission was able to build on a famous court ruling from 1979, popularly known as the Cassis de Dijon case. The German *Bundesmonopolverwaltung für Branntwein* (Federal Monopoly Administration for Spirits) had attempted to prevent a French liqueur, Crème de Cassis de Dijon, from being sold in Germany, because the drink in question only had an alcohol content of 15 to 20 per cent. German legislation, on the other hand, required that liqueurs have a minimum alcoholic content of 25 per cent. The European Court of Justice ruled that the German regulation in question did not serve 'a purpose which is in the general interest and such as to take precedence over the requirements of the free movement of goods', and that it essentially served as a barrier to trade. There was no reason why a drink that was lawfully produced and marketed in one Member State should be excluded from another.[11] In other words, the Commission was able to build on a body of law promoting the principal of 'mutual recognition' of national rules. This obviously simplified their task considerably, reducing the amount of legislation that had to be introduced in order to eliminate technical barriers to trade within the EC. But European legislation was still required in a number of areas, for example in order to establish essential health and safety standards that had to be respected across the EC. Precisely defined

European technical standards could then provide firms with a way of proving that they complied with these. As we saw in Chapter 1, one of the core purposes of European integration has been to ensure that the benefits of trade do not come at the expense of regulatory races to the bottom. It is therefore not surprising that the Single European Act, which set in train the 1992 process, and was agreed in 1986, specified that 'The Commission, in its proposals . . . concerning health, safety, environmental protection and consumer protection, will take as a base a high level of protection.'[12]

Finally, eliminating physical barriers also required eliminating the third category of barriers considered in the White Paper: fiscal barriers requiring frontier controls for tax-related reasons. Tariffs had of course already been eliminated, but states raised (and still raise) substantial amounts of money via indirect taxation – that is to say, by taxing the sale of goods and services (rather than workers' wages, landowners' rents, or investors' profits). Indirect taxes in Europe come in two main forms: Value Added Tax or VAT, and excise duties, which are straightforward taxes on the consumption of particular goods such as alcohol, tobacco and fuel. Since member states set different tax rates, there were strong incentives to check goods crossing national borders in order to ensure that tax revenue was not lost. For example, a state with a relatively high excise tax on tobacco would have an incentive to stop shoppers from buying their tobacco abroad. Less obviously, since the subject is inherently complicated (but hopefully not excessively so), border formalities were also required because of VAT. Since the issue is important for Brexit, although it is rarely if ever discussed, a brief detour is necessary.

We Have to Talk about VAT

VAT is a gift from France to the world. True, it was invented by a German, or possibly an American, but it was Jean-Baptiste Colbert, Louis XIV's Finance Minister, who famously said that 'The art of taxation consists in so plucking the goose as to obtain the largest possible amount of feathers with the smallest possible amount of hissing', and it was France that first adopted a value added tax, in 1954.[13] VAT is a sales tax. Unlike excise taxes, sales taxes are levied not on the sales of particular items, but on the sales of goods and services more generally. They come in different forms: turnover taxes, retail sales taxes and VAT. If Europe has converged on VAT as the sales tax of choice this is not just because of the French example, but because of the logic of European economic integration.

To see the differences between these different sales taxes, and begin to understand the potential problems that VAT poses for Brexit, let us start with a very simple example. Let us imagine that a farmer produces €1,000 worth of barley, which he sells to a brewer. To keep things really simple, imagine that the farmer incurs no costs: his value-added (the difference between the cost of his inputs and the value of his output) is equal to €1,000. Let us then imagine that the brewer produces beer that he sells to a pub for €3,000. His only inputs are the barley he bought from the farmer. His value-added is equal to €3,000 minus the cost of the barley (€1,000), or €2,000. Finally, let us assume that the publican sells the beer to his customers for €6,000. His value-added is equal to €6,000 minus the cost of the beer (€3,000), or €3,000.

Now let us imagine that the government wishes to impose

a sales tax of 10 per cent. A turnover tax would tax the sales of every company in the above example at the rate of 10 per cent – there would be a 10 per cent tax on the sales of the farmer, a 10 per cent tax on the sales of the brewer, and a 10 per cent tax on the sales of the publican. Do you see the problem? If the publican were to buy the businesses of the brewer and the farmer (that is to say, if the production in this example were to become 'vertically integrated' and take place within one big firm), the only sales for the government to tax would be the final sales to the consumer. If the three businesses remain separate, on the other hand, not only are the final sales to the consumer taxed, but so are the two intermediate sales in the example (the farmer's sales of barley to the brewer, and the brewer's sales of beer to the publican). A turnover tax of this sort would therefore give a strong artificial incentive to companies to vertically integrate, and hand a strong artificial advantage to bigger firms over smaller firms. For this reason, turnover taxes are generally regarded as inefficient and undesirable.[14]

A retail sales tax avoids this problem. It only taxes sales to final consumers: sales to other businesses are exempt from tax. In this example, a retail sales tax would involve a 10 per cent tax being levied on the sales of the publican to his customers, who are the final consumers. The publican would add 10 per cent to the price charged to his clients, who would thus end up paying €6,000 plus 10 per cent, or €6,600, and he would send the €600 in tax to the government. A certification scheme would need to be put in place proving that the publican and the brewer were businesses, and that the sales of beer to the pub, and barley to the brewery, were thus tax-exempt.[15] There would be no artificial, tax-based reason for the pub, the brewery and the farm to merge, since the sales from farm to brewery and from brewery to pub are tax-exempt in all circumstances.

Finally, let us imagine that the government imposes a 10 per cent value added tax. Like the turnover tax, this is imposed on the sales of each of the three businesses in the example above. However, it does not give rise to an artificial incentive for the three to merge. The farmer sells his barley to the brewer for €1,000 plus 10 per cent, or €1,100. He provides the brewer with an invoice stating that this total sum included a VAT payment of €100, and sends the €100 to the government. He ends up with €1,000 for himself, just as if there had not been a tax at all. The brewer sells his beer to the publican for €3,000 plus 10 per cent, or €3,300. Again, he provides the publican with an invoice stating that €300 of this total sum consisted of VAT. He then sends the government the money that he collected in VAT, €300, minus the money that he paid in VAT when buying the barley (€100), or €200. It is this ability of businesses to deduct from the taxes due on their sales the money that they paid in tax when buying inputs that defines a VAT. You will notice that the money that the brewer sends to the government (€200) is equal to 10 per cent of his value-added (€2,000), hence the name of the tax. Also notice that the brewer ends up with €2,000 after all of these transactions have been undertaken, just as if there had not been a tax at all (he takes €3,300 from the pub, sends €200 to the government, and pays €1,100 to the farmer). Finally, the pub sells €6,000 worth of beer to the final consumers, and again charges 10 per cent in tax. The customers pay €6,600 for their beer. The pub sends to the government the amount it received in VAT on these sales (€600) minus the money that it paid in VAT when buying the beer (€300), or €300. Again, you will notice that €300 is 10 per cent of the pub's value-added (€3,000), and that the pub ends up with €3,000 (taking €6,600 from its customers, sending €300 to the government, and paying €3,300 to the brewer) – just as if there had not been a tax at all.

The total tax take in this example is €600 – the sum of the €100 sent by the farmer to the government, the €200 sent by the brewer, and the €300 sent by the publican. The three businesses are as well off as they would have been without a tax, since it is not they who pay the tax.[16] Rather, it is the final consumers who effectively pay the tax, since they are charged €600 more than they would have been in its absence. In other words, the VAT in this example ends up having precisely the same effects on all three businesses and on the final consumers as a retail sales tax. So why bother with what seems like a very complicated way of achieving exactly the same thing? The major perceived advantage of VAT is that retail sales taxes are collected only when goods are sold to final consumers: in the example above, the entire €600 would be collected in one go when the pub sells beer to its customers. In contrast, VAT is collected in stages – three stages in our example. This makes it less easy to evade, or at least to evade entirely. Another practical issue regards who pays the retail sales tax. In principle, it is only the final consumer: that is the whole point of a retail sales tax. However, in practice this seems difficult to achieve: one study found that on average 40 per cent of American states' retail sales taxes were paid by businesses rather than consumers.[17] This implies that retail sales taxes can give rise to the distorting incentives described above, but it also implies that value-added taxes have important practical advantages when it comes to international trade – which is where European integration comes in.

The 1947 General Agreement on Tariffs and Trade, which we encountered in Chapter 2, did not just deal with tariffs and quotas. It also specified that countries could not impose indirect taxes on imported goods that were higher than those imposed on equivalent domestic goods – such behaviour would obviously constitute (badly) disguised protectionism.[18] This means in practice – again taking our example above – that a pub in France would need to impose the same sales tax (or indeed excise duty, since we are talking about alcohol) on Belgian and French beer. The GATT also prohibited export subsidies for non-primary products: countries were not allowed to give their companies unfair competitive advantages in other markets by subsidizing their sales abroad.[19] At the same time, however, countries were allowed to exempt their exports from domestic sales taxes. Otherwise, a good being exported would have to pay not only the domestic sales tax in the exporting country, but the domestic sales tax in the importing country – leaving it at an obvious disadvantage relative to local competitors in the importing country, whose goods would only be taxed once. What if domestic sales taxes had already been paid on a good being exported, because they had been paid on inputs used in the production of that good? For example, what if the Belgian brewer had already paid sales taxes on his purchases of barley? In that case, it was permissible to refund him those taxes before he exported his beer.

But in practice calculating the sales taxes that had already been paid by a producer could be tricky, even with retail sales taxes – as we have seen, these are often in fact paid on sales of inputs to businesses rather than on sales to final consumers. And turnover taxes were even less transparent from this point of view. Exactly how many sales taxes had already been paid per litre of beer, let alone on a motor car? By the 1950s France had a VAT, but other countries had a variety of sales and turnover taxes that made such calculations very difficult. If you couldn't accurately calculate the taxes embodied in a product that had to be refunded to the exporter, you had to estimate them – and this gave governments the opportunity to overestimate, to over-refund, and in effect to subsidize their companies' exports. This is why the Treaty of Rome decreed that 'The Commission shall consider how the legislation of the various Member States concerning turnover taxes, excise duties and other forms of indirect taxation, including countervailing measures applicable to trade between Member States, can be harmonized in the interest of the common market.'

Eventually, the member states converged on the value added tax as the ideal solution to these problems, and in 1967 they agreed to replace existing sales taxes with VAT. Ever since then, new member states have been obliged to adopt a VAT system, if they have not already done so. With VAT, it becomes straightforward to calculate and deduct sales taxes that have been previously paid by producers from the value of goods being exported. Let us take the example of the Belgian brewer selling to France, and let us assume that the structure of the brewing industry is exactly the same as before. However, let us also assume that the Belgian VAT rate is 20 per cent. The Belgian brewer has €3,000 worth of beer to sell, and has paid €1,200 to the farmer for his barley, of which €200 (20 per cent of €1,000) was VAT. If he sold his beer to a pub in Belgium he would charge €3,600, remit €400 (equal to €600 minus €200) to the government, and keep €2,000 for himself. What if he sells to a pub in France? Sales to other countries are 'zero rated', that is to say no VAT is charged on them. The Belgian brewer would thus sell his beer to the French pub for €3,000. He would then be reimbursed for the VAT he had paid when buying the barley, namely €200. Once again, he gets to keep €2,000. Crucially, it is very easy for the tax authorities to see how much the Belgian brewer should be reimbursed, since this is simply the amount stated on the invoice given to him by the Belgian farmer. As for the French pub, when buying the beer from the Belgian brewer it would immediately pay the French state the tax due on that purchase, but calculated at the French rate. If that rate is 10 per cent, as in the earlier example, this would amount to €300, which is the same as would have been paid if the French pub had bought its beer from a French brewer.

In principle this all works very efficiently. In practice there is scope for fraud, based on the fact that the Belgian brewer is being paid money by the Belgian government, and is not sending the government any sales-related VAT to offset this. You therefore need to make sure that the beer in question is indeed being exported, rather than being sold illegally in Belgium. You also need to make sure that French VAT is paid on the beer when it is imported into France. Before the advent of the Single Market, border controls were an important part of the administrative apparatus required to ensure that fraud was not occurring, that the goods that were supposed to be exported were in fact being exported, and that all taxes that were legally due were paid. The VAT on exports was refunded at the export stage; border controls ensured that all goods that were supposed to be exported were in fact exported; and the VAT on imports was levied at the border by customs authorities. However, all this required physical border formalities, and as we saw earlier the 1992 programme sought to do away with these. What was the solution?[20]

Back to 1992

The Cockfield White Paper had warned that 'The removal of fiscal barriers may well be contentious' and so it proved. In the end, a transitional arrangement was put in place that survives to this day. First of all, individual shoppers were allowed to cross borders, buy goods for their personal use, and return home unhindered. High-tax member states thus accepted that they would lose a certain amount of tax revenue, but since this is individual citizens buying for their own consumption rather than businesses, the losses are for the most part small, and acceptable given the benefits to everyone of abolishing frontier controls. Second, there was some limited harmonization of tax rates. The general VAT rate was to be no lower than 15 per cent, although exceptions could be made on a limited number of products. And third, physical controls at the border were replaced by the self-reporting of firms.

In order for the exporting firm to receive its VAT rebate, it had to provide the authorities with the VAT identification number of its customer in the other member state. That customer would then pay the import VAT due when making their next periodic VAT return. (In France, for example, businesses have to submit monthly returns unless they are below a certain size, in which case they can submit them quarterly.)[21] Instead of customs controls at the frontier, there is the VAT Information Exchange System (VIES), which collates all of the information provided by exporting and importing firms regarding their sales to and purchases from other member states and provides this to member state tax authorities. As we will see later in the book, this point is crucial for Brexit: without the VIES, inspections at borders would become both essential and inevitable.

The Politics of the Single Market Programme

Abolishing the 297 barriers identified in Cockfield's White Paper was an immense political undertaking, involving as it did twelve member states (Portugal and Spain having joined the European Communities in 1986) whose elected politicians were responsible to their voters and had many vested interests to worry about. As we saw in Chapter 3, ever since the 1960s the so-called Luxembourg Compromise had ensured that member states could veto European legislation whenever what they regarded as vital national interests were at stake. Since the whole point of many of the barriers to be eliminated was that they sought to protect politically influential vested interests, allowing each member state the right to veto every change required to construct a Single Market would have doomed the process from the beginning. The Single European Act therefore specified that when it came to matters concerning the construction of the Single Market, decisions should be made by qualified majority voting – a system that requires not only that a certain proportion of the member states vote in favour, but that they represent another specified proportion of the population of the member states as a whole. (The precise rules have varied over time: a qualified majority today requires at least 55 per cent of member states, representing at least 65 per cent of the total EU population, to vote in favour.)[22] In this manner, bigger member states have considerably more power in reaching decisions than smaller ones.

There were two major exceptions to the principle of qualified majority voting, reflecting their political sensitivity (not least in Britain): decisions regarding taxation and the free movement of people still had to be taken unanimously.[23] Nonetheless, the Single European Act represented a major step towards a more supranational Europe, in that it allowed for the possibility that a member state would find itself in a position where it had to implement legislation with which it disagreed. Furthermore, there was always the risk that as time progressed the list of policy areas deemed to be relevant to the Single Market would expand. And yet Mrs Thatcher and the British government were at the time strongly in favour of this shift towards majority voting, in that it helped to create a competitive and freer market across Europe: 'Thatcherism on a European scale' as the slogan went. As Hugo Young says, 'Everyone in the Thatcher Cabinet backed it, and so did almost everyone in the Thatcher Party – storing up trouble for the day when it became an inconvenient memory. For their eyes weren't open, and they couldn't really face the consequences of what they had done.'[24]

Qualified majority voting accomplished what it was supposed to do. The legislative programme identified by the White Paper was speedily accomplished, and the Single Market became a reality, at least insofar as goods are concerned – the Single Market for services has remained a work in progress, much to the occasional irritation of British politicians given the importance of services to the UK economy. The remaining capital controls between member states also came down, meaning that there were no restrictions on the ability to buy and sell financial products across borders – much to the benefit of the City of London. But symbolically, as the White Paper anticipated, the most visible consequence of the Single Market programme was the abolition of frontier controls. On 1 January 1993 these came down between the twelve member states of the European Communities – or the European Union as it was now called. That is another story to which we shall return later in this book.

One of the borders along which frontier controls were dismantled was that between Ireland and Northern Ireland, and it is to Ireland that we now must turn.

CHAPTER 6

Ireland, Europe and the Good Friday Agreement

A French rugby commentator used to ask, when Les Bleus played against Ireland, 'What is the difference between the Irish and the British?' To which the answer was, 'The Irish are not British.' The joke is reminiscent of Samuel Beckett's famous reply to a French journalist who had asked him whether he was English: 'Au contraire.'

As a kid growing up in Brussels I became used to explaining to people that I wasn't in fact British, but Irish. At the same time, however, I began to see that there was a reason why they were confused. My British friends and I spoke the same language, ate the same food, had the same slightly agricultural approach to playing football, quite distinct from the way that the Dutch or Italian kids in the school practised the sport. Viewed from further afield the similarities no doubt seem even greater, and sometimes so is the confusion. A University College Dublin colleague of mine once told an elderly American lady that he was Irish – 'Ireland,' she replied. 'Is that the little one, or the top of the big one?'

It's hard for the Irish to see any upside to Brexit. One consolation, perhaps, may be that other Europeans will be less inclined to confuse our country with our next-door neighbour.

For although Britain and Ireland must seem similar in many respects when viewed from the continent or outside Europe we are actually two quite different countries, and this will become much more apparent to everyone after 2019.

Up until this point I have been guilty of systematic inaccuracy. If you haven't noticed, this is because everybody does it, and you are no doubt used to it. Until now, I have used the terms 'United Kingdom' and 'Britain' interchangeably, as if they were the same thing. But they are not: Britain, or Great Britain, refers to the island comprising England, Scotland and Wales. The state of which Britain is a part, on the other hand, is the United Kingdom of Great Britain *and* Northern Ireland. Similarly, I have systematically used the adjective 'British', since as far as I am aware there is no adjective corresponding to the proper noun 'the United Kingdom'.[1] But as George Orwell warned us, 'the slovenliness of our language makes it easier for us to have foolish thoughts.'[2] And you do have to wonder if this quirk of the English language, this linguistic tendency to confuse Britain and the United Kingdom, not only reflects but also helps to amplify the neglect of Northern Ireland in the British consciousness.

Northern Ireland barely got a mention in the Brexit campaign of 2016. Nor did Ireland more generally. Neither 'Ireland' nor 'Northern Ireland' merits an entry in the index of Tim Shipman's gripping and authoritative account of how the 2016 referendum was lost and won, and that is an accurate reflection of what happened.[3] But if Ireland was irrelevant to Brexit before the referendum, it has turned out to be the central issue ever since. The Irish border question may lead the British government to eventually seek the softest of all Brexits – a Brexit in name only, as some critics dismissively refer to it. Or it may lead to the hardest of all Brexits – a Brexit in which the UK crashes out of the European Union without any deal at all, and in default of its existing obligations to its former European partners. At the time of writing these words (September 2018) it is impossible to know what the outcome will be, but whatever the outcome the question of Ireland will have been central to the process of getting there.

Partition

Fortunately it is not necessary to recall the entire history of British involvement in Ireland in order to understand the main issues at stake today. A little bit of background is in order, however. The story begins in the late twelfth century, with the Norman invasions of Ireland. Since the invaders owed allegiance to the King of England, they are frequently referred to as Anglo-Norman, and the King eventually became known as the Lord of Ireland. The native Irish retained control over a large part of the island, however, and it was not until the sixteenth and seventeenth centuries that the English (for at this stage we can definitely refer to them as English) established effective control over the country, and that the Lord of Ireland became its King.

Perhaps it was inevitable in a violent world that the larger of the two islands would eventually conquer the smaller. But the process was made even more violent by the divisions that appeared within Western Christianity following the Reformation, and by the fact that while Ireland remained Catholic, Britain for the most part did not. In the context of the wars of religion, which supplied the perceived need, and the colonization of America that was happening at the same time, which supplied the model, it no doubt made sense for the Crown to expropriate Irish Catholic landowners in Ulster (the northernmost of the four historic provinces of Ireland), and grant their lands to English and Scottish Protestant settlers whose loyalty to the Protestant King was guaranteed. But this led to a society in which religious and national divisions coincided, and to a cycle of atrocities and counter-atrocities amplified by political turmoil in Britain itself – the English Civil War of the middle of the seventeenth century, and the overthrow of the Catholic King James by the Protestant (and Dutch) King William a few decades later. And this religious context also made it much more difficult for Ireland to ever be fully incorporated within the larger political unit. It may come as a surprise to the French, familiar with the Revocation of the Edict of Nantes, to learn that Protestants were also capable of being intolerant when they were in power, but in fact they were, and anti-Catholic legislation persisted in Ireland for many decades.[4] Indeed, as noted earlier in this book, anti-Catholic prejudice, as opposed to legislation, survived in Britain well into the twentieth century and helped colour attitudes towards Europe.[5] This cannot have helped in making the Catholic Irish accept rule from London as legitimate, and it presumably didn't help in getting their rulers to accept the Irish as their fellow nationals either.

In 1707 England and Scotland merged to form the United Kingdom of Great Britain.[6] The monarch was now King both of the United Kingdom and (separately) of Ireland. This changed a century later: the American and French revolutions of 1776 and 1789 were followed in 1798 by a republican revolution in Ireland, supported by France, that was suppressed only after a great deal of bloodshed. While the leadership of the revolution was notable for the way in which it incorporated both Catholics and Protestants, on the ground there were once again sectarian atrocities on both sides. Partly as a consequence of the revolution, on 1 January 1801 Ireland and Britain were merged to form the United Kingdom of Great Britain and Ireland. While Irish republicanism would continue to seek independence from Britain during the centuries that followed, it would eventually become a mostly Catholic phenomenon.

By the end of the nineteenth century an alternative strand of Irish nationalism had risen to the fore. Reformist rather than revolutionary, Home Rulers such as the Southern Protestant landowner Charles Stewart Parnell sought land reform, so that Irish tenant farmers could own their own land, and Home Rule, involving a limited degree of self-government for Ireland under the British Crown. Parnell's Irish Parliamentary Party became the dominant force in Irish nationalist politics, and by the second decade of the twentieth century seemed to be on the verge of achieving its aims. However, this prospect prompted the creation in 1912 of the Ulster Volunteers, a paramilitary force with strong Protestant support opposed to Home Rule.[7] This in turn prompted the formation of the Irish Volunteers, some of whose members favoured Home Rule, and some of whom went further and supported the creation of an Irish Republic. Both the Ulster Volunteers and the Irish Volunteers imported arms into Ireland. The gathering crisis took on a potentially sinister constitutional nature when elements in the British Army made it clear that they would not be prepared to act against the Ulster Volunteers, should the politicians in London order them to do so. Who knows what might have happened had the First World War not intervened – some feared a civil war. As it was, the wider war erupted in August 1914, and Parliament agreed to Home Rule on condition that this would only come into effect at the end of the war. The Ulster Volunteers offered their services to the British war effort, as did the majority of the Irish Volunteers. But a minority refused, among them a small group of republicans led by Patrick Pearse, who in 1916 staged an armed rebellion in Dublin.

It was understandable that in the midst of a world war such an act should have been suppressed without mercy. At the same time, one has to wonder whether artillery shells would have been used to suppress a revolt in a crowded city centre in Britain itself. When the leaders of the rising were executed, public sentiment became radicalised, and the republican Sinn Féin Party gradually took over from the old Irish Parliamentary Party as the voice of Irish nationalism. In the general election of December 1918 they swept to victory, winning 73 out of the 105 Irish seats. In Ulster, however, Protestant Unionists (that is to say, people seeking to retain the Union with Great Britain) won 23 out of 38 seats.

In January 1919 those Sinn Féin MPs who were able to attend (for several were in prison) attended the first meeting of the Dáil in Dublin, which issued a declaration of Irish independence. A guerrilla war ensued, fought by the Irish Republican Army (IRA)[8] on behalf of the government that had been appointed by the Dáil. A mark of the radicalization that had occurred since 1916 is the fact that the fighters included some, like my grandfather, who had previously fought on behalf of the British during the world war. A truce was declared in July 1921, and in December of that year a treaty was signed giving Ireland 'the same constitutional status in the Community of Nations known as the British Empire as the Dominion of Canada, the Commonwealth of Australia, the Dominion of New Zealand, and the Union of South Africa'.[9] This was not the republic that had been hoped for, but it was a lot more than the Home Rule an earlier generation had aspired to. On 6 December 1922 the Irish Free State came into existence, and although the link with the British Empire and Crown survived, Ireland was effectively independent.

On the following day, however, Northern Ireland exercised its right under the treaty to opt out of the new Irish state and remain part of the United Kingdom: the United Kingdom of Great Britain and Ireland was now the United Kingdom of Great Britain and Northern Ireland. The terms 'Northern Ireland' and 'Ulster' are sometimes used interchangeably, but as in the case of 'Britain' and 'United Kingdom' this is inaccurate. Northern Ireland only comprises six of the nine counties of Ulster, the six being chosen on the grounds that they were the largest subsection of Ulster that could be relied upon to have a durable Protestant, and hence Unionist, majority. (Catholics only made up 34.4 per cent of the population in the six counties in question in 1911.)[10] Northern Ireland thus defined had its origins in the aftermath of the war, when the British government tried to figure out a way of implementing the Home Rule it had promised in 1914. Given the pre-war tensions between Irish and Ulster Volunteers, and the strong objection by Ulster Protestants to being included in a

Home Rule Ireland governed from Dublin, the solution (embodied in the 1920 Government of Ireland Act) was to set up two Home Rule Parliaments, one for Northern Ireland in Belfast and the other for the rest of the island in Dublin. Home Rule for Northern Ireland came into effect in May 1921, at which stage the island became effectively partitioned into two jurisdictions.

The political divide between North and South widened with the establishment of the Irish Free State in December 1922: the frontier between them was no longer internal to the United Kingdom but an international one. And the border between Northern Ireland and the Irish Free State was given a physical form on 1 April 1923 when the Irish Free State left the UK customs union, regaining control over its own tariffs and excise duties. Customs posts immediately appeared along the frontier. It was an April Fool's joke that would last seventy years.[11]

Ireland After Partition

South and west of the new border (for we should always remember that the northernmost county in Ireland, Donegal, is in Ulster but not in Northern Ireland – see Map 10.1 in Chapter 10) – constitutional change occurred fairly quickly. The leaders of the new state, who had in many cases been involved in a guerrilla war against the British Crown just a few years previously, set about making Irish independence a reality. At the same time, they accepted the Dominion status accorded to the Irish Free State under the treaty, and participated in the imperial conferences that we encountered in Chapter 2. The British King remained the head of state, just as in Australia, Canada or New Zealand. This continued link to the Crown prompted a vicious civil war in 1922 and 1923, with both Sinn Féin and the IRA splitting over the question of whether or not to accept the Treaty. The war was eventually won by the pro-treaty side, whose army became the official National Army of the Irish Free State; the losing side's armed forces retained the label 'IRA', and the IRA continued to exist after the civil war as an illegal organization regarding itself as the sole rightful heir of those who had fought in 1916 and the War of Independence.

Many of the new states that emerged in the aftermath of the First World War started life as democracies but soon became authoritarian. Ireland is an honourable exception. In 1932 the party representing the anti-treaty forces that had been defeated in the Civil War, Fianna Fáil, came to power and remained there for the next sixteen years. Neither the army nor the police force, which had fought and won a brutal war against their new rulers less than a decade previously, opposed the transfer of power, which occurred smoothly. The new Irish leader, Éamon de Valera, proceeded to dismantle most of the links with the British Crown. In 1936 he deleted the references to the King in the constitution of the Irish Free State: the only role now played by the monarch related to such diplomatic formalities as the presentation of diplomatic credentials and the signing of treaties. The following year a new constitution replaced the King with a directly elected President as head of state, and the name of the state was changed to Ireland, the name by which it is still known today. Since the British King continued to fulfil the diplomatic functions referred to above, there was some ambiguity about who the Irish head of state really was. In 1948, however, Ireland ended this uncertainty by unilaterally declaring itself to be a republic, thus formalizing what had in fact been the case for the previous twelve years.[12] The last vestigial role of the King was now extinguished, and Ireland left the British Commonwealth.

In response, the British government passed the Ireland Act of 1949. This recognized the legitimacy of what had happened, but also stated that 'the Republic of Ireland is not a foreign country for the purposes of any law in force in any part of the United Kingdom'. The result has been that Irish citizens resident in the UK have always enjoyed privileged conditions there, even prior to the two countries joining the EC in 1973, for example being able to vote in all UK elections.[13] The fact that we Irish can also complain about being accorded these privileges, on the grounds that the British ought to recognize our foreign-ness but don't, is of course an extra bonus.

The British Government's Ireland Act also guaranteed that 'in no event will Northern Ireland or any part thereof cease to be part of His Majesty's dominions and of the United Kingdom without the consent of the Parliament of Northern Ireland.' This guarantee to Unionists was in direct contrast with the 1937 Irish Constitution, which asserted that 'The national territory consists of the whole island of Ireland, its islands and the territorial seas.' This territorial dispute would last for a further 50 years, and was a source of constant tension between Ireland and the UK. The tension even spilled over into the way the two states referred to each other. Unlike other countries, the UK referred to Ireland (the state, as opposed to the island) as 'the Republic of Ireland', while Ireland was reluctant to use the term 'Northern Ireland', and by extension 'the United Kingdom of Great Britain and Northern Ireland', preferring to use 'Great Britain' instead. It was only after the 1998 Good Friday (or Belfast) Agreement that the two states finally started calling each other by their official names.[14]

Northern Ireland: From Partition to the Good Friday Agreement

Political development in Northern Ireland was much slower, or if you prefer, the institutional framework set up there in 1921 was much more stable: the Northern Irish Home Rule Parliament established in that year survived for a full 50 years. Northern Ireland largely governed itself, but in a society that was divided along religious lines, and in which religion and political affiliation coincided almost perfectly, this was a mixed blessing. Politics was defined by the issue of the Irish border, with Protestants almost invariably favouring its retention, and Catholics almost always opposed to it – hence the linguistic tendency to use the terms 'Protestant' and 'Unionist', and 'Catholic' and 'Nationalist', interchangeably. There was, almost inevitably, severe sectarian violence in the early 1920s coinciding with the violence on the rest of the island, and while this eventually faded away the society that emerged was deeply divided along religious lines. With demography guaranteeing a Protestant Unionist majority, the Catholic minority faced discrimination in employment and housing.[15] In 1971 the unemployment rate among Catholics was 17.3 per cent, as opposed to 7.6 per cent for the rest of the population.[16]

The 1960s saw a thaw in North–South relations, with

meetings between the Irish Taoiseach Seán Lemass and the Northern Irish Prime Minister Terence O'Neill, and proposals for cross-border cooperation. However, the decade also saw the emergence of a Northern Irish civil rights campaign modelling itself on what was happening in America at the time, which began actively protesting against anti-Catholic discrimination. It included not only representatives of the non-sectarian political left, as well as some young Unionists, but also Irish republicans (the term 'republican' in the Northern Irish context denoting at that time more militant nationalists associated with the IRA). As my colleague Seňia Paseta says, 'The leaders of these organizations emphasized their non-sectarian credentials, but whether the bulk of their supporters shared this view is questionable.'[17]

One of my earliest memories of television is the images of one of these civil rights demonstrations being brutally attacked by the Northern Irish police. My father told me that it was very serious, and he was right. The year 1969 saw the widespread eruption of violence in Northern Ireland; the Irish Taoiseach called (unsuccessfully) for United Nations intervention, and refugee camps were set up on the southern side of the border. The British Army was sent to the province to keep the peace, initially being welcomed by the Catholic population; the IRA split, with the Provisional IRA becoming the dominant faction and embarking on a murderous terrorist campaign targeting the security forces, Protestant civilians and Catholics deemed to be disloyal to the cause. That in turn prompted the introduction of internment without trial and other measures by the security forces, alienating many Catholics. Loyalist terrorists ('loyalist' being the Protestant

equivalent of 'republican') targeted their republican opposite numbers as well as the Catholic population more generally. Ian Paisley, who had led the opposition to the civil rights
movement, founded the radical Democratic Unionist Party
in 1971. In 1972 British paratroopers shot 28 unarmed civilians in Derry, of whom fourteen eventually died, and a mob
in Dublin burned down the British Embassy in response.

Those were just some of the early highlights of 'The Troubles', as they were known, and there were many more to
come. The violence lasted until 1998, and continued sporadi-
cally thereafter. Between 1969 and 1998, 3,489 people were
killed: 59 per cent by republican terrorists, 29 per cent by loyalist terrorists, and 10 per cent by the British security forces.
The violence reached both the British mainland and the Irish
Republic: there were 125 deaths in the former, and 116 in the
latter. Eighteen were killed on the European mainland.[18] The
British Royal family lost Prince Charles's great-uncle and godfather, Lord Mountbatten, murdered by the IRA in 1979; Margaret Thatcher lost her colleague and friend Airey Neave, a
British Member of Parliament, in the same year. An attempt
to murder her in 1984, at the Conservative Party conference
in Brighton, led to the deaths of five people connected with
the party, including yet another MP, Anthony Berry, and permanently disabled the wife of Norman Tebbit, a prominent
British Cabinet Minister. In Ireland Senator Billy Fox was
murdered in 1974, the same year that a series of coordinated
bombs in central Dublin and Monaghan killed 33 civilians, including a woman who was nine months pregnant. For the political classes in both countries, the Troubles were personal.

But the greatest number of victims was in Northern

Ireland itself: 3,232 in the 30 years from 1969 to 1998 inclusive. The population of Northern Ireland in 1971 was 1.5 million, as compared with a metropolitan French population in the same year of 51.3 million:[19] 3,232 deaths in Northern Ireland was thus equivalent to more than 110,000 deaths in France, or ten murders a day, every day, for 30 years. For decades TV news largely consisted of murders, condemnations by politicians and clergymen, funerals and court cases. It is what we all grew up with, even those of us fortunate enough (as far as we were concerned) to live south of the border. It was a devastating, traumatic conflict that overshadowed everything else on the island.

The Good Friday Agreement

There were several attempts by the British and Irish governments to find a political solution to the conflict, beginning as early as 1973 when the Sunningdale Agreement was signed. This proposed a new Northern Ireland Assembly, to be elected by proportional representation rather than the British first past the post system, so as to ensure the fair representation of both communities. A power-sharing executive was to be established, with representatives of both the nationalist and unionist communities, and North–South institutions were to be established: 'a Council of Ministers with executive and harmonizing functions and a consultative role, and a Consultative Assembly with advisory and review functions'.[20] The Irish government 'fully accepted and solemnly declared that there could be no change in the status of Northern Ireland until a majority of the people of Northern Ireland desired a change in that status', while the British government stated that 'If in the future the majority of the people of Northern Ireland should indicate a wish to become part of a united Ireland, the British Government would support that wish.' The agreement collapsed the following year, however, following opposition from many Unionist politicians, strikes and violence.

The years passed, and the violence continued, but beneath the surface relations between British and Irish politicians were slowly being transformed as a result of the two countries' membership of the EC from 1973 onwards. Ministers met regularly in Brussels when attending meetings of the Council of Ministers; the British Prime Minister and Irish Taoiseach met regularly at meetings of the European Council. The two countries discovered that they had many interests in common, and despite continuing tensions over Northern Ireland learned to cooperate with each other on a wide range of issues. Whereas before 1973 the two states had had what a former Irish Taoiseach described as a 'bilateral unequal relationship, which had all the difficulties that go with any bilateral unequal relationship, whether in a family, between states or between businesses', the relationship became normalized in the decades that followed. To take just one example, no British Prime Minister had visited Dublin before 1973, but this changed very soon thereafter. As the Irish Ambassador to London told the British House of Lords European Union Committee in 2016,

> There are probably 25 meetings taking place today at various levels in Brussels. At each meeting, there will be a British delegation and an Irish delegation. In most cases, they will probably have a word together in advance or

afterwards. They might have a discussion about the rugby or whatever other topic. Friendships and connections have been developed over the past 40 years.[21]

The Committee's conclusion that 'Common EU membership has been a vital ingredient in the positive transformation of UK–Irish relations in recent years, and in helping lay the groundwork for the development of the peace process' is almost universally shared.

But European integration also helped change facts on the ground. The customs frontiers that had been set up in April 1923 did not come down in 1965, when Ireland and the UK signed the Anglo-Irish Free Trade Agreement and agreed to abolish most tariffs on each other's products: as we saw in Chapter 3, a free trade area still requires customs controls. While Ireland had agreed to reduce its tariffs on imports of British goods, it had not agreed to reduce its tariffs on imports from elsewhere. Customs inspectors therefore still needed to distinguish between imports of British and Australian lamb, for example.

My colleague John FitzGerald tells the story of how an Irish delegation to London in the 1960s therefore requested that British goods exported to Ireland be clearly labelled as 'Made in Britain', or words to that effect. The British Cabinet Minister Denis Healey asked, with some irritation, whether he was supposed to stamp 'Made in Britain' on the balls of every bullock shipped to Ireland, to which the Irish Minister's retort was that bullocks don't have balls.[22] The anecdote is pedagogical in multiple ways, and provides us with an early illustration of a technological solution to border frictions that – with the best will in the world – could never have worked. To repeat, since the point is often misunderstood, mere free trade areas always and necessarily involve border checks, to ensure that goods from third countries are not given the preferential treatment enjoyed by countries party to the agreement.

Nor did border controls come down from 1973 onwards, when both Ireland and the UK joined the EEC and its customs union. As we saw in Chapter 5, there were still physical barriers to trade at borders between member states because of the technical and fiscal barriers that made frontier controls essential. But with the advent of the Single Market these controls were no longer necessary, and on 1 January 1993 they were, as already stated, eliminated across the European Union. At this stage, the only remaining checkpoints at border crossings between Northern Ireland and the Republic were those that were necessary for security reasons. If those security reasons were to vanish, there would be no need for a visible border at all.

By now a variety of informal talks were ongoing regarding how to end the violence. The Anglo-Irish Agreement of 1985, negotiated by Garrett FitzGerald and Margaret Thatcher, had already given Dublin an advisory role in Northern Ireland while recognizing that Irish unity could only come about with the consent of the people of Northern Ireland. It also promoted cross-border cooperation in a number of areas including security.[23] The Downing Street Declaration, issued by John Major and Albert Reynolds in 1993, was another important step forward. It noted that 'the development of Europe will, of itself, require new approaches to serve interests common to both parts of the island of Ireland, and to Ireland and the United Kingdom as partners in the European Union.' The Irish government agreed that it would, 'as part of a balanced constitutional accommodation, put forward and support proposals for change in the Irish Constitution which would fully reflect the principle of consent in Northern Ireland'. The British government, for its part, reiterated that it had 'no selfish strategic or economic interest in Northern Ireland' and that it was 'for the people of the island of Ireland alone, by agreement between the two parts respectively, to exercise their right of self-determination on the basis of consent, freely and concurrently given, North and South, to bring about a united Ireland, if that is their wish'.[24]

By 1997 Tony Blair was in Downing Street, and Sinn Féin, the political wing of the Provisional IRA, was involved in official multi-party talks in Belfast concerning the future of Northern Ireland.[25] The resulting agreement, signed on Good Friday 1998, and brokered with the active involvement of the American government, was a triumph of what diplomats call constructive ambiguity.[26] Ireland dropped its territorial claim to Northern Ireland, and the corresponding articles of the Irish constitution were amended following a referendum. The UK recognized that the constitutional status of Northern Ireland was a matter solely for the people of the island of Ireland. Both sides agreed that any change in the constitutional status of Northern Ireland could only come about with the consent of the people of Northern Ireland. Both political traditions in Northern Ireland were to be regarded as equally legitimate, and all born in Northern Ireland had the right 'to identify themselves and be accepted as Irish or British, or both, as they may so choose'. In practice this meant that they had the right to both Irish and British citizenship, and could choose to carry either one or both of the two passports in question.

There were three institutional 'strands' to the agreement. The first concerned Northern Ireland itself: a Northern Ireland assembly was established, to be elected by proportional representation, and a power-sharing executive representing both political communities was to manage the internal affairs of Northern Ireland. A series of safeguards was put in place to guarantee fairness and respect for human rights. The second strand established a North–South Ministerial Council to cooperate on a variety of cross-border and all-Ireland issues. And the third strand set up a British–Irish Council, including representatives of both governments and of the devolved administrations of Northern Ireland, Scotland and Wales, as well as representatives from the Isle of Man and Channel Islands In this manner, the identities of all were given institutional form: both those for whom the entire island of Ireland was a natural political unit, and those for whom the East–West links between Britain and Ireland were of paramount importance.

The Provisional IRA and various loyalist terrorist groups agreed to disarm, and eventually did so after several delays and accompanying political crises. Prisoners who were members of organizations maintaining ceasefires were released – in many cases these were people who had been convicted of serious terrorist offences including murder. This was obviously extremely difficult for many victims to accept. But against the injustice of this aspect of the agreement has to be set the end of large-scale political violence in Northern Ireland, and the many lives that have been saved as a result.

The remaining security checkpoints between North and South were eventually removed, and the Irish border became essentially invisible. As I have been emphasizing, this was thanks not only to the peace process and the Good Friday Agreement, but to the European Union's customs union and Single Market. The Good Friday Agreement guaranteed that people living in Northern Ireland who felt themselves to be Irish could be Irish, and that this was entirely legitimate. The border, moreover, was now largely irrelevant in people's lives. In such circumstances, what did it matter if the Republic had dropped its constitutional claim to the North? What did it matter if the North remained *de jure* a part of the United Kingdom?

The rise of an assertive and increasingly well-educated Catholic middle class may have been uncomfortable for many Unionists, but the Good Friday Agreement was good news for them too. The percentage of the Northern Irish population that was Catholic had declined from 33.5 per cent in 1926 to 28 per cent in 1981, but it then started to rise dramatically: to 38.4 per cent in 1991, 40.3 per cent in 2001, and 45.1 per cent in 2011. Demographers began to discuss the day when the majority of the Northern Irish population would be Catholic. But with the peace process more and more Catholics decided that they were comfortable living in Northern Ireland, whether as Irish citizens or not. And sociologists began to track the rise of a new 'Northern Irish' identity, distinct from either Britishness or Irishness. In the 2011 Census just 11 per cent of Catholics identified themselves as 'British only', as compared with 67 per cent of Protestants.[27] But 11 per cent is greater than zero, and a further 28 per cent of Catholics identified themselves as 'Northern Irish only'.[28] Demography, it seemed, might not be destiny: perhaps Northern Ireland, which had been constructed with the specific aim of ensuring a Protestant majority, might survive that majority's demise.

The European Union did not solve the Northern Irish conflict: powerful forces internal to that society were pushing all sides towards a political resolution. But the fact that both the UK and Ireland were members of the European Union was crucial in providing the context in which the conflict was eventually solved. As we have seen, it was absolutely essential in normalizing relationships between the two states involved, namely Ireland and the United Kingdom. It was also crucial in eliminating border controls, which in turn made it much easier for Northern nationalists to accept a solution in which they were still residents (but not necessarily citizens) of the United Kingdom. As the former Taoiseach John Bruton said in 2016,

> the fact that at the moment we are both members of the European Union means that there is effectively no border in terms of a barrier within the island of Ireland. That creates opportunities for people not to feel isolated.
> A sense of isolation in terms of being disregarded or in a permanent minority lay behind some of the very aggressive tactics that were adopted by republicans and indeed at times by loyalists as well.[29]

As happened elsewhere in Europe, shared membership of the EU made the boundaries between its member states less important than they had been before, and this was good for peace.

The Preamble to the Good Friday Agreement speaks of the two states 'Wishing to develop still further the unique relationship between their peoples and the close co-operation between their countries as friendly neighbours and as partners in the European Union', and the agreement contains multiple references to the EU. For Bertie Ahern, the Irish Taoiseach involved in negotiating the agreement, these references were vital.[30] As George Mitchell, Bill Clinton's envoy to Northern Ireland, who played a critical role in the process, said to the BBC, 'I don't think the European Union was essential in the [Good Friday Agreement] talks themselves, but I believe the talks would never have occurred had there not been a European Union.'[31]

And herein lies a considerable irony. The traditional British attitude towards Europe had been to welcome its economic aspects, but to be suspicious of its political aspirations and the continental rhetoric according to which its main achievement had been to make war unthinkable in Europe. But the United Kingdom itself provides us with one of the best examples of Europe as peace project. Whether it is the very success of the Irish peace process, or an occasional tendency to ignore Northern Ireland, that has blinded some in Britain to this stunningly obvious fact is a matter for debate.

We are used to seeing our politicians squabbling about financial matters in Brussels, and that is right and proper, for they are arguing on behalf of the taxpayers to whom they are accountable. The core of the EU remains its customs union and Single Market. But Europe has always been a political project. It has always been about peace. It was never just about the money.

CHAPTER 7

Europe and the Irish Economic Miracle

As we saw in the previous chapter, membership of the European Union had a profound transformative effect on Irish politics. Not only did it help in providing a background against which a decades-long territorial dispute could be resolved and a bloody conflict ended; for Ireland it was a way of getting out from under Britain's shadow and becoming more fully independent. Far from being seen as limiting Irish sovereignty, EU membership was understood as being an important contributor to both sovereignty and national self-respect. Such political considerations help to explain why Irish attitudes towards the European Union are so different from attitudes in Britain, but they are not the entire explanation. For membership of the EU also helped transform Ireland's economic fortunes, and crucially it did so largely by making Ireland less dependent on Britain. This economic history continues to shape the way in which both politicians and ordinary people in Ireland view the EU, and it helps to explain why almost no one in the country is tempted to follow Britain out of the door.

Irish economic performance under British rule was disappointing and occasionally tragic.[1] Ireland's population in 1845, on the eve of the Famine, stood at around 8.5 million.

Over the course of the subsequent five years about one million people died, and a further million emigrated. The Famine ushered in a wave of mass emigration which persisted into the twentieth century, and which led to a continuously declining population throughout the late nineteenth century at a time when Europe as a whole was experiencing a population explosion. Indeed, the population of the 26 counties that became the Irish Free State in 1922 continued to fall: it stood at 6.5 million in 1841, 3.0 million in 1926, and just 2.8 million in 1961.[2]

Ireland's history meant that the British and Irish economies were closely intertwined. The newly independent Irish Free State was overwhelmingly specialized in agricultural activities, and its agricultural exports went overwhelmingly to the United Kingdom. The Irish and British labour markets were very tightly integrated with each other. The Irish Free State, and later the Irish Republic, would share a common legal system with Britain, as well as a common currency (until 1979) and many other institutions. For much of the twentieth century it makes sense to regard Ireland as one small regional component of a broader British and Irish economy. And the problem was that this broader British and Irish economy, within which the British component was obviously overwhelmingly dominant, was a poor performer within the wider European context. Only when Ireland emancipated itself from excessive reliance on its nearest neighbour was it able to finally grow as rapidly as other poor countries around the European periphery.

Assessing Irish Performance

In order to assess Ireland's economic performance, we need a benchmark.[3] Because of Ireland's history a natural tendency is to use the UK, but that is a mistake. The UK performed poorly relative to most European economies: by using it as a benchmark we are setting the bar too low.

A second alternative is to compare Ireland with similar regions inside the UK – Northern Ireland most obviously, but perhaps also Scotland and Wales. As we will see, doing so provides us with useful insights, but again, by comparing Ireland with regions located within the slowly growing UK economy we are again setting the bar too low.

A third alternative, which makes more sense, is to compare Ireland with other relatively poor economies around the European periphery. Greece, Portugal and Spain were all as poor as Ireland at the start of the twentieth century, if not poorer. They therefore faced many of the same obstacles, but also shared the same potential for rapid growth based on catching up on the industrial core. How did Ireland do compared with these economies? Indeed, how did Ireland do compared with European economies more generally?

It is a matter of statistical fact that within Western Europe, countries that were initially poorer have grown more rapidly than countries that were initially richer during the twentieth century. In other words, poorer economies have tended to converge on richer ones, mostly as a result of importing best practice technologies already adopted elsewhere. We don't have reliable national income evidence for Ireland before 1926, so Figure 7.1 plots initial income levels, per

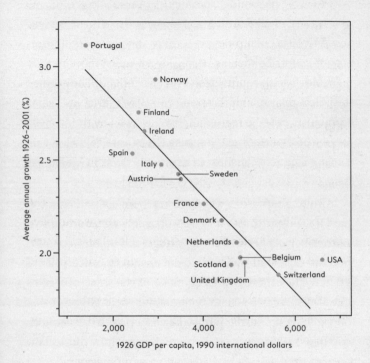

Figure 7.1

Initial income and subsequent growth, 1926–2001

Source: Broadberry and Klein (2012). GNP rather than GDP is used for Ireland, using adjustment ratios kindly provided by Rebecca Stuart. Her data go back to 1944 so I have simply assumed that GNP was the same proportion of GDP in previous years.

capita, in 1926 against average growth per annum over the course of the subsequent 75 years. I have done this for the broadest available sample of European countries that managed to avoid becoming Communist later in the century, as well as the United States. As can be seen, there is a very clear negative relationship between these two variables. Initially poor countries such as Portugal grew much more rapidly than initially rich countries such as Switzerland. The average statistical relationship between these two variables (what economists call 'the regression line') is given by the straight line in the figure. As can be seen, the 'statistical fit' of this convergence relationship is remarkably tight, in that most countries are very closely clustered around this line.

Strikingly, Ireland's economic performance during the 75 years following 1926 was *exactly* what you would have expected, given Ireland's initial income level and the tendency of poorer countries to converge on the rich: Ireland lies neither above nor below, but precisely on the regression line. There was nothing unusual about Irish growth over this period taken as a whole. The timing of Irish growth was, however, highly unusual.

The Interwar Period and the Second World War: 1922–50

During the first ten years of Irish independence the new state's trade policy was, comparatively speaking, remarkably liberal. The election of Fianna Fáil in 1932 coincided with a dramatic shift towards protection, but there was nothing unusual about this. *Everybody* adopted protectionist policies following the onset of the Great Depression in 1929. As we saw in Chapter 2, even the traditionally free-trading British moved decisively towards protection from November 1931 onward – that is to say, before Ireland.

Ireland was very protectionist during the 1930s, but not unusually so.[4] A striking feature of its economic policy during this period, given what came later, was its attempts to restrict the foreign ownership of Irish-based firms. However, Ireland was by no means alone in adopting such restrictions, and they were often evaded by means of fancy legal footwork, as indeed was the case in other countries. More unusual was the so-called Economic War with the UK, which lasted from 1932 until 1938. This had its origins in pre-independence schemes to transfer land from British landowners to Irish tenant farmers. The Irish Free State inherited the obligation to transfer money to Britain to compensate these landowners. When de Valera came to power he refused to continue the practice; the British government retaliated with measures restricting agricultural imports from Ireland; and Ireland counter-retaliated. The dispute was eventually settled on terms highly favourable to the Irish. A capitalized £100 million liability was settled with a £10 million lump sum payment, and Ireland gained control of three ports which had remained under the control of the British Royal Navy under the terms of the 1921 treaty. Even taking the undoubted costs of the Economic War (which hurt larger farmers particularly badly) into account, it is entirely plausible that its net economic impact was actually beneficial.[5]

Not only were Ireland's economic *policies* typical during this period, so was its economic *performance*. The problem, of course, was that a typical performance during the Great

Depression was very bad indeed. And the war that followed was also very difficult for the Irish economy, even though the country was spared the horrors of the fighting. Imports of energy and other essential requirements were very scarce; domestic industry suffered accordingly. As a predominantly agricultural economy, with no heavy industry to speak of, the Irish Free State did not benefit from the demand for war-related *matériel* in the way that Scotland or Northern Ireland did. Even worse, it found itself selling its agricultural output to a hard-pressed British customer, which quite understandably used its monopoly position to lower the prices it paid for Irish agricultural produce.

In common with almost all of Western Europe, Ireland experienced a strong boom between 1945 and 1950. As noted in Chapter 5, in formerly belligerent powers, especially on the continent, the boom largely took the form of reconstruction. In the Irish case it was far more consumption-driven, as consumers made up for lost time and bought American and other imported goods. Construction also benefited, as did industry.[6] Such a consumption-driven boom was surely less sustainable than the more investment-based booms experienced in continental Europe at the time. Nevertheless, the overall impression that one gets when placing Irish economic policies between 1922 and 1950 into a comparative perspective is that there was nothing unusually perverse or self-destructive about Irish policy choices during this period. Irish politicians were relatively liberal during the 1920s, and were protectionist like everybody else from 1932 onwards. They were hardly to blame for the deprivations of the Second World War, nor could they be praised for the inevitable recovery that followed. And the country's economic performance during the first 30 years of independence was also pretty typical for the time.

Ireland's not so Golden Age

In contrast, Ireland's performance during the subsequent 25 years was very disappointing. Whereas Ireland had been an average performer during the dismal interwar period, it performed well below average during Europe's 'Golden Age'. Figure 7.2 shows that Irish growth during this period was much lower than it should have been compared to others, given how poor Ireland was at the outset. The 1950s were particularly bad (Panel A), and the GNP (aggregate income) data plotted for Ireland in the figure understate the case, if it is the living standards of ordinary people that we are concerned with. Throughout post-war Europe governments erected modern welfare states, but Ireland lagged far behind. If independent Ireland can be said to have 'failed' during any period, it did so most obviously during this decade.

Irish underperformance continued during the 1960s. As can be seen from Panel B of Figure 7.2, this was the decade during which Greece, Portugal and Spain experienced their economic miracles. Ireland, by contrast, was still an underperformer. Importantly, a comparison with Britain alone would miss this: from 1960 onwards the Irish economy grew more rapidly than the British one. But growing more rapidly than an economy which was itself an underperformer was not enough to prevent Ireland from falling even further behind mainstream Europe. Why was Ireland's performance so poor during these two crucial decades? I want to highlight two reasons.[7] The first has to do with delayed liberalization, and the second with Ireland's excessive dependence on the poorly performing British economy.

A first explanation for poor Irish performance during the European Golden Age, and particularly during the 1950s, is the delay in reversing interwar protectionist policies. These policies were, as already noted, not unusual in the context of the 1930s, and were maybe even beneficial at a time when everyone was protecting their domestic markets; when an export-oriented growth strategy was therefore not feasible; and when jobs were scarce everywhere.[8] But by the 1950s protectionism was clearly no longer appropriate. As we have seen, European countries were gradually removing barriers to trade and integrating their economies with each other – first within the context of the OEEC, and later within the context of the EEC and EFTA. This meant that export-oriented growth strategies could now be, and were in fact, adopted throughout Western Europe, while the rapid growth of the period implied that protection was not needed in order to create jobs. Ireland was slower to lower its tariff barriers than core European economies, behaving instead like other peripheral European economies such as Finland, Greece or Spain. In Ireland's case this relatively slow reduction in tariffs persisted into the 1960s, which was a costly mistake. On the other hand, Ireland was relatively precocious in seeking to attract foreign direct investment. The Industrial Development Authority (IDA) was established as early as 1949, and soon started trying to attract inward multinational investment. Tax relief on export profits was introduced in 1956.[9]

The timing of trade liberalization in Ireland and the rest

A. 1950–60

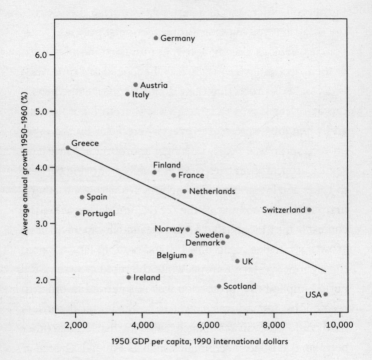

Figure 7.2
Initial income and subsequent growth
A. 1950–60
B. 1960–73
Source: as for Figure 7.1

B. 1960–73

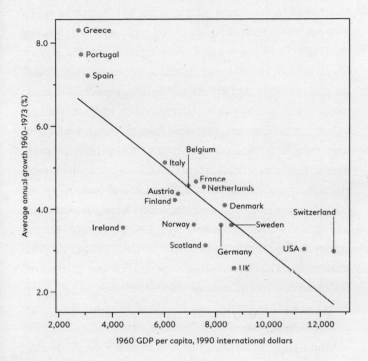

of the European periphery to a large extent reflected the impact of the formation of the EEC and EFTA. No Western European country, no matter how peripheral or economically backward, could avoid responding to this disruption of the prevailing European trade regime. Spain abandoned its long-standing autarkic trade policy regime in 1959, joining the OEEC in that year and embarking on a process of trade liberalization. In 1960 it abolished quantitative restrictions on 90 per cent of its imports, tariffs were gradually reduced over the succeeding years, and the country opened itself up, at least to some extent, to inward foreign investment.[10] Portugal became a founder member of EFTA, although it managed to negotiate a transitional deal allowing it to delay tariff reductions on sectors representing about half of its imports.[11] Finland started lowering tariffs from 1957 onwards, and signed a trade agreement with EFTA in 1961.[12] Greece signed an Association Agreement with the EEC in 1961. This granted it a 22-year transitional period leading to eventual full membership; Greece was allowed to lower its tariffs vis-à-vis the EEC gradually, but benefited from an immediate reduction of EEC tariffs on Greek exports.[13]

And so it is no surprise that Ireland also took the plunge, at more or less exactly the same time, and applied for EEC membership in 1961 along with Britain. Nor is it surprising that when Charles de Gaulle vetoed the UK bid in 1963, and the Irish application lapsed in consequence, Ireland unilaterally cut its tariffs. It did so again in the following year, and in 1965 signed the Anglo-Irish Free Trade Agreement (AIFTA). At this stage Ireland was fully committed to eventual EEC membership, which was finally achieved in 1973.[14]

What *was* unusual about Irish trade liberalization was the extent to which it remained focused on the economic relationship with Britain. To be sure, the AIFTA was seen as a stepping stone towards eventual EEC membership, but despite this European motivation the reality was that Ireland was not yet well integrated with the European economy as a whole. And this was a problem, since access to the British market alone was a far less appealing carrot to dangle in front of potential multinational investors than access to the much larger and more dynamic EEC market.

This leads us to the second explanation for Ireland's relatively poor performance during Europe's Golden Age. If the poor performance in the 1950s was due to protectionism, and if Ireland started to liberalize from the end of the 1950s onwards, why was its performance so disappointing between 1960 and 1973? The comparison with other peripheral European economies, in particular Greece and Portugal, is illuminating. As we have seen in Figure 7.2, Greece and Portugal grew extremely rapidly during this period, while Ireland remained an underperformer. And yet Greek tariffs were even higher than Irish ones during the 1960s. What can explain the superior performances of Greece and Portugal? Why did Ireland not keep pace?

A key factor in the Greek success story was the country's Association Agreement with the EEC. Foreign direct investment (FDI) had been encouraged since the early 1950s, when a series of FDI-friendly policies were introduced,[15] but tariff-free access to EEC markets provided an essential additional stimulus to inward investment. Between 1962 and 1964 more than three-fifths of all manufacturing investment was foreign; Michael Kopsidis and Martin Ivanov argue that FDI during this period 'diversified and modernised Greek industry'.[16] Continent-wide markets for cheap consumer goods produced in Greece also benefited traditional Greek-owned light industry.

In Portugal too EFTA membership is seen as having been crucial in promoting a more outward-looking and dynamic economy. According to one estimate, annual inflows of foreign direct investment were more than 30 times higher during the 1960s than they had been between 1943 and 1960.[17] Portuguese accession to the EEC in the 1980s would lead to a further step increase in inward foreign investment, as happened also in Spain.[18]

A key difference, therefore, between the Irish case on the one hand, and the Portuguese and Greek cases on the other, was that Ireland had neither an Association Agreement with the EEC, nor membership of EFTA.[19] Irish historians often assume that once Ireland had signed the AIFTA, it was to all intents and purposes a free trader, and there is something to this. Local firms had to adjust to British competition, and this was good for efficiency. But there is a big difference between accepting free trade between oneself and just one (not particularly successful) economy, and becoming part of a continent-wide customs union. Until EEC accession, the IDA had to try to sell Ireland as an export platform into the UK and Commonwealth, but this was never as effective a sales pitch as the one it was able to make after 1973. From then on, Ireland was selling into the EEC as a whole, and that made all the difference.

One very striking feature of the data between 1954[20] and

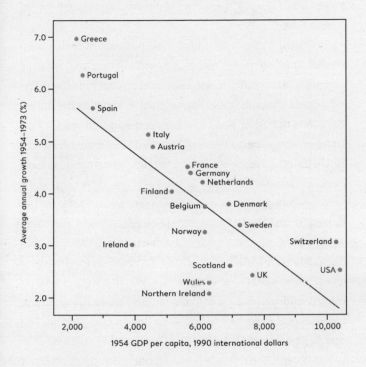

Figure 7.3

Initial income and subsequent growth, 1954–73

Source: as for Figure 7.1. Wales and Northern Ireland: data underlying Dorsett (2013), graciously provided by author. Scotland: data graciously provided by Brian Ashcroft.

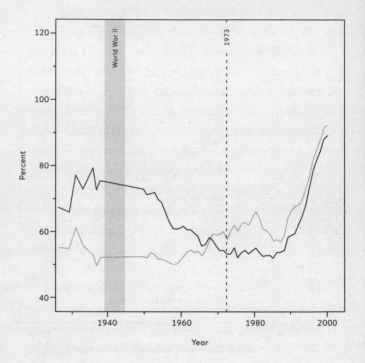

Figure 7.4
Irish GNP per capita as percentage of UK and French GDP per capita

—— As share of France

—— As share of UK

Source: as for Figure 7.1

1973 is that Ireland's growth performance was very close to those of both Northern Ireland and Wales. All three economies were underperforming in a similar way, growing less rapidly than they should have been given their initial income levels (Figure 7.3). This suggests that all three were facing a common problem or set of problems. Some of these may have been institutional in nature, such as a fragmented trade union structure that made the corporatist arrangements then in vogue on the continent difficult to achieve.[21] But an excessive reliance on the sluggish British economy is another plausible candidate.

In consequence, while GDP per capita grew more rapidly in Ireland than in the UK during the 1960s (Figure 7.4), this was not sufficient to prevent Ireland falling even further behind a major continental economy like France. This would change in 1973.

Ireland in Europe

As Figure 7.4 shows, Ireland immediately stopped falling further behind France once it entered the EEC in 1973: on one estimate membership boosted Ireland's per capita growth rate by almost two percentage points.[22] Even before the Irish economic miracle of the 1990s, Ireland was once again growing just about as rapidly as would have been predicted within a convergence framework (Figure 7.5). Foreign direct investment, based on selling into the EEC, was a major factor improving Irish performance from 1973 onwards, and the Common Agricultural Policy also helped. But as Figure 7.6 shows, another notable feature of the Irish economy after its entry to the EC was its rapidly decreasing dependence on

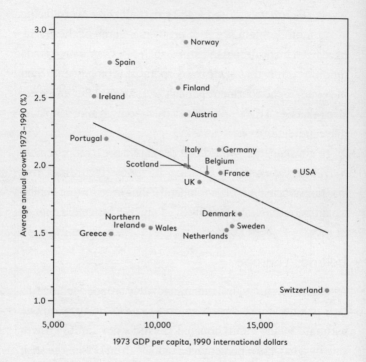

Figure 7.5
Initial income and subsequent growth, 1973–1990

Source: as for Figure 7.1

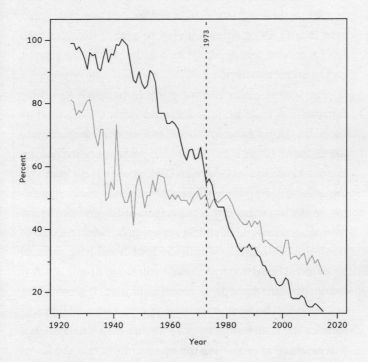

Figure 7.6
Share of the United Kingdom in Ireland's imports and exports
——— UK share of imports
——— UK share of exports

Source: Mitchell (2003) and www.cso.ie for 1972 onwards.

the UK for its imports, and especially its exports. Virtually all Irish exports went to the UK before the Second World War, and the share was still 61 per cent on the eve of entry in 1972. It had declined to just 37 per cent in 1983, stood at 31 per cent in 1992 on the eve of the Single Market, and was only 14 per cent in 2015. EC membership led to a far more diversified Irish economy, less dependent on its immediate neighbour, and healthier as a result.

The second major turning point in Ireland's economic fortunes was 1992, when the Single Market transformed its economy. During the 1990s Ireland was an extraordinary overachiever (Figure 7.7). A comparison between Ireland, on the one hand, and Northern Ireland, Scotland and Wales on the other, is informative (Figure 7.8). Ireland had been gaining ground on these UK regions from 1960 onwards, as we have already seen, which might represent a gradual process of convergence occurring within the British and Irish regional economy. The Irish acceleration from 1990 onwards, however, represents something entirely different. It seems clear, not only that the European Union was fundamental in transforming the Irish economy, but also that Irish independence was essential in exploiting the opportunities that the European Union afforded. As the figure suggests, Ireland would never have done anywhere near as well as it in fact did, had it remained a mere region of the United Kingdom.

Policy flexibility at a time of rapid change was essential, and that is what independence gave Ireland. It is important to note that Ireland is not the only small European country to have performed well in the context of a globalizing economy. There is a well-established political science literature

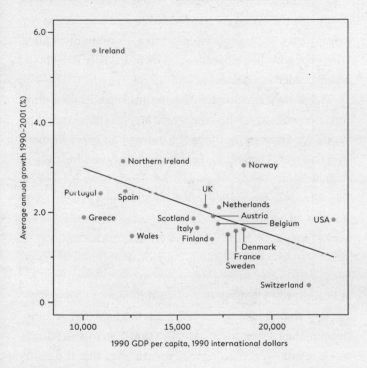

Figure 7.7
Initial income and subsequent growth, 1990–2001

Source: as for Figure 7.1

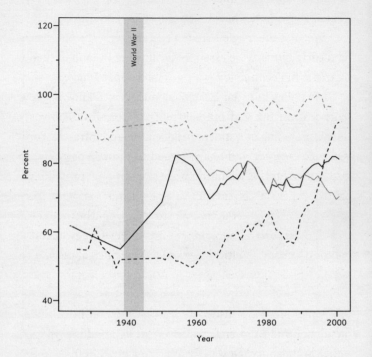

Figure 7.8
Incomes relative to UK, 1924–2001

——— Northern Ireland

——— Wales

---- Ireland (GNP)

----- Scotland

Source: as for Figure 7.3

that shows how other small European countries, in Scandinavia and elsewhere, have been able to respond nimbly and flexibly to changing international market conditions in ways that larger countries have found more difficult.[23] But EU membership, and the Single Market programme of the late 1980s and early 1990s, were essential in allowing Ireland to finally reap the full economic rewards of its independence.

The policy mix that Ireland adopted is well known: a low corporation tax and other incentives for inward investment, including investment in education and infrastructure. Cormac Ó Gráda and I have argued that social partnership was important, moderating wage growth and providing a stable industrial relations environment in a manner somewhat reminiscent of the corporatism of the continental European Golden Age.[24] Underpinning everything were two crucial factors: Ireland's political independence, which allowed it to adopt a policy mix well suited to its own circumstances; and Ireland's membership of the European Single Market, without which none of this would have worked. Political independence and EU membership were never at odds with each other in Ireland; each was required to give full effect to the other. Ireland's independence would not have worked as well as it did without the EU; Ireland's EU membership would not have worked as well as it did without independence.

2016

The year 2016 dawned on an Ireland that was both prosperous and at peace with itself, with the EU having played a crucial role in bringing this about. Anglo-Irish relations had been normalized, with Queen Elizabeth making a state visit to Ireland in 2011 and President Michael D. Higgins reciprocating three years later. The main preoccupation of the country's politicians was the 100th anniversary of the 1916 Easter Rising. Unlike the 50th anniversary in 1966 the event was not a rehearsal of traditional Irish nationalism: there were no anti-British speeches, while all those who died in the Rising were remembered, not just the Irish revolutionaries. But the event was also very different from the 75th anniversary in 1991. By that stage so many people had been killed in the Troubles that non-republicans felt nervous about paying tribute to an earlier generation of revolutionaries, lest this be interpreted as showing support for the present-day IRA and its campaign of murder. Barely anyone showed up.

Peace changed all that. To be sure, the government announced rather solemnly that the centenary of the Rising would be commemorated rather than celebrated, but many Irish people decided that they would go ahead and celebrate anyway. Hundreds of thousands of spectators crowded Dublin city centre to watch the largest military parade in the country's history, and many others watched on TV. A few weeks later there was a party on my street. Our oldest resident, Claire Molloy, born on the day that Patrick Pearse surrendered to the British, was wheeled up to a stage that had been erected in the middle of the road. Green ribbons in her hair, a smartly dressed officer from nearby Cathal Brugha barracks, where the peace activist Francis Sheehy Skeffington was murdered by British soldiers in 1916, read a copy of the Proclamation of Independence. Children sidled closer to the tricoloured cake. Everyone applauded.

Neither the American nor the French Revolution was

particularly non-violent: the origins of most countries involved bloodshed. But whatever people might think of the morality of the Easter Rising – and there were animated debates around many Irish dinner tables in the spring of 2016 – the fact remained that it was the event that eventually led to the establishment of an independent Irish Republic. And most of us were OK with that.

In retrospect, 2016 probably wasn't the best year for the UK to take a unilateral decision imperilling Irish prosperity and political stability.

But that is what then happened.

Brexit

When we left 1980s Britain at the end of Chapter 5, the Labour Party was the anti-European party, whereas Mrs Thatcher's Conservatives strongly supported the creation of the European Single Market and its suppression of border formalities. Before the 1983 general election a young Labour candidate called Tony Blair said that 'We'll negotiate withdrawal from the EEC, which has drained our natural resources and destroyed jobs.'[1] There was nothing strange or unusual about this, since it was, as we have seen, official Labour Party policy. Indeed, the commitment to withdraw from the EC was one of the factors that had led a group of Labour Party politicians, including Roy Jenkins (who had returned to the UK after a stint as European Commission President), to break away and form the Social Democratic Party in 1981. The party soon formed an alliance with the Liberals and eventually merged with them, becoming the Liberal Democrats. The 'Lib Dems' as they are known are, along with the Scottish National Party, the most pro-European of the major British political parties today.

Tony Blair won a seat in 1983, but the election was a disaster for the Labour Party and Mrs Thatcher was returned to power. The Labour Party therefore began, slowly, to

recalibrate its position on Europe as well as on other radical policy stances (such as unilateral nuclear disarmament)
that were seen as electoral handicaps. The celebrated visit in
1988 of Jacques Delors to the British Trades Union Congress
(TUC) was an important turning point: his speech suggested
to those present that Europe might not be the capitalist plot
that the British left had traditionally considered it to be. The
Single Market had to have a 'social dimension': there needed
to be 'a platform of guaranteed social rights, containing general principles, such as every worker's right to be covered by
a collective agreement'.[2] Hugo Young describes him as being
received 'as if he were a prophet', with the brothers serenad-
ing him 'as Frère Jacques, to the tune of the only French song
most of them knew'.[3] Needless to say, the event did not go
down well in Downing Street. By the mid-1990s Labour was
an essentially pro-European party, although still containing
within itself some Eurosceptic elements that have once again
become important today.

One of the reasons why it made political sense for Labour
to become less hostile to Europe is that the Conservative
Party was becoming more so. There are several explanations
for this, beginning with Mrs Thatcher herself. In 1988 she
declared as 'absurd' Jacques Delors's claims to the European
Parliament that within ten years '80 per cent of economic
legislation and perhaps even fiscal and social legislation will
be of Community origins': she had already determined that
Delors was a 'Euro-demagogue' who wished to 'belittle Britain', and by now it was clear that he had 'gone over the top'.[4]
In September 1988, less than two weeks after Delors made
his speech to the TUC, Thatcher addressed the College of

Europe in Bruges. While not questioning Britain's membership of the European Communities, she advocated 'willing and active cooperation between independent sovereign states', and denied that this required 'power to be centralized in Brussels or decisions to be taken by an appointed bureaucracy'. And then came the celebrated phrase, showing that her opposition to Delors was not just based on concerns about sovereignty but also on ideology: 'We have not successfully rolled back the frontiers of the state in Britain, only to see them re-imposed at a European level with a European super-state exercising a new dominance from Brussels.'[5]

In some British Eurosceptic quarters the Bruges speech has the status of holy writ. The following year saw the establishment of the Bruges Group, which according to its website not only 'aims to promote discussion on the European Union and to advance the education of the public on European affairs' but also 'spearheads the intellectual battle against European integration, EU federalism, centralisation and enlargement'. It became a key focal point for Eurosceptic activity in the 1990s, with more than 130 Conservative MPs eventually joining it.[6] And if so many joined, this was because of the events in the years immediately following Bruges.

The years 1989 and 1990 saw an increasingly bitter battle between Mrs Thatcher and her main lieutenants, who were becoming alarmed by the extent of her anti-European rhetoric. There was, for example, her reaction to the impending reunification of Germany which brought out her latent Germanophobia: at a European Council meeting in December 1989, with Chancellor Kohl present, she announced that 'We beat the Germans twice, and now they're back.'[7] In March of the following year a seminar of academics and politicians was held at Chequers, the Prime Minister's country residence, to discuss 'the German problem'. Participants were asked questions such as 'What does history tell us about the character and behaviour of the German-speaking people of Europe?', and 'In the light of history, how can we "satisfy" the Germans? Is there something they want and we can give them, which will neutralise their drive to extend their sway, whether politically or territorially?' According to a leaked memorandum of the meeting, the German character was characterized by, among other things, 'angst, aggressiveness, assertiveness, bullying, egotism, inferiority complex, sentimentality' – although at least one of the experts present has denied that this was an accurate account of what the meeting had concluded.[8]

Mrs Thatcher was not alone among British Conservatives in being suspicious of Germany. In July 1990 her Secretary of State for Trade and Industry, Nicholas Ridley, described European Monetary Union (EMU) as 'a German racket designed to take over the whole of Europe' , and the French as 'behaving like poodles to the Germans . . . When I look at the institutions to which it is proposed that sovereignty is to be handed over, I'm aghast. Seventeen unelected reject politicians[9] . . . I'm not against giving up sovereignty in principle, but not to this lot. You might just as well give it to Adolf Hitler, frankly.' The interviewer concluded his piece by speculating:

> Mr Ridley's confidence in expressing his views on the
> German threat must owe a little something to the

knowledge that they are not significantly different from those of the Prime Minister, who originally opposed German reunification, even though in public she is required not to be so indelicate as to draw comparisons between Herren Kohl and Hitler.[10]

Not surprisingly, the interview caused a scandal, and Ridley had to resign.

There was also a furious fight between Thatcher and her ministers about whether or not the UK should join the European Monetary System's 'Exchange Rate Mechanism', or ERM. The European Monetary System was a system of quasi-fixed exchange rates that had existed since 1979. (Ireland had joined it while the UK had not. Until that time Irish and British pounds had been equal in value to each other, and when I was a child British coins circulated freely in Dublin. Since 1979 the two currencies have been completely distinct.) The question was given a new importance by the publication in 1989 of the Delors Report, which recommended a three-stage process leading eventually to EMU. During the first of these stages all member state currencies were supposed to join the ERM, which made the issue even more sensitive in Britain than it would have been anyway. Eventually the ministers won: Thatcher later wrote that the now-departed Ridley had been 'almost my only ally in the Cabinet'.[11] To Mrs Thatcher's fury the UK joined the ERM in October 1990.

Shortly thereafter the Prime Minister reported back to the House of Commons on a European Council meeting in Rome largely devoted to a discussion of EMU. In the question and answer session following her statement she remarked that it was 'very ironic indeed that, at a time when eastern Europe is striving for greater democracy, the Commission should be striving to extinguish democracy and to put more and more power into its own hands, or into the hands of non-elected bodies.' As for Jacques Delors, he 'said at a press conference the other day that he wanted the European Parliament to be the democratic body of the Community, he wanted the Commission to be the Executive and he wanted the Council of Ministers to be the Senate. No. No. No.'[12]

It was too much for her ministers. Geoffrey Howe, a former Foreign Secretary who had become estranged after Bruges but was still a member of the Cabinet, resigned. In his resignation speech two weeks later he argued that

> the Prime Minister's perceived attitude towards Europe
> is running increasingly serious risks for the future of our
> nation. It risks minimising our influence and maximising
> our chances of being once again shut out. We have
> paid heavily in the past for late starts and squandered
> opportunities in Europe. We dare not let that happen again.
> If we detach ourselves completely, as a party or a nation,
> from the middle ground of Europe, the effects will be
> incalculable and very hard ever to correct.[13]

A week later Mrs Thatcher was gone.

From Major to Blair

This matricide at the hands of the Cabinet's Europhiles gave an extra impetus to Tory Euroscepticism. Shortly after Mrs Thatcher's defenestration she became Honorary President of the Bruges Group, and as already noted the organization became a rallying point for Eurosceptics.[14] Their cause was given a further boost by the signing of the Maastricht Treaty in 1992, even though at the time of its drafting it was viewed as a major success for the new Prime Minister John Major: 'a copybook triumph' according to the journalist Boris Johnson.[15] Perhaps Major's 'victory' – game, set and match for Britain, as it was claimed at the time – was due to the fact that he was being given constant advice throughout the summit meeting by the British Permanent Representative (that is to say, Ambassador) to the European Communities, John Kerr, who supposedly hid beneath the table at a time when all advisers were supposed to be out of the room.[16] Whatever the reason, Major secured the right for the UK to opt out of not only EMU, but also the new social chapter. This committed the other eleven member states to 'the promotion of employment, improved living and working conditions, proper social protection, dialogue between management and labour, the development of human resources with a view to lasting high employment and the combating of exclusion'. Major viewed the chapter as bad for business, and it was downgraded to a protocol that explicitly did not apply to the UK.

Despite this undoubted success the Maastricht Treaty represented a fundamental deepening of European integration. It established the European Union, which was based on three 'pillars', the first of which was the continuation of the old European Communities. The European Economic Community, one of those three Communities, was now simply the European Community, emphasizing the political nature of the enterprise. There were also pillars for foreign and security policy, and justice and home affairs, which would however be run on a more intergovernmental basis than the first. The Maastricht Treaty paved the way for EMU, and set down the guidelines for budget deficits and government debt (3 per cent and 60 per cent of GDP, respectively) that have since become all too familiar.[17] The treaty also introduced the concept of European citizenship: every citizen had 'the right to move and reside freely within the territory of the Member States', as well as the right to vote and stand as a candidate in European and municipal elections.[18] These fundamental freedoms that we share as European citizens are one of the most visible benefits of EU membership. But the notion of European citizenship is also a red rag to a certain sort of Eurosceptic bull.

Despite this, everything might have gone smoothly if it had not been for the Danes. In June 1992 my mother's homeland rejected the Maastricht Treaty in a referendum. It was a memorable month for the country. Denmark found itself being included in the UEFA European Championship finals despite not having qualified, due to the elimination of Yugoslavia which was breaking up at the time. Even better, it won the championship. Better still, it beat Germany in the final. And best of all, this all happened right under the noses of the Swedes, since Sweden is where the championship was held. The country's Foreign Minister, Uffe Ellemann-Jensen, reacted to this improbable sequence of events by commenting, philosophically, 'If you can't join them, beat them.'

The Danish referendum mattered in two ways for British politics. First, it meant that the Maastricht Treaty couldn't enter into force until the Danes had secured various opt-outs and voted again. This delayed the ratification process in Britain which had up until then been going smoothly, and also gave the Eurosceptics the hope that Maastricht might be defeated. Over time the number of Conservative MPs willing to rebel against Major's government grew, and while ratification was eventually secured this was only after a long and brutal struggle. The British Conservative Party has been split right down the middle about Europe ever since. And second, the Danish referendum result, as well as opinion polls suggesting that the French referendum, which was due to be held in September, would be tight, cast doubt over the Maastricht process for attaining European Monetary Union. One immediate consequence was that currency markets, already doubtful about the ERM's fixed exchange rate system, became even more so. Speculators like George Soros began to bet against the British pound, and in September 1992 the currency was forced out of the ERM.[19] Bringing sterling into the Exchange Rate Mechanism had been one of the main objectives of Europhile British politicians over the course of the previous few years. To many observers, both they and their cause now seemed discredited. Towards the end of the decade, Hugo Young wrote some words which summed up the transformation that had taken place within the Conservative Party since 1990: 'In 1998, it was utterly jarring to recall that the prime cause – at least the indispensable pretext – of Mrs Thatcher's removal was that Conservative Members of Parliament were unable any longer to trust her hostile conduct of British relations with Europe.'[20]

Major limped on for a few more years, with the divisions within his party over Europe overshadowing everything else. It was no surprise when in 1997 Tony Blair and his 'New'

Labour Party swept to power. While Blair – largely at the insistence of his Chancellor, Gordon Brown – eventually decided not to bring the UK into EMU, one of his first acts was to opt into the European social chapter that Major had opted out of – in deeds as well as words he was by then a pro-European politician, at least by British standards. More broadly he was a liberal internationalist who believed in the value of co-operation to solve shared problems. Viewed from the outside, Britain became a more normal country.

In retrospect the early Blair years seem like a golden age and in many respects they were. But that was not always so evident at the time.[21] An excessive dedication to political spin ended up turning off many voters – a useful lesson for other young and mediagenic leaders to take to heart. The Iraq War was a fatal blow to Blair's credibility. And the global financial crisis that began in 2008, a year after Blair had resigned as Prime Minister, ensured Labour's defeat in the subsequent general election. Nonetheless, it had in many ways been a successful premiership, during which the Tory party had at times seemed unelectable: 'the nasty party', as Theresa May put it in a speech to the Conservative Party conference in 2002.

Cameron Comes to Power

When the Labour Party had seemed unelectable, in the 1980s, this had prompted a shift to the political centre, and the replacement of the party's traditional Euroscepticism with a much more positive approach to Europe. In 2005 David Cameron was elected to the Conservative leadership after the party's third general election defeat in a row. He did try to make his party less 'nasty', for example by getting it to adopt more liberal positions on issues such as gay marriage. But there was no Blairite shift towards a more positive attitude towards Europe: by this stage it would have been difficult or impossible for an enthusiastically pro-European politician to be elected leader by Conservative Party MPs. Indeed, during his election campaign Cameron promised that he would bring the party out of the European People's Party (EPP), the mainstream conservative grouping in the European Parliament, on the grounds that it was too 'federalist'.

On the other hand, Cameron did not begin his leadership of the party with the aim of crusading against Europe: if anything, he hoped that the subject could be avoided for as long as possible. In his first address as leader to the Conservative Party conference, in 2006, he explicitly acknowledged that Tory divisions about Europe had cost them dearly: 'Instead of talking about the things that most people care about, we talked about what we cared about most. While parents worried about childcare, getting the kids to school, balancing work and family life – we were banging on about Europe.'[22] In the same year he described UKIP (UK Independence Party) members as 'a bunch of fruitcakes and loonies and closet racists'.[23] In 2007 Cameron promised that he would hold a referendum on the Lisbon Treaty (see Chapter 9), but the promise was dropped once the treaty had been ratified by everyone including the UK Labour government. Banging on about Europe was precisely what Cameron wanted to avoid, but it was not to be.

The Tory wilderness years also saw the revival of an old British intellectual tradition according to which the country's most natural allies were the other members of what was now increasingly referred to as the 'Anglosphere'.[24] Previous chapters have described various earlier variations on the theme: Joseph Chamberlain's schemes for a great imperial customs union, Churchill's determination to preserve the Empire, the view of the 1960s Labour Party that the Commonwealth should be the primary focus of British political loyalty. But the Anglosphere could also be defined as including the United States, with which Britain had a 'special relationship' as its most dependable ally. Mrs Thatcher certainly had a special relationship with Ronald Reagan, and so did Tony Blair with Bill Clinton. The fact that Blair's subsequent special relationship with George W. Bush had led to disaster in Iraq might have been expected to kill off the concept of the Anglosphere, but it did not. Historians wrote articles and books highlighting the positive contributions of the British Empire, and journalists and intellectuals speculated about ways in which the Anglosphere might be brought more closely together. In 2010 UKIP argued for a Commonwealth free trade area, while in the 2015 general election it stated that it wanted 'to foster closer ties with the Anglosphere'. And here, according to the academics Michael Kenny and Nick Pearce, is where the notion of the Anglosphere was potentially important: it 'sustained the growing belief that there was a potential answer to the difficult question posed by supporters of the UK's membership of the EU: what might be the better alternative to it?'[25]

In 2010 Cameron came to power at the head of a coalition government that included the Liberal Democrats. It was just like old times: within seventeen months there had already been 22 backbench rebellions on Europe.[26] And then came an even bigger rebellion: in October 2011, 81 Conservative MPs disobeyed orders and voted in favour of a referendum on UK membership of the EU. For Tim Shipman this was the crucial turning point: 'One of Cameron's closest aides said, "For me the pivotal moment was the eighty-one rebellion. It was clear after that that the parliamentary party would not stand for anything but a referendum by the next election. I think the PM knew instinctively that was where he was going to end up."'[27] In October 2013, concerned about the rise of UKIP in opinion polls, Cameron promised in an interview that if re-elected he would renegotiate the terms of UK membership of the European Union, and then hold a referendum on whether or not to remain a member on those new terms. After all, the strategy had worked for Harold Wilson.

This probably wouldn't have mattered had the 2015 general election gone as expected. On election nights the younger fellows in my college put up a big screen in the Old Library and bring out beer and pizza. I can remember sitting there as the results came in, and it became clear that the Conservatives were going to win an overall majority: this meant a referendum and the possibility of Brexit. Everyone had expected that Cameron would be forced to form another coalition with the Europhile Liberal Democrats, and while we will never know for sure whether a referendum would have been held under those circumstances, it seems unlikely. As it was, there was no reason for him not to fulfil his election pledge, and in any event a referendum was what a large portion of his parliamentary party demanded. And so the renegotiation began.

Enlargement

In order to understand what happened next, a little bit of context is in order. When the Maastricht Treaty came into effect, the new European Union that resulted had twelve members: the original Six, the three countries who had joined in 1973 (Denmark, Ireland and the United Kingdom), Greece, and the two Iberian countries. Soon afterwards, however, the number grew to fifteen, when Austria, Finland and Sweden joined in 1995. The Single European Act and the establishment of the Single Market were crucial in explaining this: the three countries concerned could not afford to be excluded from it for fear of being discriminated against in important export markets. Nor, for that matter, could the other EFTA states: Iceland, Liechtenstein, Norway and Switzerland. In the late 1980s, therefore, the EC and EFTA started to explore whether it would be possible for the latter group of countries to benefit from the Single Market without becoming members of the EC, with all of the implications for sovereignty that this would inevitably entail. In 1989 Jacques Delors suggested that 'a system based on Community rules' might indeed be possible, but that there could be no picking or choosing. Because of the similarities with today's debates about Brexit, it is worth quoting him at length:

> It becomes clear in fact that our EFTA friends are basically attracted, in varying degrees, by the prospect of enjoying the benefits of a frontier-free market. But we all know that the single market forms a whole with its advantages and disadvantages, its possibilities and limitations. Can our

EFTA friends be allowed to pick and choose? I have some
misgivings here. The single market is first and foremost
a customs union. Are our partners prepared to abide by
the common commercial policy that any customs union
must apply to outsiders? . . . The single market also implies
harmonization. Are our partners willing to transpose
the common rules essential to the free movement of
goods into their domestic law and, in consequence,
accept the supervision of the Court of Justice, which
has demonstrated its outstanding competence and
impartiality? . . . But the Community is much more than
a large market. It is a frontier-free economic and social
area on the way to becoming a political union entailing
closer cooperation on foreign policy and security . . . It
is extremely difficult, within this all-embracing union, to
provide a choice of menus.[28]

The outcome was an agreement in 1992 to set up the European
Economic Area (EEA) to which all EU and EFTA member
states (except for Switzerland) belong. Delors didn't get his
customs union, but he did get 'a system based on Community rules'. The EEA extended EU legislation concerning the
so-called four freedoms – that is to say, the free movement
of goods, services, persons and capital – to all its member
states. The goal of gaining access to the Single Market while
remaining outside the EU (which as we have seen replaced
the EC from 1993 onwards) had been achieved. So why did
Austria, Finland and Sweden, as well as Norway and Switzerland, almost immediately afterwards apply to join the European Union? (The Norwegians voted against membership yet

again, and remained in EFTA and the EEA. In consequence, a hypothetical arrangement whereby post-Brexit Britain would remain within the European Single Market is frequently known today as a 'Norway-style' deal. The Swiss voted against EEA membership, suspended EU membership negotiations, remained in EFTA, and developed an extremely cumbersome mechanism for essentially mirroring most EU laws relevant to EEA membership while remaining formally outside it.) The answer to this question is straightforward: remaining outside the EU retained notional sovereignty, but at the expense of being obliged to adopt legislation over which the country concerned had had no say.[29] Even a small country inside the EU has a vote at the table, but even a big country outside has none.

The 1995 enlargement is thus very relevant for helping us to think about life after Brexit. But it was the next enlargement that was important in helping Brexit to come about in the first place. The UK had always favoured 'widening' the EU over 'deepening' it: it was more in favour of admitting new members than of deepening integration. And if widening made deepening more difficult, so much the better! There was of course a compelling moral and strategic argument in favour of admitting to the EU countries who had suffered for so long under Soviet oppression, who desperately wanted to belong to the West, and who feared renewed domination by Russia. Tony Blair was a leading advocate of rapid enlargement to the east, and in 2004 ten new member states joined the EU: eight former Communist countries (the Czech Republic, Estonia, Hungary, Latvia, Lithuania, Poland, Slovakia and Slovenia) plus Cyprus and Malta. Bulgaria and Romania joined in 2007, and Croatia joined in 2013, bringing the total number of members to 28.

Thus after 2004 citizens from Eastern Europe were in principle entitled to live and work anywhere in the Union. In practice twelve of the fifteen existing member states exercised their right to postpone opening up their labour markets for a period of up to seven years. Only three countries – Ireland, Sweden and the United Kingdom – allowed free movement from the new member states immediately. For the first time since independence Ireland became a country of large-scale net immigration: a truly historic change. But the political effects were far greater in Britain, and more particularly in England.

Brexit

David Cameron had promised that he would renegotiate the terms of the UK's membership of the European Union. But what should he be aiming for in the renegotiation? Immigration, both from Eastern Europe (which was not under the control of the British government after the expiration of the aforementioned seven-year transition period, since it was guaranteed by the treaties) and the rest of the world (which was just as important, and which the British government could control as it saw fit), was provoking a political backlash and helping UKIP in opinion polls and elections. In 2014 UKIP got the largest share of the vote in the European elections. That October Cameron told his party conference that 'I will go to Brussels, I will not take no for an answer and – when it comes to free movement – I will get what Britain needs.'[30] But there was never any chance that Cameron's European colleagues were going to be willing to renegotiate the treaties guaranteeing free movement just to satisfy the British Prime Minister. By claiming that he would achieve something that was in fact unachievable Cameron had set himself up for failure. And by claiming that he would renegotiate free movement he had conceded that UKIP and others hostile to free movement were in fact right.

In the event Cameron obtained a number of concessions.[31] Free movement itself was not restricted, but member states would have the right to apply an 'emergency brake' for up to seven years to in-work benefits paid to migrants from the rest of the Union, in cases where 'exceptional' levels of immigration were placing undue strain on the social security system, the employment market or public services. Child benefits paid to immigrants whose children lived in other member states could be tailored to conditions in those other countries, rather than to conditions in the country in which the immigrant was working. And the United Kingdom, which already enjoyed opt-outs from EMU, the Schengen system that allows passport-free travel, and a variety of other initiatives, was now granted the greatest opt-out of them all: the commitment of all EU member states to 'an ever closer union' no longer applied to the UK. On this basis Cameron returned home and announced that he was going to campaign for a 'Remain' vote in the referendum, due to be held in June.

The story of the campaign is too detailed to be recounted here at any great length: Tim Shipman's book on the subject, which describes all the twists and turns, runs to more than 600 pages and manages to be interesting throughout. I will limit myself here to some of the more important facts.

There were two 'Leave' campaigns. The first was Vote Leave, which regarded itself as the official Leave campaign, and was eventually designated as such by the Electoral Commission. This is the organization to which leading Eurosceptic MPs from the Conservative Party, Labour Party and Northern Ireland's Democratic Unionist Party (DUP) belonged. Many of these people had campaigned for years for British withdrawal from the EU: there was never any doubt as to what side they were going to be on. And then there was Boris Johnson, who – and it is hard to remember this now – was at the time one of Britain's most popular politicians, and who decided at the very last moment to campaign for Leave rather than Remain. It is commonly assumed that this decision was made for careerist reasons, and who am I to suggest otherwise. The second Leave campaign was Leave.EU, associated with the businessman Arron Banks and the leader of UKIP, Nigel Farage. It was Farage who unveiled an infamous poster showing vast numbers of Syrian refugees hoping to enter Europe, and whose slogan was 'Breaking Point'. The poster was widely denounced as racist, including by leading members of Vote Leave.

Shipman cites 'a key figure' in Vote Leave who argues that the Farage campaign cost them votes by alienating floating voters. But Shipman also suggests that having two 'Leave' campaigns may have been beneficial. On the one hand, there was a 'respectable' campaign, and on the other, a campaign delivering what Shipman describes as 'edgier messages designed to appeal to working-class voters'.[32] Many of these edgy messages were populist, nativist and anti-immigrant: they appealed above all to a fairly unreconstructed English (as opposed to British) nationalism.[33] But the official campaign was also guilty of bad behaviour. Their official slogan was 'Take back control', but they will always be remembered for their letterbox-red bus on which it was stated that 'We send the EU £350 million a week, let's fund our NHS instead'. The claim that EU membership was costing the UK £350 million a week, which could be diverted to the UK's National Health Service in the event of withdrawal, was simply not true. Vote Leave itself produced a poster claiming that 'Turkey (population 76 million) is joining the EU'. There were no pictures on the poster of hordes of Muslims waiting to enter Europe, and by extension the United Kingdom, but the message was clear. And Boris Johnson compared the EU's attempts to unify Europe to those of Adolf Hitler.[34]

The official 'Remain' campaign was Britain Stronger in Europe. The Labour Party, however, set up its own Remain campaign, Labour In for Britain. The campaign was handicapped by the fact that the party's new leader, Jeremy Corbyn, like Tony Benn and Michael Foot before him, was a long-standing Eurosceptic. Corbyn did campaign in favour of Remain, but is widely viewed as having done so in a half-hearted and lacklustre way.

The gist of the official Remain campaign was that leaving the EU would be economically costly: 'Project Fear' is how the Brexiteers described the claims, despite the fact that most experts agreed. (This led to the famous statement by leading Brexiteer Michael Gove that 'the people in this country have had enough of experts from organizations with acronyms saying they know what is best and getting it consistently wrong.')[35] Two features of the campaign in particular struck

me as odd, coming as I do from a country which has benefited so greatly from EU membership and whose population
is overwhelmingly pro-European. First, the main messages
coming from the Remain camp were for the most part negative: beware of withdrawal because it will cost you money.
In fairness, it was a strategy that had worked for Cameron
in the Scottish independence referendum of 2014, but the
failure to represent the European Union, its citizenship and
the freedoms that this entails as something fundamentally
positive was striking not just to me but to many Europeans.
And second, as already mentioned in Chapter 6, the campaign
barely mentioned Ireland.

On the evening of 23 June 2016 I found myself once again
in front of the big screen in my college's Old Library. Most
people were still expecting a Remain victory despite opinion
polls showing that it would be very close. Indeed, at 22.03
Nigel Farage announced that it looked as though Remain
was going to win; shortly afterwards he said that whether or
not this particular battle had been won or lost, the war for
Brexit would continue.[36] It soon became clear, however, that
Leave was doing better than expected, and we woke up the
following morning to the news that the United Kingdom was
leaving the European Union. Sixty-two per cent of Scots had
voted in favour of remaining in the EU. So had 55.8 per cent
of the population of Northern Ireland, where four out of the
five major political parties had advocated Remain (the DUP
being the odd man out). Ninety-six per cent of the population of Gibraltar voted Remain, as did 59.9 per cent of Lon-
doners. But every other major region of England, as well as
Wales, voted to Leave. The overall margin was tight: 51.9 per

cent to 48.1 per cent. Two of the United Kingdom's four constituent nations had voted to Remain. But the UK was on its way out.

What struck me forcibly on 24 June was how genuinely upsetting the news was for several colleagues of mine who had voted Remain. This had nothing to do with economics, even though the Remain campaign had been about virtually nothing else. My colleagues were just as European as I, and also felt themselves to be strongly British. But their identity as European citizens was about to be taken away from them, while their British identity seemed to be in danger as well – for Brexit was something that English nationalism was doing to the rest of the UK, and who knew how Scotland might react.

We tend to take European citizenship for granted. It is only when you are deprived of it that you realize just how precious it is.

CHAPTER 9
Explaining Brexit

What explains Brexit? The question will keep many academics happily employed for years. If you have read thus far, the answer may seem obvious to you: Britain's relationship with Europe was always an ambivalent one. It had always looked towards its imperial past and its relationship with America. It initially tried to sabotage European integration, and when the government eventually decided that entry was in the UK's best interests it did so in a less than whole-hearted fashion. The British traditionally valued the economic opportunities afforded by Europe, but were much less enthusiastic about the supranational ambitions of the European Communities. And when the European Communities made way for the European Union, a Conservative Party civil war erupted: for many within the party this was a dilution of sovereignty too far. Add to this the ambivalence of a small but influential section of the Labour Party, and in particular its leader since 2015, as well as the rise of UKIP, and Brexit was unsurprising.

But Brexit was not inevitable: Leave only won by a small majority. Thirty-three million six hundred thousand people voted in the referendum. If just 635,000 of these had voted to Remain rather than Leave I would not be writing this book. And so one important distinction is between structural explanations that emphasize the deep underlying roots of the phenomenon, and explanations emphasizing the roles of chance and contingency. If you had to generalize, you would say that social scientists tend to favour the former, and historians the latter. And if you are an economic historian, as I am, with one foot in each camp, you are probably going to conclude that both deeper historical forces (structure) and chance events from 2010 onwards (contingency) mattered.

Another important distinction is between explanations focused solely on the United Kingdom, and explanations that view Brexit as part of a bigger story. As we know, 2016 was marked not only by the UK referendum but also by the election of Donald Trump in the United States. The following year saw an uncomfortably strong showing for the French National Front, which made it into the second round of the presidential election, and the arrival to power (albeit as part of a coalition) of the far-right FPÖ (Freedom Party of Austria) in Vienna. In 2018 a populist government was elected in Italy. There are strong populist parties elsewhere in Western Europe, and populist governments in Hungary and Poland. When you see common trends of this sort in many countries a common explanation seems in order.

What form might such a common explanation take? There is a raging debate today in both Britain and the United States regarding whether Brexit and Trump reflect 'economics' or 'culture'. For some, both phenomena are the product of globalization, or technological change, or other impersonal economic forces that are damaging vulnerable communities. (When using the word 'globalization' in what follows I will be using the term in its economic sense, referring to the international integration of markets through trade, migration, international borrowing and lending, and multinational investment.) For others, they are the product of racism, xenophobia, nationalism and other forms of extreme cultural conservatism. The question of whether economics or culture explains these two watershed political events is in many respects an ideological one. Some on the left are reluctant to admit that either Brexit or Trump might have an economic explanation, for fear of justifying those who voted for them. Some on the right are happy to parade their solidarity with those who have been left behind, and to portray the political upsets of 2016 as a victory for the common man, although neither the UK Conservatives nor the US Republicans have traditionally distinguished themselves by their concern for the poor.

Schematically, one could envisage a catalogue of structural explanations as in Table 9.1, distinguished by whether they are Anglo-centric or international, and economic or cultural. The Anglo-centric and cultural explanation suggested by the previous chapters of this book is one possibility, listed here in the top left-hand cell of the matrix;[1] the alternative argument that both Brexit and Trump represented a revolt against globalization is listed in the bottom right-hand cell (it is both international and economic). One could imagine explanations that are both international and cultural – the systematic use of the Internet by Russia to destabilize Western democracies, the spread of fake news by far-right organizations such as Breitbart News, international networks of populist politicians and pundits, or the abuse of personal data by companies such as Cambridge Analytica (which

	Cultural	Economic
Anglo-centric	British Euroscepticism	Austerity
International	Russian interference Breitbart, fake news	Globalization

Table 9.1
Structural explanations for Brexit

worked for both the Trump Campaign and Leave.EU). And there are explanations that are both British and economic, such as those emphasizing the role of the UK government's radical austerity drive under David Cameron and his Chancellor George Osborne.

Finally, there is a distinction that matters greatly to economists and a certain sort of political scientist – were voters rational or not? If a voter in the American rustbelt supported Donald Trump because he or she was suffering as a result of international trade, and thought that Donald Trump would be protectionist, then you could view their vote as a rational one. Alternatively, you could view both Donald Trump's supporters and those who voted in favour of Brexit as having been fooled by unscrupulous politicians. Economists tend to believe that people behave in their own best interests, and in ordinary life it usually makes sense to assume that those with whom you are dealing are going to do what's best for them. But just because something is usually true doesn't mean that it always is, and in any event if it is costly to acquire information about the costs and benefits of European integration or globalization then a rational person may decide to remain ignorant.

People often assume that economic explanations of voting behaviour must imply rational behaviour, but that isn't so. To be sure, our hypothetical rustbelt voter is voting in his or her own best economic interests, which is what economists tend to define as 'rational' behaviour. But what about a hypothetical British voter supporting Brexit because of Conservative Party austerity? It would be difficult to argue that this wasn't an economic reason to vote for Brexit, but it would hardly be a rational one, given that Osborne's austerity policies had little or nothing to do with Europe. The UK is not a member of European Monetary Union, nor is it bound by the European Fiscal Compact, nor are the avoidance of excessive deficits and debt and the associated numerical fiscal rules mandated by the Stability and Growth Pact directly binding upon it (more UK opt-outs).[2] Like Denis Healey's bullocks, George Osborne's austerity was Made in Britain. If our hypothetical voter supported Brexit because he was unhappy with austerity, he was aiming at the wrong target.

If I were teaching Brexit in 50 years' time, this is probably how I would introduce the subject. My students would then write essays debating whether the causes of Brexit were cultural or economic, British or international, rational or irrational, structural or contingent. These distinctions make pedagogical sense, and they help in understanding what is a complex social phenomenon. But my guess is that, having gone through all the arguments, and assessed all the empirical evidence, and read the authoritative histories of Brexit that would have been written at that point, the conclusion would be that Brexit was complicated, and that all of the reasons mentioned above mattered. Because that is nearly always the conclusion that you reach in questions such as this one.

Only two years have passed since 2016, not 50, and it's too soon to give a definitive account of why the British, or more accurately the English and Welsh, decided that it would be a good idea to leave the European Union. But here are some of the factors that seem likely to have mattered.

The European Context

I haven't said anything yet about what was happening in the rest of Europe in 2015 and 2016. It was very difficult period. Figure 9.1 plots GDP in the USA, Germany, the UK, and the Eurozone excluding Germany. As can be seen, the financial crisis in 2008 led to a sharp contraction in economic activity in all four economies in 2009, which was followed by rapid recovery in 2010. (Both the initial contraction and subsequent recovery were greater in Germany than elsewhere.) But after 2010 the performance of the Eurozone outside Germany diverged sharply from that of Britain, America and Germany. Recovery continued in the latter three countries, including, interestingly enough, the UK. In the Eurozone, in contrast, growth ceased altogether.

The reasons for this are well known. The initial recovery in 2009 was due to a coordinated policy of reflation: in the face of a collapse in output rivalling that of the Great Depression of the 1930s, governments around the world slashed interest rates and allowed their budget deficits to grow, rather than cutting expenditure and raising taxes at the worst possible moment. Both the UK and US embarked on a programme of 'quantitative easing', with central banks directly expanding the money supply by buying a variety of assets.[3] (The European Central Bank, on the other hand, was much too conservative in its response to the Great Recession before Mario Draghi's arrival in Frankfurt in 2011.) This coordinated effort was aided by a successful G-20 summit hosted in London by Gordon Brown, the Labour Party Prime Minister who

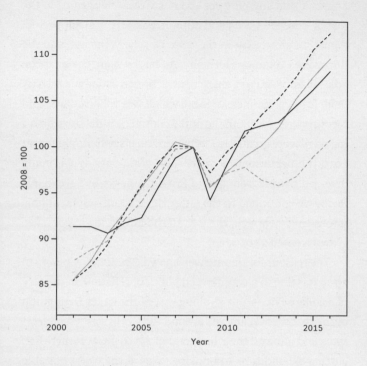

Figure 9.1
GDP 2001–16 (2008=100)
— Germany
— UK
---- USA
---- Eurozone outside Germany

Source: AMECO Macroeconomic Database (European Commission)

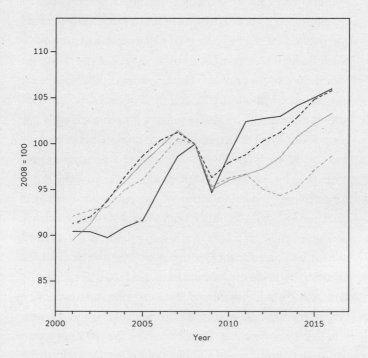

Figure 9.2
GDP per capita 2001–16 (2008=100)

—— Germany

—— UK

---- USA

----- Eurozone outside Germany

Source: AMECO Macroeconomic Database (European Commission)

succeeded Tony Blair: this was New Labour liberal internationalism at its most effective.

But then in 2010 the Greek government was revealed to have falsified its public finance statistics: its budget deficit and public debt were significantly higher than had previously been thought. This gave fiscal conservatives in the Eurozone the excuse that they needed. The reflationary policies of 2009 were replaced with austerity at a time when economies had not yet recovered: they still required a lot more stimulus but got policies that cut demand instead. The predictable result was that whereas the US economy had recovered to its pre-crisis peak by 2011, and the UK economy by 2012, the Eurozone economy – outside Germany – only got back to where it had been in 2016, a full eight years later. I showed an earlier version of these numbers to a seminar audience in Oxford in 2015, and an eminent German public figure chastised me for using GDP: clearly I should have used GDP per capita, he said, which would have shown the Eurozone in a much more favourable light. So in case he is reading this, and to show him that I was listening, Figure 9.2 gives the GDP per capita data and it doesn't make a blind bit of difference. Indeed, the Eurozone outside Germany does even worse on this score: it only recovered to its 2008 pre-crisis peak in 2017.

This was a truly pathetic and utterly avoidable performance. To make matters worse, there were the Troika interventions in Ireland, where taxpayers were forced to bail out large private sector investors who had lent money to bankrupt banks;[4] Portugal; Cyprus, where bank depositors (as opposed to investors) ended up losing money; and above all Greece, which experienced bank closures, capital controls, and a constant battle between the IMF, which (correctly) regarded the Greek debt as unsustainable, and European authorities who were at every stage reluctant to admit the obvious truth. The impact on Greek GDP was and remains catastrophic, and there have been serious repercussions for ordinary people, including severe health consequences.[5]

The year 2015 also saw the peak of the European refugee crisis, as over a million asylum seekers crossed the Mediterranean to seek refuge in Europe. Roughly half of these were fleeing the war in Syria. People in many European countries felt that governments were losing control, and European unity was placed under enormous strain – whatever one thinks about Mrs Merkel's decision to open Germany's borders to refugees, it was a unilateral one that had consequences for her neighbours. Other countries responded by taking unilateral decisions of their own. Passport controls reappeared along several borders inside the Schengen area, which in principle allows people to travel without passports. An important and visible dimension of European integration seemed to be crumbling (although such measures are in fact consistent with the Schengen rules in certain circumstances).

What does any of this have to do with Brexit? After all, the United Kingdom was not a member of the Eurozone, was not forced to adopt austerity policies by Brussels, had a central bank that was much more proactive in combating the Great Recession than the European Central Bank, and recovered much more quickly as a result. And as for the refugee crisis: some of those admitted into Germany migrated north into Scandinavia, but Britain is an island and the UK is not a member of the Schengen area. Migrants cannot simply wander into Britain uninvited, as the residents of Calais know only too well. So neither the Eurozone crisis nor the refugee crisis was particularly relevant in Britain.

However, they provided the context in which the referendum campaign was fought. The refugee crisis provided Nigel Farage with the opportunity to produce his infamous Syrian refugee poster, and the more 'respectable' Vote Leave campaign with the opportunity to warn voters about the supposedly imminent admission to the EU of Turkey with its 76 million Muslims. Brexiteers always glossed over the distinction between the free movement of European citizens between member states, and the immigration of non-Europeans to the United Kingdom that was always solely a matter for the British government. The refugee crisis, which was undoubtedly a crisis for the European Union, made it easier for them to maintain this confusion in the public mind. And both the refugee crisis and the Eurozone crisis helped to create the impression that the European Union was incompetent and crisis-ridden: this was not an organization that Britain should be scared to leave. The timing of the referendum was therefore highly beneficial to the Brexiteers – it would have been much more difficult for them to have fought the campaign in 2018.

Globalization

Every January the great, the good and the self-important descend on the Swiss Alps, sporting their best parkas and a variety of silly hats and opining about the state of the world. If there's one thing that people agree about in Davos, it's that globalization is a Good Thing. And indeed so it is, if the alternative is the autarky of the interwar period. No one can deny that exporting has been the key to growth in China and other developing countries in recent years, or that this growth has raised hundreds of millions of our fellow human beings out of poverty. If you are even slightly cosmopolitan in your ethical outlook you should want this to continue. But it always makes sense to ask whether you can have too much of a good thing.

Standard international trade theory teaches us that trade increases overall incomes, but that not everyone benefits: instead trade helps some groups in society and hurts others. The textbooks then make the point that, since overall incomes have increased, the losers could be compensated by the winners, leaving everyone better off. If this were the way the world actually worked, then we would not have to worry about the income distribution effects of globalization; but of course that is not the way the world works. 'The Davos lie' is how former US Treasury Secretary Larry Summers characterized the argument in 2007.[6]

Since 23 June 2016 it has become commonplace even in Davos to argue that globalization can leave people behind, and that this can have severe political consequences. While this belated acceptance of the blindingly obvious is welcome it has come much too late. For the disasters of 2016 did not appear out of nowhere, like lightning in a clear blue sky. Widening inequality, especially in the US and UK, and tensions associated with globalization, have been with us for years if not decades. The only wonder is that we got away with it for so long.

The present wave of globalization has been under way since the 1980s, and accelerated sharply at the start of the

twenty-first century.[7] In 1995 the GATT, which we first encountered in Chapter 2, became the World Trade Organization (WTO). Whereas the GATT dealt with trade in goods,
WTO rules also concern trade in services and intellectual
property. Even more importantly, the WTO created new settlement dispute procedures helping to ensure that disagreements
between nations over trade would be settled by the rule of
law rather than the law of the jungle. As the experience of the
1930s suggests, the benefits of a mutually agreed-upon dispute
settlement mechanism go far beyond economics: they make
the world a safer and more peaceful place.

In 2001 China became a member of the WTO. The European Union had accorded China most-favoured-nation (MFN)
status in 1985, and by the end of the twentieth century the
United States had done the same, but there was constant uncertainty over whether the Americans would continue this
policy in the future. WTO membership eliminated that uncertainty, since as we saw earlier all GATT (and therefore WTO)
members are obliged to offer each other MFN status. It was
now illegal to discriminate against Chinese exports (although
transitional arrangements were kept in place for textiles).
Globalization seemed an unstoppable force.

Economic historians, on the other hand, have always understood that globalization is neither new nor irreversible. They
know this because globalization existed and was reversed in
the past. In 1999 Jeff Williamson and I wrote a book making
the point in the context of the globalization of the nineteenth
century that we encountered in Chapter 2. Among the losers
from trade at that time were European landowners, who found
themselves competing against an abundant supply of cheap

New World land: food prices in Europe fell and with them the incomes of landlords and farmers. The result was that in Germany and France, Italy and Sweden, the move towards ever-freer trade that had been ongoing for several years was halted and replaced by a shift towards protection that benefited not only agricultural interests but industrial ones as well. Meanwhile, across the Atlantic, immigration restrictions were gradually tightened, as highly paid American workers found themselves competing with European migrants coming from ever-poorer source countries.

In our concluding chapter, we wrote:

> A focus of this book has been the political implications of globalization, and the lessons are sobering. Politicians, journalists, and market analysts have a tendency to extrapolate the immediate past into the indefinite future, and such thinking suggests that the world is irreversibly headed toward ever greater levels of economic integration. The historical record suggests the contrary . . . unless politicians worry about who gains and who loses, they may be forced by the electorate to stop efforts to strengthen global economy links, and perhaps even to dismantle them.[8]

The reason why Jeff and I framed our historical argument in this way is that the 1990s saw a vigorous debate about whether globalization was responsible for the growing inequality experienced in the United States at that time. The obvious late twentieth-century counterparts of those late nineteenth-century European landowners were unskilled workers in rich countries, who found themselves competing against large supplies of very cheap unskilled labour in Asia. And by the 1990s unskilled workers in countries like the US had been doing badly for a long time: average hourly real wages had stopped growing a full quarter of a century earlier. As Figure 9.3 shows, average real wages only surpassed their early 1970s levels in a sustained fashion from 2007 onwards, and as late as 2016 they were only 7.6 per cent higher than in 1972.[9] Since the US economy had grown substantially over that 45-year period, the almost complete failure of average workers' wages to grow necessarily implied that they were falling behind those groups who gained the most: high-skilled workers and owners of capital.[10]

This is not just a story of stagnant real wages, nor is it confined to the United States. According to recent estimates by the economists Thomas Piketty, Emmanuel Saez and Gabriel Zucman, between 1946 and 1980 the real incomes of the poorest 50 per cent of the American population rose by 102 per cent. Between 1980 and 2014 they rose by just 1 per cent, even as top incomes soared.[11] Median household incomes* are lower today in the United States than they were in 1999. In the United Kingdom the real wages of the median worker have fallen by 10 per cent since 2008.[12] These figures are a damning indictment of the economies concerned and of the politicians in charge of them.

During the 1980s and 1990s the consensus was that this

---

* That is to say, the incomes of those households sitting slap in the middle of the income distribution, with as many households being richer than them as there are households that are poorer than them. Median incomes are a better indicator of 'typical' living standards than average (or mean) incomes, since extremely high incomes at the top end of the scale can drag the average up a lot.

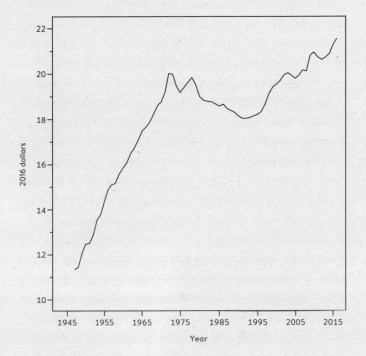

Figure 9.3

Average hourly real wages for private production and
nonsupervisory workers, USA 1947–2016

Source: Economic Policy Institute, State of Working America Data Library,
Historical Wage Series, 2018, based on data taken from the Bureau of Labor
Statistics Current Employment Statistics.

growing inequality was due not so much to international trade as to technological change that was systematically favouring skilled over unskilled workers. One strike against the globalization explanation was that the skill premium (the gap between skilled and unskilled wages) was rising in developing economies such as Mexico as well: if rich-country inequality was being increased as a result of rising exports of unskilled-labour-intensive goods from the developing world, then those same exports should be driving up unskilled wages in poor countries and lowering inequality there. That is not in fact what happened.

More recently, however, the debate has swung back towards the view that trade is important in explaining rising inequality, not only in rich countries, but potentially in developing economies such as Mexico as well. For one thing, Mexico is competing against countries like China, not just against countries like the United States. For another, the outsourcing activities of multinational firms may be reallocating labour tasks between countries in ways that traditional trade theory did not take account of. For example, very-low-skill service jobs, and high-skilled jobs involving abstract tasks, may be difficult to outsource, but middle-ranking routine tasks may be much more easily so. And indeed there seems to have been a 'hollowing out' of the income distribution in the US in recent years: wages at the top have been pulling away from average wages, while in some cases low wages are converging somewhat on the average. But the most influential work linking trade and income distribution today is, deservedly, a remarkable series of papers by the economists David Autor, David Dorn and Gordon Hanson.[13] They show that US regions which were more heavily exposed to rising Chinese import competition between 1990 and 2007, in the sense that they were specialized in producing goods that would face Chinese competition in the years to come, experienced higher unemployment, lower labour force participation and lower wages. Similar results have been found for a number of European countries.

In explaining Brexit what matters, of course, is the political consequences of globalization. And we have known for a long time that unskilled workers in rich countries are on average more protectionist than the more highly skilled. This has been extensively documented by academics using survey evidence, but we also have direct evidence from other European referendums. As you will recall, in 2005 a French referendum rejected the so-called 'European Constitutional Treaty' by a convincing margin. Although the reforms the treaty was supposed to introduce were largely procedural, the debate ended up being largely about the nature of the European integration process, seen as a regional example of globalization more generally. Left-wing opponents of the treaty pointed to the outsourcing of French jobs to Eastern Europe, and denounced the plans by Frits Bolkestein, an EU commissioner, to create a Europe-wide market for services. Fears were raised about Polish plumbers, and it was argued that unfair competition from low-tax, light-regulation economies would lead to 'social dumping' which would ultimately place the French welfare state under threat.

These arguments proved decisive, and in a major shock for Europe's political establishment voters rejected the Constitutional Treaty by a margin of 55 per cent to 45 per cent.

A few days later Dutch voters rejected the Constitutional Treaty by an even bigger margin. What is particularly striking about the French results is the way that voters divided along class lines. Only 35 per cent of professionals voted against the treaty, while the figure was 53 per cent for middle management, 67 per cent for clerical workers, 70 per cent for farmers, and an overwhelming 79 per cent for blue-collar workers.[14]

The response was to preserve many of the treaty's substantive reforms, while studiously avoiding any suggestion that the EU might be on its way to eventually becoming a federal state.[15] There was of course no referendum on what became the Lisbon Treaty in France, but there was in Ireland in 2008 and once again a clear class divide opened up. In affluent areas of Dublin's south side over 60 per cent of voters supported the treaty, while more than 60 per cent of voters in working-class areas opposed it.

There are at least two ways of interpreting such patterns. The first would hold that well-educated voters are more politically sophisticated, and better able to understand the issues involved in a complex amendment to the institutional underpinnings of the European Union. I believe that academics should be reluctant to accept arguments that are from their point of view so obviously self-serving as this one, and economists should be especially reluctant since they typically assume that people are rational. The second interpretation is that, on the contrary, both rich and poor are capable of correctly discerning where their economic interests lie and vote accordingly. The argument would be that globalization generally, and European integration more narrowly, has overwhelmingly favoured skilled workers, at least in affluent countries such as France, Ireland and the Netherlands. Unskilled workers, by contrast, feel under threat from Romanian (or Asian) competition, or immigration from Eastern Europe and further afield.

Subsequent analysis of survey data carried out on behalf of the Irish government found some support for both of these positions.[16] On the one hand, there was clear evidence that the more information people had about the contents of the treaty the more likely they were to vote in favour of it. On the other hand, concerns about low wages were an important factor leading people to vote no – but only if they were in the labour force. Similarly, university education led people to vote yes, but again only if they were in the labour force. If a university education mattered for voting behaviour only by allowing people to understand complex issues, it should have led to university graduates voting yes whether or not they were active in the labour market. The fact that university education and concerns about lower wages only influenced the votes of workers and the unemployed – that is to say, people whose living standards were potentially affected by European integration and globalization more generally – suggests to me that economic interests were playing an important role in these referendums.

In the United States economists have found that those regions most exposed to the 'China shock' experienced greater political polarization from 2000 onwards: 'Trade-exposed districts initially in Republican hands become substantially more likely to elect a conservative Republican, while trade-exposed districts initially in Democratic hands become more likely to elect either a liberal Democrat or a conservative Republican.'[17] Take this in conjunction with the evidence cited earlier, on the impact of Chinese imports on local labour market outcomes, and you have a compelling empirical argument linking globalization to both economic deprivation and Donald Trump. The precise mechanism is unclear, however. Some Trump supporters were presumably voting in favour of protection, in the manner of nineteenth-century European landowners. However, populist voters in the US could also have been voting for politicians promising a greater slice of the public service pie for white voters, at a time of increased competition for government services: it is sometimes difficult to disentangle purely economic explanations for populism from those emphasizing racism.[18]

Strikingly there is also compelling evidence that both trade and immigration were associated with the vote for Brexit. In an important recent contribution, Italo Colantone and Piero Stanig find that 'the Leave share was systematically higher in regions that have been more exposed to the Chinese import shock, due to their historical sectoral specialization.'[19] They point out that this could be because voters actually wanted protection against Chinese imports, but that it could also just reflect the fact that their regions were doing badly, and that they therefore wanted to punish the government and business leaders. Another study by Sascha Becker, Thiemo Fetzer and Dennis Novy finds that areas with low pay, high unemployment, a tradition of manufacturing, and lower-skilled workers were all more likely to vote for Brexit, as were areas that had experienced a recent influx of Eastern European migrants.[20] These findings are all consistent with the notion that Brexit had something to do with the stresses of globalization.

Austerity

If globalization is hurting particular regions in the West, and causing voters to express their frustration by voting for populist parties or causes, then the question arises as to what can be done to prevent this. The traditional answer is that the government has an important role to play by providing safety nets for individuals, families and regions. The evidence suggests that governments can make a difference, and that there is nothing inevitable about growing inequality in a globalizing world. This is an important point to stress. In many continental European countries states have been far more protective of workers than in the US or UK, and this has mattered for outcomes. In France, for example, Piketty, Saez and Zucman estimate that the incomes of the poorest 50 per cent of the population have increased by 32 per cent since 1980, a sharp contrast with the situation in the United States described earlier.

One of the problems in the UK was that local communities were left to cope with the consequences of globalization with much less help from the government. As already mentioned, Cameron and Osborne imposed a radical austerity programme on the British economy, and their aim was not just to borrow less: their stated goal was to shrink the size of the state. One of the most comprehensive studies of the referendum has found extensive evidence that the Brexit vote was related to austerity and the poor provision of public services. Furthermore, austerity was much more important in driving the Brexit vote than immigration from Eastern Europe: while even a very large reduction in the inflow of immigrants would have been insufficient to overturn the result, a modest reduction in austerity could have sufficed to produce a different outcome.[21]

A comprehensive and careful study by Thiemo Fetzer documents the austerity connection in even greater detail. His conclusions are striking:

> Austerity-induced welfare reforms are a strong driving factor behind the growing support for the populist UKIP party . . . contributed to the development of broader anti-establishment preferences and are strongly associated with popular support for Leave. The results suggest that the EU referendum either may not have taken place, or . . . could have resulted in a victory for Remain, had it not been for austerity.

Austerity-driven welfare reforms had an especially important political impact in regions where rising inequality meant that vulnerable populations were becoming increasingly reliant on the state. Prior to 2010 the welfare state muted the rise in inequality, but it stopped doing so after the switch to austerity: 'austerity was key to *activating these grievances*, converting them into political dissatisfaction culminating in Brexit.'[22]

Austerity created the conditions in which that red campaign bus, with its promise to bring back money from Brussels and invest it in the health services, was so effective. There is a considerable irony here, and also an important cautionary tale. The irony is that, presumably, when the Conservatives came to power in 2010 they thought that it would be a good idea to shrink the state because this would be beneficial for business: less state, lower taxes, greater competitiveness. But what they actually achieved was the greatest catastrophe to hit British business since the war. The debacle is a textbook demonstration of a point that the distinguished Turkish economist Dani Rodrik has often made. Political debates between left and right frequently make it sound as though the market and the state are substitutes: more market means less state and vice versa. But once you take the politics into account this turns out to be wrong. You need an effective state to protect citizens against the risks associated with the market. Undermine the state and you risk undermining political support for the market. In the British context a small-state agenda helped to bring about Brexit, which as we will see risks bringing about a historic destruction of previously integrated markets.

The cautionary tale is obvious. Political leaders who want to retain the efficiency of markets need to maintain political support for them. Too many unpopular reforms and you are potentially opening the door to every populism. Too big a reduction in state safety nets and you may ultimately end up hurting the market you want to promote.

Chance and Contingency

By now some readers may have concluded that Brexit was inevitable (and Trump as well). It is in the Anglo-Saxon economies that the pendulum has swung the most towards markets in recent decades, and away from interventionist states that can protect workers when things go wrong. In the context of a rapidly globalizing world this ended up being unsustainable, and a populist political backlash was the result. On top of that there were the many British voters who had traditionally been Eurosceptic because of worries about parliamentary sovereignty or for other reasons: the resulting Brexit coalition was unstoppable. But as Dominic Cummings, the mastermind of the Vote Leave campaign puts it, 'Reality has branching histories, not "a big why".'[23]

Cummings and Tim Shipman list several factors that helped history to branch in favour of Brexit. Boris Johnson might easily have decided to campaign for a Remain vote: he even wrote an article explaining why this was a good idea (although he never published it). According to Cummings, 'Without Boris, Farage would have been a much more prominent face on TV during the crucial final weeks, probably *the* most prominent face . . . It is extremely plausible that this would have lost us over 600,000 vital middle class votes.' Jeremy Corbyn might not have been elected leader of the Labour Party: a more pro-European leader might have campaigned more effectively for Remain in working-class areas. David Cameron might have called the referendum later, and as I suggested above this might have helped him. And he could have avoided obvious mistakes, such as suggesting that he could obtain a fundamental reform of the rules of the Single Market by removing the rights of European citizens to live and work wherever they like. This was never a possibility, and it meant that Cameron had set himself up for failure before the campaign had ever begun.[24]

Above all, you can question whether Cameron really did have to promise a referendum in 2013. As I indicated in the last chapter, Shipman believes that the referendum became inevitable after the backbench rebellion in 2011, but Cummings strongly disagrees and he is worth quoting at length:

> I also thought it foolish of Cameron to cave in to the pressure and promise a referendum in 2013. So did Gove and Osborne, both of whom told Cameron not to do it. He mistakenly thought it would take the wind out of UKIP's sails and did not understand why it would actually boost UKIP and Farage . . . The idea that there was an irresistible force for a referendum is pushed by Farage's and Cameron's supporters. They are both wrong. The country supported one but without any passion outside the small fraction who had long been passionate about it. Most Tory MPs did not want it. Most Tory donors thought the timing was wrong . . . Those MPs who did want it could mostly have been bought off or distracted in other ways – a mix of some policy, gongs, bribes, and so on in the usual fashion.

In a closely fought referendum campaign everything matters. Cummings believes that 'If Boris, Gove, and Gisela had not supported us and picked up the baseball bat marked "Turkey/NHS/£350 million" with five weeks to go, then 650,000 votes might have been lost', and he is better qualified than most to make this judgement.[25] Deeper structural factors – deprivation in former manufacturing areas, old-fashioned English nationalism, or the deeply held belief of many that EU membership undermined British parliamentary sovereignty – surely mattered also. And so did the long-standing civil war within the Tory party, and the choices that a handful of ambitious men made as a result. In 2012, as David Cameron was edging his way towards a commitment on a referendum, he told Nick Clegg, the Liberal Democrat leader, 'I have to do this. It is a party management issue.'[26]

Rarely does a political gamble fail as spectacularly as Cameron's. He assumed that he would win the referendum but lost it. And as for party management, which was the object of the exercise: as we will see in the following chapters, the Tory civil war is still with us.

CHAPTER 10
The Aftermath

The twenty-fourth of June 2016 dawned on an uncertain Europe. In the UK David Cameron arrived at Downing Street at 7 a.m. acknowledging 'Well, that didn't go according to plan!' Kenneth Clarke had predicted that Cameron wouldn't last 30 seconds if he lost the referendum and he was almost right: Cameron was gone an hour later.[1] A leadership race ensued in which Boris Johnson initially appeared to be the frontrunner, but many Conservative Remainers were horrified by the prospect. They soon settled on Theresa May as an alternative candidate. May was the Home Secretary, and like many other Home Secretaries in the UK and elsewhere was hostile to immigration. In October 2015 she had made a strongly anti-immigration speech to the Conservative Party conference in which she stated baldly that 'the numbers coming from Europe are unsustainable and the rules have to change.' She also explicitly linked the question of refugee flows and illegal immigration into Europe with the EU's rules on free movement for European citizens.[2] Such considerations led her to strongly support Cameron's pledge to renegotiate the principle of free movement of people, for as she had written earlier, 'the biggest single factor preventing us from meeting our objective [to reduce net immigration] is net migration from the European Union.'[3]

You might not think that such a person would be a logical candidate for Remainers to unite behind: her 2015 conference speech led one MP to describe her as 'Enoch Powell in a dress'.[4] But May had in fact backed Remain, if only in the most half-hearted of ways. This made her potentially capable of uniting the Leave and Remain factions within the party, and above all it made her potentially capable of stopping Boris Johnson. That task was made easier on 30 June when Johnson's main backer, Michael Gove, announced that he had come to the conclusion that Johnson was not up to the job and would be running instead. In the end Mrs May was the last woman standing, and on 13 July 2016 she succeeded David Cameron as Prime Minister. The question was: what kind of Brexit would the new government be pursuing?

Apart from the UK itself, the country where the answer to that question mattered most was Ireland. As we saw in Chapter 6, the fact that both Ireland and the UK were members of the European Union had been crucial in helping to resolve a long and bloody conflict in Northern Ireland. The two communities there remained deeply divided, but there had been some moving symbols of reconciliation over the years, one of the most striking being the friendship that emerged between Ian Paisley, founder of the DUP and opponent of the 1960s civil rights movement, and Martin McGuinness, a former IRA member. The two served together as First Minister and Deputy First Minister of Northern Ireland between 2007 and 2008. The border between Ireland and Northern Ireland had become essentially invisible, bringing important practical benefits to ordinary people. What would Brexit mean for the Northern Irish peace process, or for communities on both sides of the border? And what would it mean for the rest of Ireland? As we saw in Chapters 6 and 7 Irish independence and prosperity had both been enhanced by EU membership, so there was never any question of Ireland following Britain out of the EU. But Britain remained a very important trading partner for an economy that had only just recovered from a devastating banking crisis, so British choices mattered a lot for Ireland.

In addition to the UK and Ireland, the other immediately affected parties were the other 26 member states and the European institutions. In France Jean-Marie Le Pen congratulated the British electorate on its courage and called for a referendum in France. His daughter Marine tweeted: 'Victory for liberty! As I have been demanding for years we need similar referendums in France and the countries of the EU.'5 The result was also immediately welcomed by the far-right Alternativ für Deutschland (AfD) party in Germany and the Dutch populist Geert Wilders.

Not surprisingly, the reaction of President François Hollande in France was very different. He described the referendum result as 'a painful choice that I deeply regret, for the United Kingdom and for Europe. But it is their choice and we must respect that, taking on board all its consequences . . . There is a great danger of extremism and populism. It always takes less time to dismantle than to assemble, or to destroy than to build.'6 There were similar reactions elsewhere on the continent. But apart from regretting the UK's decision, the question remained: how would the EU as a whole respond to the challenges posed by Brexit? Since Brexit was a unilateral British decision, the answer to that question would largely depend on what the UK government decided to do next.

What Does the UK Want?

The UK had voted to leave the EU, but it remained to be seen what sort of a future relationship with the EU the UK had in mind for itself. The referendum did not provide much guidance on the issue, since voters had merely been asked 'Should the United Kingdom remain a member of the European Union or leave the European Union?': there was nothing on the ballot paper about either the customs union or the Single Market, and different Leave voters presumably had different views on those issues. On the face of it, the electoral logic seemed to imply that the government should pursue what soon became known as a 'soft Brexit', that is to say a Brexit that involved the United Kingdom remaining inside the EU's Single Market, or a customs union with the EU, or both. After all, no less than 48 per cent of voters had wanted to remain inside the EU, and several Leavers had indicated before the referendum that they had no problem with remaining in the Single Market. It seemed reasonable to suppose that, given the choice between different types of Brexit, a majority of voters would therefore have backed a version that left the UK as closely tied to the EU as possible, and that a 'soft Brexit' along these lines might provide a way of uniting a bitterly divided society.

That was certainly what many outside Britain hoped for, especially in those countries heavily dependent on trade with the UK such as Denmark, the Netherlands and above all Ireland.

But the initial signs were not hopeful. Mrs May took the extraordinary step of appointing Boris Johnson as Foreign Secretary. As we saw in Chapter 8, Johnson had just compared the European Union to Adolf Hitler; he also had a history of saying things that could have been condemned as racist coming from anyone else.[7] The French Foreign Minister, Jean-Marc Ayrault, reacted by reminding his compatriots that 'During the campaign he lied a lot to the British.'[8] May also appointed two further leading Brexiteers to key positions: David Davis was to head the new Department for Exiting the European Union (DExEU), while Liam Fox became Minister in another new department, the Department for International Trade. Davis had argued during the referendum campaign that the UK would be able to negotiate trade deals with individual EU member states after Brexit. In May he tweeted that 'The first calling point of the UK's negotiator immediately after #Brexit will not be Brussels, it will be Berlin, to strike a deal.'[9] At this late stage Davis was apparently unaware that individual EU member states are not allowed to negotiate their own bilateral trade deals with other countries: as you will recall from Chapter 3, a customs union commits all members to having the same external tariffs vis-à-vis third countries, and all EU member states are therefore bound by the EU's common external trade policy. As for Fox, his department was set up to strike trade deals with non-EU countries, one of the main supposed benefits of Brexit, despite the fact that the UK cannot legally do this until it has finally exited the EU. Giving Fox this job was a strong signal that Mrs May did not believe that the UK should remain inside a future EU–UK customs union.[10]

That left the option of the Single Market. But in the summer of 2016 even former Remainers seemed to be accepting the fundamental premise of the Leave campaign, namely that there were too many Europeans in Britain. Not only commentators, but also public figures such as Gordon Brown, argued that the UK should be aiming for a deal that kept it inside the European Economic Area, which we encountered in Chapter 8, and the European Single Market, but which allowed it to restrict the free movement of people. After all, Liechtenstein (population 37,000) had a special deal in place when it came to immigration.[11] With Remainers like this, who needed Leavers?[12]

Mrs May herself was, as we have seen, instinctively hostile to free movement, and one of her chief advisers was Nick Timothy – a keen admirer of none other than Joseph Chamberlain.[13] Another indication that the UK government might not be seeking a soft Brexit. But it was still a shock to this Irishman to hear Mrs May telling the Conservative Party conference in October 2016 that the UK was now going to be free to make its own decisions

> on a whole host of different matters, from how
> we label our food to the way in which we choose
> to control immigration . . . It is not, therefore, a
> negotiation to establish a relationship anything like
> the one we have had for the last forty years or more.
> So it is not going to [be] a 'Norway model' . . . We are
> not leaving the European Union only to give up control
> of immigration again. And we are not leaving only to
> return to the jurisdiction of the European Court of
> Justice.[14]

It was when Theresa May started talking about food labelling that it became clear: she no longer wanted the UK to be bound, like Norway, by the common rules that made border formalities redundant in 1993. And the reference to the European Court of Justice (ECJ) confirmed that first impression, since wherever you have common rules you need a form of arbitration to ensure that they are being respected. The message was stark: as far as the British Prime Minister was concerned, the UK would be leaving the Single Market. And the bad news for Ireland was that – as we saw in Chapter 5 – this would mean the re-introduction of border controls between the EU and UK.[15]

Mrs May's hard-line vision was spelled out even more explicitly on 17 January 2017. The Prime Minister gave a speech in Lancaster House that in retrospect feels like one of the last hubristic expressions of Brexiteer triumphalism before reality started to sink in. She reminded her audience of the UK's historic links with the Commonwealth, and explained to any Europeans who might be listening that 'Many in Britain have always felt that the United Kingdom's place in the European Union came at the expense of our global ties, and of a bolder embrace of free trade with the wider world.' As a friendly neighbour, she advised the EU to cherish difference and reform itself, rather than dealing with different interests by 'tightening a vice-like grip that ends up crushing into tiny pieces the very things you want to protect'. And most importantly, she set out a series of clear red lines that the UK would adhere to in the negotiations to come. The UK would 'bring an end to the jurisdiction of the European Court of Justice in Britain', since 'we will not have truly left the European Union if we are not in control of our own laws.' The UK would not be a member of the Single Market, since it could not accept the four freedoms (of goods, services, capital and people), could not accept regulations that had been decided elsewhere, and could not accept the jurisdiction of the ECJ. The UK would therefore no longer be making 'vast' financial contributions to Brussels every year. And since the UK wanted to make free trade deals across the world, it would no longer be bound by the EU customs union's Common Commercial Policy and Common External Tariff. The EU would be foolish to seek a 'punitive deal': 'No deal for Britain,' she warned, 'is better than a bad deal for Britain.'[16]

The Brexiteers loved it, but there was a problem: large sections of the British economy depended on the Single Market. There was the City of London, of course: since the early 1990s increasing numbers of financial services had gained passporting rights, 'based on the principle of mutual recognition and harmonised prudential measures'. Passporting meant that 'a European financial institution which has been authorised by its domestic authority has the right to establish a branch or provide services in any other European Economic Area (EEA) Member State without the need to seek further authorisation or another licence.' For example, a French bank wishing to operate in Belgium could simply open a branch there, rather than setting up a Belgian subsidiary. Since a subsidiary would be a new and separate legal entity, subject to Belgian supervision and regulation, and with its own obligations regarding, for example, how much capital it had to hold, passporting was clearly a much more efficient option. And it was not only banks that benefited from passporting: so did investment funds, rating agencies, brokers, firms involved in securities and derivatives markets, and many others.[17]

If UK financial services companies lost passporting, their ability to continue to do business within the EU would be thrown into doubt. Some might potentially be allowed to continue as before if the European Commission decided that UK regulations were 'equivalent', but such equivalence for third-country providers is established on a far more piecemeal basis, and the Commission would be free to determine that UK regulations were no longer equivalent at any point in the future. Such uncertainty would inevitably harm the City of London. For this reason the British government's position was that the UK and EU should continue to recognize that their financial regulations were equivalent: in other words, the UK wanted 'mutual recognition' of financial service regulations to continue into the future. As the new Chancellor, Philip Hammond, put it as late as March 2018,

> the EU's established third-country equivalence regime . . . would be wholly inadequate for the scale and complexity of UK–EU financial services trade. It was never meant to carry such a load. The EU regime is unilateral and access can be withdrawn with little to no notice. Clearly not a platform on which to base a multi-trillion pound trade relationship. But the principle of mutual recognition and reciprocal regulatory equivalence . . . could provide an effective basis for such a partnership.[18]

And then there were cars, and other manufacturers depending on complex international supply chains. Take Honda, for example, which manufactures the Honda Civic near Swindon.[19]

According to the *Financial Times*, 2 million components flow 'like water' from suppliers in the UK and the rest of the EU to its production line each day, but the warehouses at the plant only have parts for 36 hours' worth of production. Just-in-time production methods mean that these components are only ordered when they are needed: components from other EU member states can arrive in as little as five to 24 hours. If border controls were re-introduced between the EU and UK, those delivery times would range between two and nine days: if Honda tried to stock enough components to keep production going for nine days this would require a warehouse of 300,000 square metres, equivalent to 42 football pitches. The costs would be astronomical and give rise to doubt about whether important employers such as Honda, Nissan and Airbus, all of whom are reliant on pan-European supply chains, could continue manufacturing in Britain. There was particular political sensitivity regarding Nissan, a major employer in Sunderland – a city that had voted to leave the EU. In consequence, in October 2016 the UK Business Secretary Greg Clark wrote a secret letter to the company offering up to £80 million in aid on condition that Nissan's Qashqai and X-Trail models were produced in Sunderland. Ensuring that car makers' ability to trade with the EU would not be 'adversely affected' would be a 'critical priority' for the government, the letter promised.[20] In the same month there were suggestions in the media that the UK would indeed seek a sectoral deal with the EU, allowing industries that particularly benefited from the EU Single Market and customs union to continue to do so in the future.

But it wasn't only large car and aerospace companies that

felt threatened by the possible re-introduction of border controls: the consequences of only minimal border controls, in a situation where previously there had been none, were potentially enormous for all businesses engaged in international trade. Officials at the Port of Dover have estimated that a border delay of only two minutes per truck would imply a 27-kilometre queue on the M20 motorway. So it is no surprise that in her January 2017 Lancaster House speech Mrs May also said that she wanted trade with the EU to be 'as frictionless as possible'.

That is of course what many former Tory Remainers wanted as well. And so the British government's opening position was that it wanted to restrict immigration from the EU, regain control over its own laws, leave the jurisdiction of the ECJ, and therefore leave the EU Single Market; despite this, it also wanted to preserve the City of London's privileged access to European markets; it wanted to do free trade deals around the world, and therefore did not want to join a new post-Brexit EU–UK customs union; and yet at the same time it also wanted to maintain frictionless trade with the EU – or at least, trade that was as frictionless as possible. In other words, the UK wanted to keep the bits of EU membership that it valued and get rid of the rest: it wanted to have its cake and eat it. Famously Boris Johnson had once said as much, and in November 2016 an aide leaving DExEU was photographed clutching a notepad on which the words 'What's the model? Have cake & eat' were clearly visible to photographers.[21] A new word has thus entered the European political lexicon: 'cakeism', the policy of wanting to have your cake and eat it.

Viewed from a cakeist perspective a Norway-type solution,

in which the UK remained inside the EEA (see Chapter 8), was unacceptable: this would involve the free movement of people, financial contributions to the EU, and acceptance of EU regulations. But a free trade deal with the EU, such as the EU–Canada Comprehensive Economic and Trade Agreement signed by Justin Trudeau in 2016, was also unacceptable, since it would not guarantee a privileged position for the City of London in European markets and would involve border controls. Switching from food to fashion metaphors, the UK government argued that such 'off the shelf' arrangements were inappropriate and that an entirely new, 'bespoke' deal was what was required.

There then followed a series of proposals from British politicians, each more fanciful than the next, outlining how Britain could indeed manage to have its cake and eat it: how it could leave the Single Market, pursue an independent trade policy, and at the same time avoid the re-introduction of border controls with the EU, preserve frictionless trade, and save the jobs that depended on it. Such a deal would be easy to achieve: 'one of the easiest in human history', as Liam Fox put it in July 2017. But early on ministers displayed a worrying lack of understanding of the rules, not only of the European Union, but of the World Trade Organization. Take for example the notion that there could be special sectoral deals for cars and the City: this would involve the UK and EU granting each other preferential access to each other's markets for just these sectors. But as you will recall from Chapter 2, GATT (and hence WTO) rules do not allow the EU to treat UK imports more favourably than imports from other WTO members. The only exception to this most-favoured-nation non-discrimination rule is if the UK and the EU agree to form either a free trade area or a customs union, and crucially, such arrangements have to involve 'substantially all the trade'. There is some debate about exactly what that means, but there is no doubt that an arrangement involving just a few sectors would not be legal, and other WTO members would presumably object. In consequence the sectoral approach never went anywhere, at least as regards industrial sectors – as we have seen there have been long-standing British efforts in the negotiations to protect the interests of the City of London.

But there was an even more fundamental inconsistency at the heart of the British position. As already noted, in order for the UK to preserve frictionless trade with the EU it would need to remain in the EU Single Market; it would need to remain in the EU VAT regime; and it would need to form a new post-Brexit customs union with the EU. Mrs May's red lines ruled all of this out. Her government might well prefer to have its cake and eat it, but in the end it was always going to have to choose. And while Lancaster House suggested that if forced to it would choose a 'hard Brexit' and the re-introduction of border controls, the British government continued to insist that it would be possible to obtain a trading relationship with the EU that was frictionless – or at least 'as frictionless as possible'. It had to do so because of internal Conservative Party divisions – Leavers wanting regulatory independence and swashbuckling new British trade policies, Remainers wanting frictionless trade with the EU – but this was only putting off the moment when decisions would have to be made. And it was still unclear what way the British government would jump when that moment arrived.

Nevertheless, on 29 March 2017 the UK's Permanent Representative to the EU delivered a letter to Donald Tusk, President of the European Council, informing him of the UK's intention to leave the European Union. The letter stated that the UK wanted to retain a 'deep and special partnership' with the Union, and it apparently wanted this so badly that the phrase was used no less than seven times in the six-page document.[22] How did the European Union respond?

The EU Reaction

The EU approach to Brexit has been remarkably consistent. On the morning of 24 June 2016 Donald Tusk, the Presidents of the European Parliament (Martin Schulz) and European Commission (Jean-Claude Juncker), and the Dutch Prime Minister Mark Rutte (since the Netherlands at that time held the Presidency of the Council of the European Union) set out some basic principles regarding what had to happen next:

> We now expect the United Kingdom government to give effect to this decision of the British people as soon as possible, however painful that process may be. Any delay would unnecessarily prolong uncertainty. We have rules to deal with this in an orderly way. Article 50 of the Treaty on European Union sets out the procedure to be followed if a Member State decides to leave the European Union. We stand ready to launch negotiations swiftly with the United Kingdom regarding the terms and conditions of its withdrawal from the European Union . . .

The four went on to point out that the concessions obtained by David Cameron in February, and on the basis of which he had fought the referendum campaign, were now null and void. And then they continued: 'As regards the United Kingdom, we hope to have it as a close partner of the European Union in the future. We expect the United Kingdom to formulate its proposals in this respect. Any agreement, which will be concluded with the United Kingdom as a third country, will have to reflect the interests of both sides and be balanced in terms of rights and obligations.'[23]

This immediate reaction by European leaders made several important political points. First, Brexit would have to take place in accordance with the rules of the Union. Second, Brexit should happen quickly. Third, it was up to the UK to decide what it wanted the nature of its future relationship with the EU to be. But fourth, any future relationship between the EU and UK would have to be in the interests of the EU, and would have to balance 'rights and obligations'.

What rules had to be followed regarding Brexit? The Lisbon Treaty had for the first time spelled these out explicitly: this is the famous Article 50 referred to in the statement above. It was drafted by none other than John Kerr, whom we last encountered hiding under a table in Maastricht, and it states that:

A Member State which decides to withdraw shall notify the European Council of its intention. In the light of the guidelines provided by the European Council, the Union shall negotiate and conclude an agreement with that State, setting out the arrangements for its withdrawal, taking account of the framework for its future relationship with the Union . . . The Treaties shall cease to apply to the

State in question from the date of entry into force of the withdrawal agreement or, failing that, two years after the notification referred to [above], unless the European Council, in agreement with the Member State concerned, unanimously decides to extend this period.

In other words, first the UK would have to notify the European Council that it was leaving. The EU would negotiate a Withdrawal Agreement, based on guidelines agreed upon by the European Council (that is to say, the heads of state or government of the 27 remaining member states). This agreement would above all set out the arrangements under which Britain would leave the EU. It only had to 'take account of' what the future relationship between the UK and EU might be. If a Withdrawal Agreement had not been negotiated within two years of the UK's formal notification that it was leaving, the UK would automatically crash out without any deal at all – unless all 27 remaining member states agreed to extend the deadline. The implication was that unless the UK requested an extension, and everyone agreed to this, it would leave the EU no later than 29 March 2019.

Article 50 suggests a sequence of events: first notification, then negotiation. It may not say explicitly that this is the way things have to happen, but at a minimum it suggests that the remaining member states are under no obligation to negotiate until notification has been received, thus triggering the withdrawal process.[24] And in fact a statement issued by the heads of state or government of the remaining 27 Member States on 29 June was explicit on the subject: 'there can be no negotiations of any kind before this notification has taken place.' This made logical sense: why negotiate before you have been officially notified that the UK wants to leave the EU? It also implied that the UK would be under extreme time pressure: it would only have two years to negotiate its exit or else it would crash out without a deal. Indeed, it would have less than two years, since the 27 leaders also decided that the European Council would only agree on its negotiating guidelines after the notification had been received: again, why bother to agree these before it was certain that the UK government in fact wanted to proceed with Brexit? The Article 50 process is therefore stacked against the interests of the withdrawing country, as you would expect.

The Withdrawal Agreement only has to 'take account' of the future relationship. But many in Britain were shocked to learn that it would in fact be impossible to agree the future trade relationship between the two sides until after exit had occurred.[25] There was some debate about the point in 2016, with the British arguing that trade negotiations should take place in parallel with negotiations about withdrawal, but they eventually conceded the point. It was not clear what the legal basis would be for negotiating a trade agreement with a soon-to-be-non-member that was currently a member, nor how this could happen in practice: it is the EU as a whole that negotiates trade deals with third countries, and how could you have a situation in which the EU, including the UK, negotiated a deal with the UK? But the implications of this were potentially very disturbing, since it takes years for free trade agreements to be negotiated – for example, the Canada–EU free trade deal was only signed after seven years of talks. In the period between Brexit and the successful negotiation and ratification of a new free trade deal, the EU and UK would be forced to impose tariffs on each other's goods, since otherwise they would be breaking the most-favoured-nation provisions of the WTO.

There is a logical solution to this dilemma. It involves agreeing a post-Brexit transition period during which the UK would no longer be a member of the EU but in practice everything would remain the same. In particular, during the transition period the UK would remain a member of the EU customs union and Single Market. The hope would then be that a new trade deal between the two sides could be negotiated during this transition period. In this manner businesses would only have to adjust once to the new trading environment, when the UK exited the transition phase and entered into the new relationship with the EU, whatever that might be. Whether the transition phase would be long enough to permit this new relationship to be negotiated is of course another matter.

And what about the requirement that any future relationship would have to be balanced in terms of 'rights and obligations'? The 29 June statement spelled this out in precise terms: 'Access to the Single Market requires acceptance of all four freedoms.' The UK could aim for a future relationship that implied high levels of rights and obligations: it could remain within the Single Market for goods, services and capital if it wished, but it would then have to accept the fourth freedom associated with the Single Market, that regarding the free movement of persons. Or it could aim for a future relationship implying low levels of rights and obligations, and leave the Single Market entirely. It could not remain in just those bits that were of interest to it: as European politicians have frequently put it, the UK cannot have the rights of Norway and the obligations of Canada. The sentence regarding the four freedoms was inserted at the insistence of Angela Merkel: none of the other member states objected. Cakeism would not be tolerated. To use another food metaphor, there was to be no cherry picking.[26]

This insistence that the UK cannot simply pick and choose those bits of the Single Market that it likes and disregard the rest is easy to understand. The Single Market was negotiated at a time when the European Communities only had twelve members, but even so it was an astonishing diplomatic and political achievement. A complex international deal like this is by definition something that everyone has decided they can live with: allow countries to avoid the bits they dislike and the whole thing risks collapsing. To allow a member state to cherry pick would therefore be dangerous enough (as well as illegal under the treaties); to allow a non-member or 'third country' to do so would be absurd. This is simple self-preservation on the part of the EU, which is defined by the treaties: take them away and it ceases to exist.

The insistence that any future trade relationship would have to balance rights and obligations had immediate logical consequences when combined with Theresa May's Lancaster House red lines. Since Mrs May was ruling out membership of a customs union, and did not want to remain inside the Single Market, the best that could be hoped for was a Canada-style free trade agreement. This would, as frequently stressed in this book, bring frictionless trade between the EU and UK to an end. On the other hand, if Mrs May's red lines were to evolve, then a deeper relationship would become possible.

Another obvious EU interest is to preserve its own decision-making autonomy. If there is one thing that gives the EU influence on the world stage it is surely its Single Market and the fact that the EU decides what the rules for that market should be. If firms from other countries want to participate in the Single Market they have to follow EU rules. And so any proposals that might undermine that regulatory autonomy posed an existential threat to the European Union. This has been the rock on which UK proposals for mutual recognition of financial service regulations have foundered, for example. The notion that the EU would not retain complete discretion regarding the rules applying to financial services was never going to fly, especially in the aftermath of the 2008 financial crisis.

The EU was also concerned about the possibility that the UK would use its new-found regulatory freedom to deregulate, cutting costs for British businesses and giving them a competitive advantage in the European market. As we saw in Chapter 1, one of the main purposes of supranational European institutions was that they could help to prevent a damaging regulatory race to the bottom, but you will also recall Mrs Thatcher's fear, expressed in Bruges, of British deregulation being undone by EU legislation. There was therefore every reason to worry about what her heirs in the Conservative Party might do after Brexit, and those fears were given tangible form in January 2017 when Philip Hammond raised the possibility of the UK abandoning the European social model.[27] Ensuring a 'level playing field' as a condition for the UK being granted deep access to the European Single Market was thus another important negotiating objective for the EU:

this goes beyond adherence to Single Market regulations, with implications (for example) regarding post-Brexit UK tax policy.

There were also more mundane matters of concern to the EU, in particular money. The EU had previously agreed a budget that was to run until the end of 2020; the UK had agreed that budget along with everyone else and had assumed financial obligations as a result. Since the UK is a net financial contributor to the EU, the EU had an obvious interest in making sure that the UK paid as much as possible, and preferably all, of what it had signed up to. And then there were the interests of the more than 3 million EU citizens living in the UK to take account of: how could their rights after 2019 be ensured?

The Irish Border

Finally, EU negotiating objectives have been shaped to a remarkable extent by the interests of one small country, namely Ireland. This reflects outstanding work by the Irish diplomatic service, but you also have the sense that Ireland was to a large extent pushing on an open door, for most other European governments instinctively understand that the EU is above all a political project and a peace project. The fact that Fine Gael, the governing party in Dublin, was a member of the European People's Party that David Cameron had previously abandoned was useful in creating links with governing parties elsewhere in Europe. It surely also helped that the EU's chief Brexit negotiator was Michel Barnier. A Savoyard, he instinctively understood the concerns of the rural communities who would be most affected, and this French background was complemented by his experience as EU

Commissioner when he oversaw the signing of the second EU Programme for Peace and Reconciliation in Northern Ireland and the Border Region of Ireland (2000–2004).

By the autumn of 2016 Irish politicians, businesses and commentators were becoming increasingly worried by the hard Brexit signals coming from London. There were concerns about the future of small Irish-owned, labour-intensive businesses exporting to the British market, and outright alarm about the potential consequences for the Irish border. Because if the UK did indeed leave the EU Single Market, or did not form a new customs union with the EU after Brexit, then border controls would inevitably return. Indeed they would also return if the UK left the EU's VAT regime, although it took some time for commentators to realize this.[28] And this would have potentially catastrophic consequences for small businesses, ordinary citizens, and perhaps even for the peace process itself.

The British were making it clear that they did not want to see border controls returning either, and at first this reassured some in Ireland – but as we have seen these comforting sentiments didn't necessarily mean very much since the British apparently believed that they could combine a hard Brexit with frictionless trade with the EU in general. There were also worrying indications that the Brexit Secretary, David Davis, was not taking either the problem or the Irish government particularly seriously. In July he referred to 'the internal border we have with southern Ireland', which did not go down particularly well in Dublin,[29] while in the same month an Irish official received a now-famous email from DExEU which read: 'the Secretary of State has told me he wants to meet Kenny.

Please let us know if Kenny is available.' 'Kenny' was Enda Kenny, the Irish Taoiseach, and the Irish immediately replied to DExEU to inform them that you didn't refer to another country's head of government by his surname in this manner, and that in any event the Taoiseach's interlocutor was Mrs May, not one of her ministers.[30]

In July 2016 Enda Kenny did meet Theresa May, and both sides agreed that they wanted to keep the Irish border open. But when an EU negotiator asked UK officials how a hard border could be avoided, were the UK to leave the customs union, the response was that 'We don't know. We don't have an answer.'[31] Tony Connelly's gripping book on the Brexit negotiations gives many examples of Irish businesses which could be devastated by the return of border checks – mushroom growers, beef farmers, cheddar cheese producers and others. But the potential impact on rural communities living on either side of the border is even more alarming.

I am writing these words in Saint Pierre d'Entremont, a small village in the Chartreuse. Saint Pierre is divided in two by the Guiers Vif, a river separating the departments of Isère and Savoie and which was until 1860 an international border.[32] The departmental frontier is both ubiquitous and irrelevant. It makes our lives more interesting, it occasionally causes a little inconvenience, and it essentially doesn't matter: we have two communes but one school, one post office, one postal code, one set of associations, one cinema, one parish, and so on. There are similar rural communities straddling the Irish border – Pettigo for example, a village divided between County Fermanagh in Northern Ireland and County Donegal in the Republic (see Map 10.1). An old customs hut still stands beside the

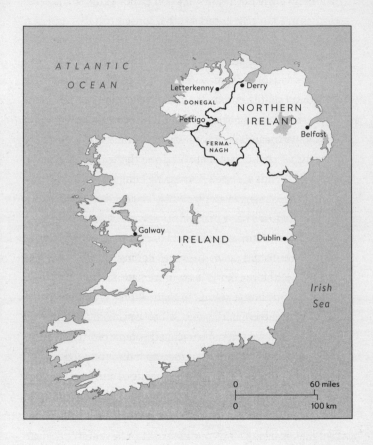

Figure 10.1
The Irish Border

river that marks the frontier. The border obviously matters more than the border in Saint Pierre – there are different currencies and educational systems on either side of it, for example. But it matters a lot less than it used to.

The 500 kilometre-long Irish border is famously irrational, which makes complete sense since it was never designed to be an international frontier in the first place. Instead it reflects centuries-old county boundaries. Rather than following a major river, like the Rhine, with a limited number of border crossings, it meanders across the Irish countryside dividing communities that naturally belong together, and on occasion bisecting individual farms or even buildings. There are more border crossings between Northern Ireland and Ireland than there are between the European Union and all the countries to its east,[33] and it would obviously never have been possible to have established customs checks along all of them. The solution found after 1923 was to designate sixteen crossings as 'approved': all dutiable goods, including motor vehicles, had to cross the border at one of these sixteen points.[34] All other crossings were unapproved, and could only be used by people travelling 'by foot, cycle or horse drawn vehicle' or by farmers (but only if they were carrying 'exempt farm produce'). A small number of clergymen, doctors and vets were also issued with permits allowing them to drive across unapproved crossings. As a local inhabitant in Pettigo told Susan McKay in 2017, 'When the customs was here it was just a substation – the trucks were not allowed to use it . . . They had to go through one of the main clearance stations. You had to be careful what you bought on either side. You had to have a special pass and if it was after hours you had to make special arrangements.'[35]

Life along the border was obviously even tougher during the Troubles. Customs posts were the targets of bomb attacks. Unapproved border crossings were now seen as potential security threats and were cratered or otherwise destroyed by the British security forces. People wishing to cross the border had in many cases to make long detours, and were forced to wait at heavily armed military checkpoints before crossing. The impact was dramatic: as one witness living close to the border later told researchers,

> living in a cul-de-sac is not a healthy thing to do . . .
> Because basically when I left my house there was only one
> way you went, you only ever went up the road. Unless you
> were delivering cattle or something. You didn't do anything
> else, because there was nothing there. But a hole. But I
> mean that is crazy when you think about it, isn't it, you just
> go somewhere and then there's a massive hole . . . I think
> that's probably worse than a wall.[36]

One particularly important way in which life along the border has changed for the better in recent years concerns healthcare. Today patients can access medical services on both sides of the frontier, but it was not always so easy. The RTÉ journalist Tony Connelly tells the story of a man from Donegal whose life was saved in 2016 because when he suffered his heart attack he was taken from Letterkenny to the hospital in Derry (in Northern Ireland) 35 kilometres away. The nearest hospitals in the Republic with acute services are in Galway or Dublin, more than 200 kilometres away: if he had had to be transported to either he would have died.[37] Such cross-border cooperation relies on a host of common EU rules, for example data protection rules making it possible to share patient details with healthcare providers across the island. Regulatory divergence making such cooperation legally impossible, or indeed border formalities of any kind delaying ambulances (assuming that these would be allowed to cross the border in the first place), would obviously place patient lives at risk.

But it is the potential political and security implications of a return to a hard border in Ireland, with customs posts once again appearing along approved crossings, that made politicians particularly nervous. The re-emergence of a border would give dissident republicans opposed to the peace process the excuse to resume violence, and it would also give them targets. Asked about the prospect of installing cameras along the border that could scan number plates with a view to making customs procedures more efficient, a Northern Ireland Office official told Tony Connelly that 'We're not even contemplating hardware like that along the border. Because the day it goes up, it will be down that night. There will be guys out with an angle grinder. The PSNI* have already said they will not be policing any customs infrastructure along the border because it will make them sitting ducks.' The PSNI itself concurs with this assessment. Its chief constable, George Hamilton, told the Sunday Times that physical infrastructure and border officials would be be targeted by dissident republicans and thus require PSNI protection: the result would be that

---

* Police Service of Northern Ireland.

The purpose for which those checking points and border controls would be put in place would become less and less relevant because they would move away from issues of trade or movement of people to old-fashioned security on a national frontier. That was done during the period of the Troubles rather unsuccessfully, and was sadly the subject of attacks and many lives lost.[38]

Imagine that whatever village you are most familiar with found itself in a situation in which border controls might suddenly appear along major departmental roads, and in which you were no longer allowed to transport goods along smaller departmental roads or communal roads. Imagine that heart attack patients would no longer be able to access the nearest acute service 30 minutes away, but would be forced to travel to a hospital that was almost four hours away. And imagine that there was even a risk that violence might erupt in the countryside in which you lived. It is no surprise that people living in Irish border communities viewed the return of a hard border as simply unthinkable. But just because something is unthinkable does not mean that it will not happen.

The EU Negotiating Guidelines

Even though the European Council would only adopt its Brexit negotiating guidelines after Britain had officially notified it of its intention to leave, negotiations *among* the 27 remaining member states regarding what should be in those guidelines obviously started much sooner. Many of the guidelines were uncontroversial, and followed directly from the EU's initial statements on Brexit and its fundamental interests as discussed above. The Irish border raised more complicated issues however, and it took more time to hammer out a common position on these.[39] The process involved Ireland progressively distancing itself from the country that had up until then been its greatest ally inside the EU, namely the United Kingdom.

It took a while for this to happen. As already noted, the Irish were initially somewhat reassured by Britain's repeated promises that it wanted no return to 'the borders of the past', but eventually people started to realize that even if the borders of the future were not the same as the borders of the past they would be borders nonetheless. There was some rather dangerous commentary in sections of the Irish media to the effect that surely the EU wouldn't make Ireland reinstate border controls, even if the UK as a whole decided to leave the customs union and/or Single Market: the impression was occasionally given that Ireland now faced being squeezed between two behemoths, the UK and EU, and would end up being badly damaged as a result. Academics such as myself pointed out that not enforcing the EU's external customs border would be both impossible and illegal in such circumstances, but chlorinated chicken proved a far more persuasive argument: in the spring of 2017 reports started to emerge that in the event of a post-Brexit UK–US trade deal the Americans would insist that the British import chicken carcasses that had been washed in chlorinated water.[40] The practice is banned in the EU, and the controversy helped people to understand exactly why it is that the EU has to enforce its external borders in order to preserve the Single Market. From then on there were fewer suggestions in the Irish media that there should be an Irish exception to the general requirement that EU member states check imports coming into the Single Market. But that left the question of how to avoid the return of a hard border unresolved.

The first months after Brexit saw a phase in which the Irish tried to come up with solutions to the problems Brexit posed for them. As in Britain, a certain amount of learning was involved. According to Connelly, at one stage in 2016 the Irish Department of Agriculture suggested a bilateral UK–Ireland free trade agreement for agriculture, which would obviously have been illegal.[41] The idea was immediately squashed by Phil Hogan, the Irish Agriculture Commissioner in Brussels. When the UK House of Lords Committee referred to in Chapter 6 suggested in December 2016 that 'in the event that the UK leaves the customs union' there should be a bilateral 'customs and trade arrangement between the two countries', the Irish government wasted no time in dismissing the proposal. This represented progress, but the Lords were disappointed.

Irish and European officials spent many hours trying to work out if there were technical ways of avoiding border controls in Ireland, while at the same time ensuring that the Irish border did not become a conduit for smuggled goods entering the European Single Market. Eventually they realized that they were doing the work of the cakeist British who had caused the problem in the first place. If there were indeed purely technical solutions to the Irish border problem it made sense for the British to come up with these; the Irish government was however increasingly of the view that any solution had to be political, not technical. Interest thus started to focus on the question of whether it might be possible to grant some sort of special status to Northern Ireland. As it became clear that Ireland was on the side of the 27, not a lone player trying to bridge the divide between the UK and the 26, relationships between Dublin and London started to cool.

On 15 December 2016 the heads of state and government of the remaining 27 member states confirmed that the European Commission would be negotiating on behalf of the European Union. On 29 April 2017, meeting as the European Council, they adopted the EU's negotiation guidelines which the Commission then had to follow. They did so unanimously, and the guidelines could only be changed if the 27 countries concerned agreed to this. There were compelling practical and legal reasons why it should be the Commission that negotiated on behalf of all 27: you could hardly have 27 separate bilateral negotiations taking place, or even have all 27 member states in the room at once across the table from the UK. It is the Commission that negotiates accession treaties with new member states and trade deals with third countries, and so it made sense that it be the Commission that negotiated Brexit. It is hard to see how else it could be done even if it were legally possible, but it is important to insist on the point since from the beginning the British government was frustrated by the European insistence that the Commission be its only interlocutor. Indeed, it periodically tried to circumvent the Commission and negotiate with individual countries. And that frustration of course highlights another good reason for Europe to negotiate with a single voice: it increased its bargaining power. As the April negotiation guidelines put it, 'So as not to undercut the position of the Union, there will be no separate negotiations between individual Member States and the United Kingdom on matters pertaining to the withdrawal of the United Kingdom from the Union.'

But it was also important that the Commission, which is unelected as the Brexiteers constantly remind us, not be allowed to make its own decisions on fundamental matters of principle. Rather, it received its instructions from the democratically elected heads of 27 countries, and it had to follow these instructions. Again, it is hard to see how it could be done any other way, but again this obviously increased the European Union's bargaining power. Even if the Commission wanted to give in to the British government on some point, it would not be able to do so if this meant going against the agreed negotiation guidelines. Once again this proved intensely frustrating to British politicians, who fulminated against the 'legalistic' or 'theological' negotiating team in the Commission. Sometimes they went on to express a desire to bypass the Commission and negotiate directly with individual member states, on the basis that they would be more flexible (which presumably meant being more amenable to British demands). But if the Commission was being inflexible, this was because the member states had asked it to be so. Coordinating the activities of 27 very different countries can be difficult and frustrating. But Brexit is a good example of how the rigidities of the European decision-making system can on occasion be a source of considerable bargaining power.

The April 2017 negotiating guidelines were thus an important document, limiting what would and what would not be possible in the future.[42] They stated clearly that the 'main purpose of the negotiations will be to ensure the United Kingdom's orderly withdrawal so as to reduce uncertainty and, to the extent possible, minimize disruption caused by this abrupt change': this took precedence over reaching an understanding about what sort of relationship the UK and EU might enjoy in the future. To that end the guidelines mandated a phased approach to negotiations. The first phase would focus on what became known as divorce issues: it would 'settle the disentanglement of the United Kingdom from the Union and from all the rights and obligations the United Kingdom derives from commitments undertaken as Member State [sic].' Three divorce issues came to dominate subsequent discussions. The first priority was to ensure that EU citizens living in the UK, and UK citizens living in the EU, retained the status and legal rights to which they were entitled before Brexit. The second was to reach agreement on the money owed by the United Kingdom to the EU. And the third was to do with Ireland:

> The Union has consistently supported the goal of peace and reconciliation enshrined in the Good Friday Agreement in all its parts, and continuing to support and protect the achievements, benefits and commitments of the Peace Process will remain of paramount importance. In view of the unique circumstances on the island of Ireland, flexible and imaginative solutions will be required, including with the aim of avoiding a hard border, while respecting the integrity of the Union legal order.

The European Union was willing to engage in 'preliminary and preparatory discussions' about the nature of the future EU–UK relationship, but only in a second phase of negotiations, after the European Council had decided that 'sufficient progress' had been made in resolving these 'first stage' divorce issues. There could be no question of the UK being allowed to use the divorce issues as leverage in any negotiations about a future trade relationship. Since the UK was above all interested in discussing the future relationship, and since there was less than two years in which to negotiate, this would hopefully give it a strong incentive to deal adequately with the divorce issues as quickly as possible. The Union was willing to consider transitional arrangements, on the basis that they be 'clearly defined, limited in time, and subject to effective enforcement mechanisms'. If the UK wanted to remain within the customs union and Single Market during the transition, this 'would require existing Union regulatory, budgetary, supervisory, judiciary and enforcement instruments and structures to apply'.

The European Council reaffirmed that 'the four freedoms of the Single Market are indivisible' and that there could be no 'cherry picking'; that there had to be 'a balance of rights and obligations'; that there could not be deals for specific sectors; and that any deal had to 'ensure a level playing field, notably in terms of competition and state aid, and in this regard encompass safeguards against unfair competitive advantages through, inter alia, tax, social, environmental and regulatory measures and practices'. And finally, any agreement could only apply to Gibraltar with the agreement of Spain.

The negotiating guidelines were a remarkable display of European solidarity towards a small country. The Irish government had succeeded in making the Irish border issue one of the three key divorce issues on which 'sufficient progress' had to be made before the talks could move on to the second stage. To be sure, avoiding a hard border was only an 'aim': no guarantees were provided, and it was made clear in the guidelines that any solution, no matter how 'flexible' or 'imaginative', would have to preserve the integrity of the Union's legal order, including its Single Market. But singling out the border issue in this manner was remarkable nonetheless. Furthermore, when the European Council assessed whether sufficient progress had in fact been made on the Irish border question (and the other divorce issues), it would do so on the basis of unanimity.[43] This meant that the Irish government would have to agree that sufficient progress had been made, in effect giving it (and every other member state) a veto over whether or not talks could proceed to the second stage.

And that was not all. The European Council also agreed that, in the event that Northern Ireland decided to join a united Ireland, it would automatically become a member of the European Union, just as East Germany had automatically become a member of the EC when Germany was reunified in 1990. The British were furious and tried to get the 'unity clause' dropped from the minutes of the Council, but to no avail. As a senior Council source told Tony Connelly, 'Our line was that this is for the Irish . . . If the Irish request this, they will get it. It's as simple as that. We said upfront to the Brits, "If this is what the Irish want, we're going to do it. They are around the table. You are not around the table."'[44]

Ireland might indeed have a veto over whether or not the UK could proceed to the second stage of the negotiations, but the signs were that European solidarity was so strong that it would never need to use it. As we will see in the next chapter, the Irish border issue subsequently became the crucial sticking point in the negotiations.

The Negotiations

Once the European Council had agreed its negotiating guidelines the two sides could get down to work. As stressed in the previous chapter, it was in the interests of the UK that this happen as soon as possible, since time was limited. But in fact negotiations did not begin for another seven weeks, and the reason that it took so long had nothing to do with the European Union. On 18 April 2017 Theresa May astonished everyone by calling a snap general election. Her stated reason was that this would strengthen her hand in negotiations with the EU, giving her a bigger majority in Parliament and undermining the efforts of opposition parties to destabilize her approach to Brexit. There was also the point that unless a snap election was held the next election would be due to take place no later than May 2020, less than a year after Brexit: Mrs May expressed the fear that the instability associated with an impending election might hand a negotiating advantage to the EU. As she said to the *Sun* newspaper, 'When I became Prime Minister, I thought the most important thing to do for the country was to have a period of stability.'[1] Some observers hoped that the election would bolster her position, not so much vis-à-vis the EU as vis-à-vis the more extreme elements in her own party: with her bigger majority she would be better able to ignore them. And many commentators thought that her decision was simply a rational and opportunistic response to the collapse of Jeremy Corbyn's Labour Party in opinion polls.

On 8 June 2017, for the third time in three years, the big screen was once again set up in my college's Old Library. Everyone assumed that there would be a Conservative landslide, even though the Tory campaign, with its repetitive promises of 'strong and stable leadership', had been poor. And so it came as a shock when the first exit polls announced that there would be a hung parliament. The Conservative Party lost its majority, and while Mrs May eventually formed a new government, this was only with the support of the Democratic Unionist Party. The implications for the Brexit negotiations were varied and complicated. On the one hand, it would be difficult to argue that the election results provided a clear mandate for the hard Brexit policy enunciated by the Prime Minister at Lancaster House. Mrs May also faced a more powerful opposition than she had done before the election. Both considerations seemed to point towards a potentially softer Brexit, although it was far from clear that the Labour Party under Jeremy Corbyn would be willing to push hard for such an outcome. But on the other hand, the fact that the Conservative Party had lost its majority made its backbench MPs more powerful. A small number of these were hard-core Remainers, but more were hard-core Brexiteers. And then there was the new dependence on the Democratic Unionist Party, which as previously noted had been the only one of the five major political parties in Northern Ireland to support the Leave campaign. Some in Ireland hoped that the DUP might push for a solution that avoided a hard border in Ireland, but it was also clear that it would oppose any solution that in its view undermined the union of Great Britain and Northern Ireland.

The first issue that had to be resolved was the agenda for the negotiations. As we saw in the previous chapter, the EU wanted negotiations to proceed in a clear sequence: divorce issues first, future relationship second. The UK was not happy about this and in May 2017 David Davis promised 'the row of the summer' over the issue. 'How on earth do you resolve the issue of the border with Northern Ireland and the Republic of Ireland unless you know what our general borders policy is, what the customs agreement is, what our trade agreement is?' he asked. 'It's wholly illogical.' But when the two sides met for the first time on 19 June 2017 the UK accepted a timetable that was sequenced in the manner that the EU had asked for. It was now locked into a process which required it to make 'sufficient progress' on the three key divorce issues – citizens' rights, the financial settlement, and the Irish border – before talks could move on to discussing transitional arrangements and the future EU–UK relationship.

Citizens' Rights

The insistence of the European Council that the first priority in the Brexit negotiations should be to secure the futures of EU citizens living in the UK, and British citizens living in the EU, is easy to understand. There are more than 3 million EU citizens living in the UK, and they did not move there as immigrants but as European citizens exercising their right to move freely within the European Union. The EU therefore aimed to ensure that they and their families – current and future – would continue to have the same level of legal protection after Brexit as they currently enjoy, for life. This included the right to permanent residence after five years, and the right to be treated equally as compared with UK citizens. In the EU's view any EU citizen living legally in the UK before Brexit should be considered legally resident there, even if they did not have documents to prove this, and EU citizens' rights had to be legally enforceable by the European Court of Justice. There should be reciprocal rights for the more than 1 million UK citizens residing in other EU member states. So-called frontier workers, residing in an EU member state but working in the UK, should also have their rights protected by the agreement.[2]

The UK agreed with much but not all of this.[3] It agreed that those living in the UK before a given cut-off date should be able to continue to live there, but it did not agree that the cut-off date necessarily be the date of Brexit – presumably for fear that there would be a stampede of Europeans seeking to enter Britain over the course of the next two years.[4] It did not want the ECJ to oversee the rights of European citizens in the UK after Brexit. And it argued that future family members of EU citizens resident in the UK – for example, future spouses – should only be allowed to come to live in the UK if a minimum income requirement was satisfied. This would obviously restrict a very basic freedom that EU citizens living in other EU member states, including the UK, currently enjoy: the right to live with whomever they marry, regardless of their financial circumstances. As Directive 2004/38/C of 29 April 2004 puts it, 'The right of all Union citizens to move and reside freely within the territory of the Member States should, if it is to be exercised under objective conditions of freedom and dignity, be also granted to their family members, irrespective of nationality.'[5] The logic behind the UK position was that its own citizens are only allowed to bring non-EU family members into the UK if minimum income requirements are fulfilled: this is not inconsistent with EU law since the freedom referred to above applies to EU citizens living in *other* countries, not EU (and therefore UK) citizens living in *their own* country. And it would seem strange if EU citizens living in the UK after Brexit enjoyed more rights than UK citizens. The EU response to this argument was that no EU citizen currently living in the UK should lose rights that they currently enjoy under EU law just because of Brexit.

Despite these differences it proved relatively easy for negotiators to make 'sufficient progress' on citizens' rights. In particular, a speech given by Theresa May in Florence on 22 September 2017 opened the way for a creative compromise regarding the role of the ECJ.[6] She announced that the agreement regarding citizens' rights would be incorporated into UK law and that EU citizens could have those rights enforced by UK courts. But those courts should in turn be able to 'take into account the judgments of the European Court of Justice'. The eventual agreement reflected this proposal: since the rights of EU citizens 'followed on' from the rights they had enjoyed under EU law UK courts should have 'due regard' to the rulings of the ECJ when arriving at their own decisions. They should also be able to ask the ECJ to clarify issues of European law when they felt that this was necessary.[7]

The UK accepted too that the cut-off date should be the

date on which Brexit took place. However, in a subsequent note to the European Council the Commission expressed the view that if a transition were eventually to be agreed the cut-off date should be the end of the transition, since otherwise EU citizens would not enjoy the same rights during the transition period as before: this was a matter to be negotiated in the second phase when transitional arrangements were discussed. Finally, both sides agreed that the question of whether future spouses should be allowed to join their partners would be determined by national law, implying that the UK could impose financial requirements as it had originally wanted to do. This represented a climb-down by the EU, although the Commission continued to believe that the issue should be addressed in the second phase of talks, and would 'inevitably be linked to the level of ambition of the future partnership between the EU and the United Kingdom'.[8]

'It's All About the Money'

If I had a euro for every time I heard a British politician, journalist or commentator telling us in 2017 that the Brexit negotiations were 'all about the money', I would be a rich man. And making 'sufficient progress' on the financial settlement was indeed more difficult. The UK government viewed money as one of its main bargaining chips: if it were not to pay the money demanded by the EU this would leave a sizeable hole in the EU budget. Surely this would help in securing a favourable trade deal in the future? But on the other side of the table there was complete unanimity that the UK should live up to its financial commitments: otherwise other net contributors to the EU budget like Germany would have to pay more, or net beneficiaries like Poland would have to receive less. And the EU side did not view a financial settlement as a quid pro quo for anything else: it was simply ensuring that the commitments of the past were lived up to. This was why, as with the other divorce issues, money had to be satisfactorily addressed before any discussion of the future relationship could begin: there was to be no question of the British being allowed to link the two issues. This interpretation was rejected by many in the UK, where that red campaign bus had promised that financial transfers to Brussels would stop. The UK should not pay any more money after Brexit unless Britain got something back in return.

The European position on the financial settlement was that there should be a single agreement, covering not only UK obligations under the terms of the 2014–20 EU budget, but the UK's share of all EU liabilities, such as those relating to pensions. On the other hand, the UK also had claims to a share of EU assets, and these should be taken account of when calculating its total net liability. The EU approach was thus to determine on *a priori* grounds which assets and liabilities should be taken account of, and only then to calculate the final figure that would be owed by Britain. UK politicians were much more focused on the amount that would be owed. During the summer of 2017 there was much discussion of the possibility that the UK might owe as much as €60 to €100 billion – this was denounced by many in London as being far too much, and the British media carried reports that the government there would not be willing to pay more than €40 billion. Such a cap would obviously have been inconsistent with the EU approach that focused on what it saw as legal obligations.

In her Florence speech Theresa May said that she did not want other member states 'to fear that they will need to pay more or receive less over the remainder of the current budget plan as a result of our decision to leave. The UK will honour commitments we have made during the period of our membership.' This was a step forward by the British, and was taken to mean that at a minimum the UK would pay the roughly €20 billion remaining out of its contribution to the budget ending in 2020. However, the EU view was that the UK had other existing commitments and liabilities, and in any event a few lines in a speech were not what was required: as a senior EU official later told the *Financial Times*, 'The British don't realize that we cannot simply look at what the Prime Minister said in a speech. We have to look at what is actually being put on the table in Brussels. And on the latter we have seen no movement.'[9]

Mrs May also faced opposition at home. Six days before the Florence speech her own Foreign Secretary, Boris Johnson, wrote an article resurrecting the referendum campaign's £350 million a week claim, and arguing that the UK should not pay for EU Single Market access. By the end of the fifth round of negotiations, on 12 October 2017, the UK was still not willing to confirm exactly which commitments Mrs May had been referring to in Florence. The initial hope had been that the European Council, due to meet that month, would be able to recommend that 'sufficient progress' had been made on the divorce issues, and that the talks could therefore proceed to the second phase in which transitional arrangements and the future trade relationship would be discussed. But with negotiations on the financial settlement still deadlocked the EU's chief negotiator, Michel Barnier, announced that he would not be recommending to the October Council that negotiations move to the second stage. The announcement came as a blow to the British government since the next Council meeting was only scheduled for December – this meant that there would be two months less in which to negotiate a final deal.

By this stage the two-year Article 50 timetable, and the phased nature of the negotiations, was placing severe time pressure on the British government. Faced with the possibility that companies based in the UK would soon start relocating staff to the EU, it accepted that a transition period was necessary, and that the sooner this was agreed to give businesses some certainty the better. And so former Remainers in the UK government, like the Chancellor Philip Hammond, argued in favour of going further on the financial settlement, while hard-line Brexiteers opposed this. Nor did it help the cause of the pragmatists that David Davis was still arguing that the UK should only spell out what financial commitments it was willing to meet once the second phase of negotiations had begun. The British government might have agreed to a two-phase negotiation, but the notion that the financial settlement should be a quid pro quo for a favourable deal, rather than a reflection of pre-existing liabilities, was a hard one to shake off.[10]

In the end the pragmatists won: if the December European Council were to decide that sufficient progress had not been made this would be a catastrophe for the British government. By the end of November reports appeared in the press that the UK had agreed to honour its financial commitments as defined by the EU. Officials were working hard to present the figures in as favourable a light as possible, making it easier for Mrs May to sell the deal back home: as one told the *Financial Times* 'They [the British] have promised to cover it all, we don't care what they say their estimate is . . . We're happy to present it.'[11]

A transition seemed assured, or at least so London thought. But then it turned out that it really wasn't all about the money after all.

The Irish Backstop

In principle it should have been easy to resolve the third divorce issue, namely the Irish border. Everybody agreed what the objective should be: to keep the border invisible and frictionless. But there was a problem: the UK government wanted to keep *all* of its trade with *all* of the EU as frictionless as possible, despite leaving both the customs union and the Single Market. The fact that it believed that this might be possible suggested that it had not yet fully grasped the issues involved. Alternatively it suggested that what the British actually wanted to do was to use the Irish border issue as a Trojan horse. If the European Union were to accept the principle that there not be border checks in Ireland, for political reasons, then London would be able to argue further down the line that the same arrangements should be put in place to facilitate frictionless trade between the UK and the rest of the EU, despite the UK being free to set its own rules and strike trade deals with the rest of the world. In this manner the UK would be able to have its cake and eat it.[12]

David Davis gave some credence to this view in early July

2017 when he was reported in the *Financial Times* as telling worried business leaders that the Irish border should be the negotiating priority for the summer, since it could be a 'test border' for the rest of the EU.[13] A few weeks earlier senior DUP figures had told Sky's Faisal Islam that they were comfortable with leaving both the customs union and Single Market, since they believed that 'the EU will feel obliged to guarantee a softer border with Ireland, and that the Republic is the European Union negotiator's Achilles Heel.'[14] The EU side, for its part, was clear that any solution for Northern Ireland should not serve as a precedent for other EU–UK borders, and that it should not undermine the integrity of the Single Market: it would be intolerable if American chlorinated chicken, for example, could cross the border from Northern Ireland to Ireland unhindered, and from there pass freely into the rest of the EU.

How did the British think that border controls could be avoided? A constant theme throughout 2017 was the potential of technology to make border controls redundant. Exactly what technologies were involved was unclear, and the list varied over time: cameras and automatic number-plate recognition; blockchain; even airships were at one stage mentioned as a possibility, although the Legatum Institute which promoted the idea and was influential among Brexiteers conceded that Irish weather conditions might pose a problem.[15] Perhaps such technological solutions might not be completely watertight, but there were frequent suggestions in the British media that in any event the EU should be willing to tolerate a bit of smuggling in the interests of the Irish peace process. According to Tim Shipman even government ministers had spent months 'assuming that the nature of the post-Brexit border could be resolved through fudge, remote technology to track consignments of goods and a casual blind eye turned to smuggling.'[16]

As we saw in the previous chapter, the EU negotiating guidelines had called for 'flexible and imaginative solutions' to avoid a hard border, but there is a limit to anything. And it did not help the British case when in August 2017 the EU's anti-fraud office found that UK customs authorities had repeatedly ignored warnings that criminals were illegally bringing Chinese textiles and footwear into the EU via Britain, costing the EU and member states billions of euros in lost customs and VAT revenue.[17] Finally, there was the point highlighted in the previous chapter: cameras or any other physical infrastructure along the Irish border were liable to be destroyed by terrorists.

On 15 August 2017 the British government issued a position paper on how to secure the cakeist objective of 'the freest and most frictionless trade possible in goods between the UK and the EU' while at the same time allowing the UK 'to forge new trade relationships with our partners in Europe and around the world'.[18] Customs procedures could be streamlined, including by the use of technology; alternatively the UK could seek a 'new customs partnership' with the EU. Under such a partnership the UK would continue to levy EU tariffs on goods imported into Britain but destined for EU markets. It would on the other hand levy its own tariffs on goods whose final destination was the UK. Thus a consignment of beef from the US would pay different tariffs depending on whether the beef was to be sold in the UK or the EU. Presumably if some of the beef were to be sold in the UK and some in the EU different tariffs would be levied on each bit of the consignment. Exactly how it would be possible, in a free market economy, to track all imported goods to their final destinations so as to ensure that the correct tariffs were paid remained unclear. Nor was it clear how the proposal would avoid the need for border controls to check that goods being shipped from Britain to France, say, complied with EU regulations: was the beef hormone-free or not, for example? The British government recognized that the approach was 'innovative and untested'; EU officials were widely quoted as saying that it represented 'magical thinking'.

The following day the UK government published a second position paper, this time on how to avoid a hard border between Northern Ireland and Ireland. This repeated the previous day's proposals, but also made the further suggestion that smaller traders could be exempted from border controls altogether. How this could happen without encouraging smuggling was not explained. While welcoming aspects of the paper, such as the acknowledgement that technological fixes such as cameras at the border would not work, and that the aim should be 'to avoid any physical border infrastructure in either the United Kingdom or Ireland, for any purpose', the Irish Foreign Minister Simon Coveney described the new customs partnership proposals as 'totally unworkable'.[19] The fact that the Northern Irish border proposals had been published by the British government immediately after its proposals on the broader trade relationship, and largely reflected those, heightened suspicions that the British were trying to use the Irish issue to advance their cakeist ambitions. It was also an obvious attempt on their part to circumvent the two-phase negotiation structure, and indeed the British government repeatedly argued during 2017 that it would be impossible to resolve the Irish border issue without dealing with the future trade relationship. This made sense from their point of view since they hoped that the Irish issue would provide them with negotiating leverage. But for the very same reason the EU was determined to stick to what had been agreed: divorce issues first, future relationship second.

In early September Michel Barnier said that he was worried by the UK's Northern Irish proposals: 'The UK wants the EU to suspend the application of its laws, its Customs Union, and its Single Market at what will be a new external border of the EU. And the UK wants to use Ireland as a kind of test case for the future EU–UK customs relations. This will not happen.'[20] On 21 September 2017 the European Commission published its own guiding principles for the negotiations on Northern Ireland: they stated that the aim should be not only to avoid a hard border, including any physical border infrastructure, but to 'respect the proper functioning of the internal market and of the Customs Union as well the integrity and effectiveness of the Union legal order'.[21]

By this stage the relationship between Dublin and London had deteriorated significantly. The Irish were increasingly frustrated by what they saw as a lack of seriousness on the part of the British: Theresa May's government repeatedly offered reassuring platitudes, but showed no sign of coming up with plausible proposals regarding how to avoid the reintroduction of a hard border. The British for their part were

irritated with the EU insistence that the sequence of negotiations that had been agreed in June be adhered to, and that
sufficient progress be made on the Irish border issue *before*
talks on the future trade relationship could begin. They were
especially irritated with the Irish, who were of course influential in determining the EU negotiating strategy on the border
issue, and who were defending their country's interests far
more stubbornly than the British had anticipated. The UK
government clung to the hope that the Irish could be isolated
on the issue: British diplomats engaged in a widespread campaign across Europe designed to undermine support for the
Irish government and its new Taoiseach Leo Varadkar, who
had succeeded Enda Kenny as leader of Fine Gael and head of
government in June 2017. If anything, such attempts to split
the 27 merely strengthened the bloc's solidarity.

Nor did such tactics endear Theresa May to the Irish government, who were of course fully aware of what she was up
to. On 21 November, as reports emerged that the UK was prepared to double its financial offer to the EU, Simon Coveney
warned, 'Anybody who thinks that just because the financial settlement issue gets resolved . . . that somehow Ireland
will have a hand put on the shoulder and be told, "Look, it's
time to move on." Well, we're not going to move on.'[22] Three
days later Donald Tusk warned Mrs May that if she wanted to
move to the second phase of negotiations, she needed to 'sort
out your problem with Ireland'. Her response was telling:
'One country cannot hold up progress.' The UK was a 'much
bigger and much more important country than Ireland'.[23] The
problem for Mrs May was that Ireland was a member of the
European Union, and the UK was on its way out. Whether

the Prime Minister liked it or not this meant that Irish views counted for more in Brussels than British ones.

The Irish – and EU – view was that guarantees were needed at this stage that would ensure that there would be no hard border in Ireland, irrespective of whatever trade deal the British and the EU would agree at a later stage. Mrs May's Lancaster House red lines suggested that such a trade deal would involve border checks somewhere: it was vital that these not occur along the border between Northern Ireland and the Republic. And so Ireland and the EU required a 'backstop' solution that would prevent this from happening even if the British continue to insist on those red lines. As Leo Varadkar put it in Gothenburg on 17 November, the British had 'unilaterally taken the customs union and Single Market off the table'; Ireland therefore wanted 'taken off the table any suggestion that there will be a physical border, a hard border, new barriers to trade on the island of Ireland' *before* the negotiations moved to phase two.[24] If the Irish were to get a backstop this was the moment to insist on it since this was the time of maximum leverage: like all other member states Ireland had a veto over whether or not talks could progress to the second stage, and the British were desperate to start talking about transitions and trade deals.

Views in Dublin and Brussels regarding *how* to avoid a hard border had crystallized nine days before the Gothenburg meeting, and they will not come as a surprise to any reader who has made it this far in the book.[25] Simon Coveney spelled out the issues succinctly on 14 November 2017:

> The Government in London has repeatedly outlined three
> ambitions which simply cannot all be delivered. These are,

firstly, that the UK leaves the Single Market and customs union; secondly, that all parts of the UK jump together, so to speak; and thirdly, that they want no return to any hard or visible border on this island. Well, we fully share that final objective, which, to be blunt, is the most important – it's the bedrock for peace and stability on this island. We just don't see, and the EU doesn't see, how it is compatible with the other two ambitions.[26]

The only way to avoid a hard border was for either the UK as a whole, or just Northern Ireland, to remain, *de facto*, in the EU's customs union, Single Market and VAT regime. There were other good reasons why this had to happen as well.[27] As you will recall, the Good Friday Agreement had promoted North–South cooperation, and all sides were agreed that this should continue. In September 2017 British officials reported to their negotiating counterparts that there were 156 distinct areas of North–South cross-border cooperation: these included health, as we have seen already, but also waterways, electricity supply, education, transportation, agriculture, tourism and a host of other policy areas including, to take just one example, greyhound and pigeon racing. The question then became: to what extent was this cooperation dependent on EU law? A 'mapping' exercise soon made it clear that the answer was: a lot. An EU official's explanation to Tony Connelly is worth quoting at length since it gets to the heart of the matter:

North–South cooperation mostly covers things like health, waterways, and so on. The mapping meant combing through every single possible example that you can think

CHAPTER 11

of: child cancer, heart surgery, waterways management,
education. If you take the health area alone, it's easy to
explain the single-market dimension. Not only do you have
all the equality of rights, but things like single standards
for medical devices, the approval of medicines, mutual
recognition of qualifications, ambulance services, etc.
All of this is completely aligned at the moment.

The conclusion was that regulations needed to remain 'aligned'
on both sides of the border for cooperation under the terms
of the Good Friday Agreement to continue: there could be no
'regulatory divergence'.[28]

British hopes that Ireland could be isolated on the issue
were dashed on 1 December when Donald Tusk visited the
Irish Taoiseach in Dublin. He reassured the Taoiseach that

the EU is fully behind you and your request that there should
be no hard border on the island of Ireland after Brexit. The
Irish request is the EU's request. Or as the Irish proverb
goes: 'Ni neart go cur le chéile' [there is no strength without
unity]. The United Kingdom's decision to leave the EU has
created uncertainty for millions of people in Europe. Perhaps,
nowhere is this more visible than here. The border between
Ireland and Northern Ireland is no longer a symbol of division,
it is a symbol of cooperation. And we cannot allow Brexit to
destroy this achievement of the Good Friday Agreement.

It is the UK that started Brexit and now it is their
responsibility to propose a credible commitment to do
what is necessary to avoid a hard border . . . I asked Prime
Minister May to put a final offer on the table by 4 December

so that we can assess whether sufficient progress can be made at the upcoming European Council . . . I will consult the Taoiseach if the UK's offer is sufficient for the Irish government. Let me say very clearly: if the UK's offer is unacceptable for Ireland, it will also be unacceptable for the EU. I realize that for some British politicians this may be hard to understand. But such is the logic behind the fact that Ireland is an EU member while the UK is leaving. This is why the key to the UK's future lies – in some ways – in Dublin, at least as long as Brexit negotiations continue.[29]

The British had no choice but to concede. On 8 December they issued a Joint Report with the EU that included agreements between the two sides on all three divorce issues. The Joint Report's Paragraph 49 on Ireland is reproduced below:[30]

The United Kingdom remains committed to protecting North–South cooperation and to its guarantee of avoiding a hard border. Any future arrangements must be compatible with these overarching requirements. The United Kingdom's intention is to achieve these objectives through the overall EU–UK relationship. Should this not be possible, the United Kingdom will propose specific solutions to address the unique circumstances of the island of Ireland. In the absence of agreed solutions, the United Kingdom will maintain full alignment with those rules of the Internal Market and the Customs Union which, now or in the future, support North–South cooperation, the all-island economy and the protection of the 1998 Agreement.

In other words, the UK hoped to solve the Irish border issue by negotiating a future trade relationship that would do away with the need for borders. If this proved impossible, for example because of Mrs May's Lancaster House red lines, then the UK would propose 'specific solutions' for Northern Ireland – this allowed them to continue the search for the technological solutions that they favoured. But if this also proved impossible, as everyone outside the UK expected it would be, then Ireland had a backstop guarantee: the UK would ensure that all of the rules necessary to maintain not only North–South co-operation and the protection of the Good Friday Agreement, but also the all-Ireland economy and the 'overarching' requirement to avoid a hard border, would remain aligned with those of the EU. *De facto*, this seemed to imply that Northern Ireland would stay within the EU customs union and Single Market for goods after Brexit, although taken on its own the language was ambiguous: it seemed to leave open the possibility that it was the UK as a whole that would remain fully aligned with EU regulations.

The UK also agreed to respect Ireland's rights and obligations flowing from its membership of the EU (Paragraph 45). This ruled out the suggestion that Ireland and the EU should be willing to turn a blind eye to cross-border smuggling. The British further agreed (Paragraph 46) that the Irish backstop should not be viewed as a precedent for the broader UK–EU trade relationship, and would be 'specific to the unique circumstances on the island of Ireland'. On the face of it this seemed more consistent with a Northern-Ireland-only than with a UK-wide interpretation of Paragraph 49. London also agreed that the December commitments should be upheld 'irrespective of the nature of any future agreement between the European Union and United Kingdom'.

But the Joint Report also included a paragraph (50) that had been inserted at the very last moment at the insistence of the Democratic Unionist Party:

> In the absence of agreed solutions, as set out in the previous paragraph, the United Kingdom will ensure that no new regulatory barriers develop between Northern Ireland and the rest of the United Kingdom, unless, consistent with the 1998 Agreement, the Northern Ireland Executive and Assembly agree that distinct arrangements are appropriate for Northern Ireland. In all circumstances, the United Kingdom will continue to ensure the same unfettered access for Northern Ireland's businesses to the whole of the United Kingdom internal market.

In other words, if the Irish backstop were to be triggered, and Northern Ireland regulations remained aligned with those of the EU's customs union and Single Market, the UK guaranteed that it would not allow new 'regulatory barriers' to develop between Northern Ireland and Britain unless the Northern Ireland Executive and Assembly agreed to this.[31] Importantly, this was *not* a commitment made by the EU to the UK, but a commitment made by the UK to itself (or perhaps more accurately to the DUP). The EU therefore subsequently argued that it was up to the UK to decide whether or not it wanted to honour its Paragraph 50 commitment to itself; what mattered from an EU perspective was that it honour its Paragraph 49 commitment to the EU, which was in the eyes of the latter to maintain regulatory alignment between Northern

Ireland and the EU.[32] But the two paragraphs taken together seemed to many British commentators at the time to imply that in the absence of any other solution, the UK as a whole would have to remain inside the customs union and Single Market. This would obviously involve Mrs May dropping her Lancaster House red lines. Remainers were as pleased by this prospect as Leavers were furious.

The more important point was that the UK had cornered itself into a logically untenable position. The EU would insist that it uphold its backstop commitment to Ireland, no matter what. Given that, the UK was faced with a choice. It could choose to uphold its Paragraph 50 commitment to the DUP, in which case it would be forced to drop the Lancaster House red lines; or it could uphold those red lines, in which case it would be forced to drop its Paragraph 50 commitment to the DUP. It could not uphold both commitments at once without reneging on its Paragraph 49 commitment to Ireland and the EU, and so it was going to have to choose. But none of the choices were particularly appealing.

If the government reneged on Paragraph 50 there was the risk that the DUP would bring it down. If it reneged on the Lancaster House red lines there was the risk that hard-line Tory Brexiteers would bring it down. And if it reneged on Paragraph 49 there was not merely the risk, but according to the EU the certainty, that the UK would crash out of the EU in March 2019 without any deal at all. The logic was simple: the first phase divorce issues had to be satisfactorily dealt with, or there could be no Withdrawal Agreement. And that in turn would mean a chaotic rupture in UK relations with the EU, since without a Withdrawal Agreement there could be no transition period.

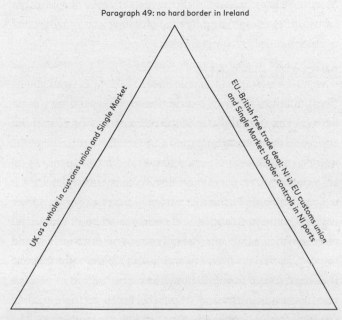

Paragraph 49: no hard border in Ireland

UK as a whole in customs union and Single Market

EU-British free trade deal: NI in EU customs union and Single Market: border controls in NI ports

UK as a whole leaves customs union and Single Market: hard border in Ireland

Paragraph 50: no regulatory barriers between Northern Ireland and Britain

Lancaster House red lines: UK leaves customs union and Single Market

Figure 11.1
The Coveney trilemma

As Simon Coveney had pointed out in November, there were three things that the UK could not do at once: uphold Paragraph 49, uphold Paragraph 50 and uphold Lancaster House. It could do any two out of these three things, but not all three (Figure 11.1). It would have to choose. The year that followed was dominated by the ways in which the UK tried to respond to this logical trilemma.

2018: A Deal is Struck

The European Council quickly issued negotiating guidelines for the second phase of the negotiations (15 December 2017) and the transition period (29 January 2018).[33] The EU wanted this transition period to be time-limited, ending on 31 December 2020, the end of the current budgetary cycle. The UK would remain inside the customs union and Single Market during this period, and would continue to be bound by all relevant EU regulations. The only practical difference would be that it would no longer participate in EU decision-making. It is hard to see how you could have a situation in which a non-member helped shape EU policies, but nevertheless David Davis wanted the 'right to object' to new EU legislation. The UK also asked the EU to consider a longer transition period, which made sense since 21 months was hardly enough time to negotiate a new free trade arrangement.

In March the two sides agreed a transitional arrangement on EU terms: it would end on 31 December 2020; the UK would have no influence on EU decision-making; and EU citizens would continue to enjoy their free movement rights in the UK during the transition. The agreement was widely denounced by Brexiteers who argued that the UK would be no more than a 'vassal state' or a 'colony' of the EU during the transition, implementing laws over which it had no say.[34] But of course the problem would only arise in the first place if a transition period were agreed, and a transition period would only be agreed if there were a withdrawal deal. And that would require the UK upholding the commitments it had made on all three divorce issues in the December Joint Report.

The initial signals were worrying. Just two days after the Joint Report had been agreed David Davis took to the airwaves to say that the agreement on Ireland was not legally binding, but was merely a statement of intent. He also said that the UK would not be paying any money to the EU unless it got a trade deal. On the same day the *Sunday Telegraph* reported that prime ministerial aides had reassured Brexiteers that the agreement was 'meaningless' and had just been inserted to get Ireland to sign off on the document.[35] Needless to say, such comments caused considerable irritation in Brussels and Dublin, and leaders sought ways to 'David Davis-proof' the advances that they thought had been made the previous week. On 13 December 2017 a European Parliament resolution noted that Davis's comments risked 'undermining the good faith that has been built up in the negotiations', and stated that the UK had to 'fully respect' its Joint Report commitments which had to be made 'fully enforceable'.[36] Two days later the European Council's negotiation guidelines stressed that 'negotiations in the second phase can only progress as long as all commitments undertaken during the first phase are respected in full and translated faithfully into legal terms as quickly as possible.' It probably shouldn't have been necessary to point this out, but it evidently was.

Translating the Joint Report commitments on Ireland into legal terms proved difficult, however. On 19 March 2018 the two sides issued a colour-coded Draft Withdrawal Agreement: green meant that the two sides agreed; yellow meant that they agreed on the objective but were still working on the drafting; and white meant that the EU had proposed a text with which the UK still disagreed.[37] The vast majority of the text was green, including the sections on citizens' rights (where the EU had dropped its insistence that future spouses be covered) and the financial settlement. On the Irish border issue, however, all that the two sides were able to agree was that 'a legally operative version of the "backstop" solution for the border between Northern Ireland and Ireland, in line with paragraph 49 of the Joint Report, should be agreed as part of the legal text of the Withdrawal Agreement, to apply unless and until another solution is found.' There was some progress here: the backstop would reflect the UK's paragraph 49 commitments to the European Union, not its paragraph 50 commitments to itself, and the backstop would be the default solution that would apply 'unless and until' a better solution was found. It was thus open-ended rather than time-limited and was to have the force of law, which was obviously crucially important from an Irish point of view. But there was as yet no agreement between the negotiators about exactly what form the backstop should take.

The European Union had already (on 28 February) suggested a text for the backstop protocol that should have come as no surprise to anyone who had been paying attention to the issues. Northern Ireland and the European Union would form a 'common regulatory area', and Northern Ireland would remain part of the customs territory of the EU. It is hard to see how else a hard border could be avoided, but seeing things spelled out in this manner caused outrage in many British quarters, and not only among Brexiteers. Mrs May rejected the text on the same day that it was issued: speaking in Parliament she said that it threatened the 'constitutional integrity' of the United Kingdom, and that 'no UK Prime Minister could ever agree' to it.[38] It remained unclear, however, how else the UK government would fulfil its commitment to providing a legally enforceable backstop based on the December agreement.

The EU's proposed backstop was sometimes referred to as creating a 'border in the Irish sea', a somewhat surreal image. The proposal would indeed involve checks on goods entering Northern Irish ports from Britain to ensure that they satisfied EU regulations, and if necessary to levy customs duties on them. There were already some checks in place on goods being brought into Northern Ireland from Britain: all live stock had to be imported through Larne Harbour, and both animals and paperwork were inspected there.[39] Michel Barnier therefore repeatedly called for the issue to be 'dedramatized', but with little success.

On 23 March 2018 the European Council issued its negotiating guidelines for the future relationship.[40] This was good news for the UK, since it gave Michel Barnier a mandate to finally start discussing the future EU–UK trade relationship. But the guidelines also contained several unwelcome statements of the obvious. First, the two sides could not negotiate a new trade deal before Brexit: the most that could be done in accordance with Article 50 would be to reach an

'overall understanding of the framework for the future relationship, that will be elaborated in a political declaration accompanying and referred to in the Withdrawal Agreement'.
An 'overall understanding' regarding the contents of a 'political declaration' was a lot less than the new trade deal many
in the UK had initially hoped it could agree.

Given the Lancaster House red lines, the only possible
future trading relationship was some sort of a free trade
agreement, and as we saw in Chapter 10 even that would
only happen if there were sufficient guarantees regarding
a level playing field. The guidelines also stated that 'In the
overall context of the FTA, existing reciprocal access to fishing waters and resources should be maintained'. EU member
states can export fish to each other tariff-free, but have also
signed up to a system managing fish stocks, and granting
fleets from across the Union access to all EU fishing waters.
There was to be no question of the UK being able to pick and
choose: if it wished to continue to export fish tariff-free to
the EU it would have to grant EU fleets continued access to
British waters. Indeed, given the political sensitivity of the
issue, the negotiating guidelines seemed to make such access
a condition, not just of tariff-free British fish exports, but
of a free trade agreement more generally, giving the EU (it
hoped) maximal leverage on the issue.

And there was a clear statement regarding the UK's
cakeist ambitions more generally:

> Being outside the customs union and the Single Market will
> inevitably lead to frictions in trade. Divergence in external
> tariffs and internal rules as well as absence of common

institutions and a shared legal system, necessitates checks
and controls to uphold the integrity of the EU Single
Market as well as of the UK market. This unfortunately will
have negative economic consequences, in particular in the
United Kingdom.

In other words, the Lancaster House red lines meant that
there would have to be border controls somewhere. And
the implication was that since they could not be between
Northern Ireland and Ireland they would have to be
between Northern Ireland and Britain. UK politics subsequently became largely dominated by the question of
how to wriggle off this logical hook. By and large Conservative
Remainers sought to avoid border controls between Northern Ireland and Britain by softening the Lancaster House
red lines, proposing UK-wide relationships with the EU
which would make border controls anywhere unnecessary. A
Northern-Ireland-only backstop could then be safely agreed
since it would never need to be used. The EU negotiating
guidelines gave Remainers some hope, since they stated that
if the UK red lines were to 'evolve' then so would the EU's
offer regarding a future relationship. Conservative Leavers,
on the other hand, continued to insist that technology could
solve the problem; in some instances they argued that the
Irish backstop be abandoned altogether. Remainers pointed
out that this would mean the UK crashing out without any
deal at all. Leavers replied that this would not be a catastrophe, and that a clean break would have its own advantages:
no deal was better than a bad deal. Mrs May's problem was
to try to find a way of bridging this gap within her own party,

and not surprisingly this is what she ended up focusing on. The problem for her was that solutions sufficiently cakeist to be acceptable to both factions tended to be unacceptable to the EU, which was after all the party with which she was actually negotiating.

On 7 June 2018 the UK government proposed that instead of a Northern Irish backstop there be a temporary, UK-wide backstop: if a backstop was required the UK as a whole would apply the EU's common external tariff, in effect joining a customs union with it. This was consistent with an all-UK reading of the Paragraph 49 backstop commitment, but as we have seen the EU rejected such a reading: Paragraph 46 had said that the backstop should be specific to the unique circumstances of Ireland, and in any case, if Paragraph 49 had been intended to imply a UK-wide commitment, then why had London insisted on Paragraph 50?[41] The suggestion was immediately rejected by Ireland and the EU: not only should the backstop be Northern Ireland-specific, but the UK government had previously agreed that it should be open-ended, applying 'unless and until another solution' had been found. A temporary, UK-wide backstop represented unacceptable backsliding on the part of the British. Nor did the proposal deal with the question of regulatory standards, although it did at least acknowledge that this would need to be addressed.[42]

As noted above, an alternative approach was for the UK to seek a future EU–UK relationship that would make the Northern Irish backstop, whatever form it might take, redundant. After all, a frequently stated UK objective was to keep trade with the EU 'as frictionless as possible'. But there was a problem here, and also a paradox: the UK had from the begin-ning argued that negotiations about the future trade relation-ship should begin as soon as possible. It had chafed against the EU insistence on dealing with the divorce issues first, even though it had agreed to this on the very first day of ne-gotiations. It was now finally possible to begin negotiations on the future relationship, but in order to negotiate the UK needed a negotiating position. And because of the divisions within the Conservative Party it had not yet agreed on one.

A future trade relationship that made the Northern Irish backstop redundant would, as previously stressed, require abandoning some or all of the Lancaster House red lines, but which ones exactly? One suggestion floated by journalists, policy wonks and academics became known as the 'Jersey' scheme since it mirrored current arrangements for that island. The UK as a whole would remain a member not only of the EU customs union, but also of the Single Market – but only for goods.[43] This would allow the UK to control migration from the EU, but the cost to Britain would be that it would lose priv-ileged access to EU markets for capital and services. As part of the deal it would naturally have to accept the jurisdiction of the European Court of Justice, make financial contributions to the EU budget (in the same way that Norway does), and so on. This made the scheme unacceptable to Brexiteers even though it would allow them to restrict the free movement of people.

The idea was rejected out of hand by the EU on the basis that it involved cherry picking, and indeed it did: as we have seen the EU had from the very beginning stressed the indi-visibility of the four freedoms. However, if the EU wanted to cherry pick these are probably the cherries it would have chosen. The EU runs a trade surplus with the UK when it comes to goods, and the proposal would allow trade in goods to continue unhindered as at present. The UK, on the other hand, is a service-based economy, and its service exports to the EU, including those of the City of London, would not be protected under the scheme. The EU's counter-argument was that many modern manufactured goods such as the iPhone involve a large service component, and that when companies such as Rolls-Royce export physical products they often bundle these with services such as maintenance. In a modern economy it is not easy to separate trade in goods and services, and so the EU argued that the proposal would not work.

On 6 July 2018 Theresa May summoned her Cabinet to her country residence at Chequers in an attempt to decide on a common British negotiating stance on the future relationship. According to several newspapers Ministers were told that if they resigned in protest at what was agreed they could take a taxi home or walk to the nearest train station: their official cars would no longer be available to them. The Prime Minister managed to get her Cabinet to approve a more cakeist version of the Jersey scheme, which it was hoped would ensure that the backstop – which the meeting agreed would be part of the Withdrawal Agreement – would never be needed.[44] The UK would mirror EU regulations for goods, insofar as this was necessary to maintain frictionless trade.[45] But rather than propose an EU–UK customs union, the Chequers Plan resurrected the 'new customs partnership' that we encountered earlier, now relabelled a 'facilitated customs arrangement'. The UK would collect EU tariffs on imports destined for EU markets, but would set its own tariffs on goods whose final destination was the UK. Despite this revival of what the EU had earlier described as 'magical thinking' the Chequers Plan was clearly a step in the direction of a softer Brexit, recognizing as it did that regulatory alignment was in fact necessary for frictionless trade. David Davis therefore resigned, but only a couple of days later, meaning that he avoided having to take a taxi home. This prompted Boris Johnson to follow suit, and open warfare now erupted between Brexiteers, determined to bring the Chequers Plan down (and, Johnson hoped, Theresa May with it), and Remainers who wanted to keep it alive.

The fact that Chequers seemed to signal the beginning of a potential shift towards greater British realism led EU officials and politicians to be restrained in their criticism of the proposals. Everyone outside the UK understood that they were never going to be acceptable to the EU, but the hope was that they might at least form the basis for negotiations. But then on 16 and 17 July a series of manoeuvres in the House of Commons halted the impression of forward momentum. Hard-line Brexiteers forced through a series of amendments to the government's Trade Bill whose obvious purpose was to make the Chequers Plan unworkable. One made it illegal for the UK to collect customs tariffs for the EU unless the EU did the same for the UK; this made the 'facilitated customs arrangement' unworkable, but since it had been unworkable anyway that was perhaps not such a problem. But another ruled out the possibility of the UK being part of the EU VAT area, which as we have seen would on its own be enough to ensure a hard border in Ireland. And a third stated that 'It shall be unlawful for Her Majesty's Government to enter into arrangements under which Northern Ireland forms part of a separate customs territory to Great Britain.' This ruled out the EU's Northern Irish backstop.[46]

By the end of August EU officials no longer felt they could be silent about the shortcomings of the Chequers Plan. In early September Michel Barnier came out strongly against the proposals: the EU could not 'relinquish control of our external borders and the revenue there to a third country – that's not legal'; the British proposal was not practical, since for example 'sugar is transported by the tonne in 25-kilo sacks, so you cannot trace every sack to its destination. That would only be possible with insane and unjustifiable bureaucracy. Therefore, the British proposal would be an invitation to fraud if implemented.' And there were services embodied even in 'every litre of milk and every apple'.[47] Hard-line Brexiteers who were also opposed to Chequers, but for very different reasons, were delighted.

On 3 September Barnier and his deputy negotiator, Sabine Weyand, appeared in front of the House of Commons Exiting the European Union Committee. Barnier told the committee that he was 'very concerned about Ireland': given that there would be no hard border on the island, and given the UK government's decision to leave the customs union and Single Market, there needed to be checks on goods coming into Ireland. Otherwise there would be 'a breach in the single market and customs union', with the EU unable to 'guarantee the safety of goods entering into the European Union and circulating in it'. Furthermore, 'on the ground' it was impossible to distinguish between customs checks and regulatory checks, since these were 'intrinsically linked in the technical physical organization of what happens when things are checked on that border for the single market': this practical issue had not even been covered by the Chequers proposal.

Weyand gave three concrete examples of why border checks would be needed to protect the Single Market and customs union, which nicely summarize one of the main themes of this book:[48]

> Here we are talking very practically about – imagine – an import of shrimps from an Asian country where they treat shrimps with antibiotics, which are prohibited in the EU because they can lead to blindness. Now this shipment arrives in Liverpool and is destined for the market in Northern Ireland and also the EU27. At what moment and how do we check that there are no residues of prohibited antibiotics? . . .
>
> The second example is bicycles imported from China on which the EU levies anti-dumping duties.* Maybe the UK in the future decides not to have such anti-dumping duties because you want to have your own system on this, so how can we ensure that bicycles, arriving in Liverpool again or somewhere else, do not end up undermining the anti-dumping duties that the EU is levying? How can we avoid that this becomes an entry point into the single market? . . .
>
> The third issue – and a very important one – is VAT. How can we ensure that VAT is levied correctly? That is a

---

* Anti-dumping duties are tariffs levied on the importation of particular goods from particular countries, in circumstances where these goods are being sold abroad for less than in their home market. They obviously infringe the principle of non-discrimination, but are legal under WTO rules if there is genuine ('material') injury to the competing domestic industry. Needless to say their use is controversial. See https://www.wto.org/english/thewto_e/whatis_e/tif_e/agrm8_e.htm.

major source of revenue for all our member states and is also a major source of fraud in the EU but also in the UK. Therefore, we will need to have a system where we can protect the integrity of the single market and the customs union, in a situation where we do not have a hard border between Ireland and Northern Ireland. It is on these very precise and concrete issues that we need to find a solution.

Unfortunately for the British government, in the EU's view Chequers did not provide such a solution.

And that is where things stood in mid-September 2018. The UK accepted that there should be a backstop, but on the basis of its 7 June all-UK customs proposals. The EU insisted that the backstop involve Northern Ireland remaining in the customs union and Single Market. Without agreement on this outstanding divorce issue the UK would crash out of the EU without a transition deal, or any other deal, on 29 March 2019. As for the future relationship: the EU still argued that UK red lines meant that nothing more than a free trade agreement would be possible. The UK government argued that its Chequers proposals would maintain frictionless trade while allowing it to strike its own free trade deals, and avoid the need for a backstop. And Tory Brexiteers such as Jacob Rees-Mogg agreed with Michel Barnier that the Chequers Plan was unworkable while denouncing it as an affront to British sovereignty.

On 9 September 2018 Boris Johnson, who was widely expected to make a bid for the leadership of the Tory party, denounced the humiliation of Theresa May's Chequers Plan, blaming it on

Northern Ireland, and the insanity of the so-called 'backstop'. We have opened ourselves to perpetual political blackmail. We have wrapped a suicide vest around the British constitution – and handed the detonator to Michel Barnier . . . We have been so mad as to agree, last December, that if we can't find ways of producing frictionless trade between Northern Ireland and the Republic of Ireland, then Northern Ireland must remain in the customs union and the Single Market: in other words, part of the EU. And that would mean a border down the Irish Sea. That outcome is completely unacceptable . . . We are now proposing our own version of the backstop: that if we can't find ways of solving the Irish border problem, then the whole of the UK must remain in the customs union and Single Market . . . It means we can't do any real free trade deals. It means we are a vassal state.[49]

Johnson's use of the suicide bomber metaphor was widely condemned, but he was not wrong to suggest that the Irish border issue, and the trilemma it implied, had been the key driver of British government policy since the December 2017 Joint Report. Not surprisingly, his 'solution' was to deny that there was a trilemma and to suggest that technology could eradicate the need for borders. He also argued that the back-stop should be scrapped.

The Endgame

On 19 September 2018 Theresa May wrote an article for the leading German newspaper *Die Welt*, in which she defended her Chequers proposals and attacked the EU's backstop: the UK had 'evolved its position' and now the EU needed to do the same.[50] The piece didn't go down well among EU leaders, whom she was due to meet in Salzburg that evening. Mindful of the fact that Mrs May was facing a potentially difficult Tory Party conference in Birmingham at the end of the month, they were still trying to be publicly polite about a plan they regarded as unrealistic and unworkable, and they didn't appreciate being told that the choice was, effectively, Chequers or nothing. Nor did it help when Mrs May continued to lecture them in this vein at a pre-summit dinner that night, or when she informed Leo Varadkar the following morning that she did not think that agreement could be reached on the Irish border issue before the next EU Council meeting, due to be held in October. It seemed to those present as though the UK was trying to run down the clock in the hope of forcing the EU to soften its stance on the backstop at the last moment. And feelings were further heightened when a report, later strongly denied, claimed that Liam Fox was planning to scrap European food standards in connection with a UK–US trade deal.[51]

The other 27 EU leaders therefore decided that it was time for some straight talking about the Chequers Plan. Donald Tusk said on their behalf that 'the suggested framework for economic cooperation will not work. Not least because it risks undermining the Single Market.' A 'solid, operational and legally binding Irish backstop' was a prerequisite for a Withdrawal Agreement, and the October Council would be a 'moment of truth' for the negotiations.[52] Tusk's message was echoed by Emmanuel Macron and other leaders. The British reaction was furious: the following day Mrs May complained that Tusk had not explained in any detail why the Chequers plan would undermine the Single Market, or offered any alternative. This was unacceptable: 'I have treated the EU with nothing but respect. The UK expects the same . . . At this late stage in the negotiations, it is not acceptable to simply reject the other side's proposals without a detailed explanation and counter proposals.' Nor would the UK accept Northern Ireland's staying in the customs union, since from a British point of view this would mean 'breaking up our country.'[53]

The claim that the EU had not explained its objections to Chequers, or provided any alternative, must have irritated EU negotiators: Tusk responded by pointing out that the UK had been aware of the EU's objections for many weeks.[54] British newspapers described the summit as a disaster, an ambush and a humiliation, but Mrs May's robust response may have helped her in the short term. The DUP leader, Arlene Foster, praised her toughness, and the Prime Minister made it relatively unscathed through a Conservative party conference that was otherwise notable for Boris Johnson's successor, Jeremy Hunt, comparing the EU to the USSR.[55]

However, while Mrs May might not acknowledge it, the Chequers plan was dead as a basis for the future relationship between the UK and EU. As we have seen it had attracted widespread Brexiteer hostility for having moved too far in the direction of what the EU regarded as a simple recognition of reality. May's problem was that if she wanted a deal with the EU she would have to go even further. In particular, if she wanted the future relationship to be such as to avoid border controls between both Britain and Northern Ireland,

and Northern Ireland and Ireland, she would need to relax her Lancaster House red lines even more. The question was how far this relaxation would go. For example, the UK might seek to remain in the EU Single Market and join a new EU–UK customs union: this would solve the Irish border issue making the backstop redundant, and in general maintain the existing economic status quo. But such a 'Norway plus' option would also mean accepting all four freedoms, paying into the EU budget, having no say over EU regulations, and not being able to strike independent trade deals with the rest of the world.[56]

Nor was the Jersey plan acceptable to the EU as we have seen. However, over the summer reports had started to emerge describing a less cakeist version of the Jersey model, which for want of a better term I will label 'Jersey minus': the UK as a whole would stay in a customs union with the EU, while Northern Ireland only would remain inside the Single Market for goods. The plan's main attraction was that it seemed to be consistent with an impressive number of red lines. It allowed the UK to end the free movement of people, the crucial red line for Mrs May.[57] Unlike the Jersey plan it did not involve British (as opposed to Northern Irish) cherry picking: Britain would not be in the Single Market for goods only, a crucial red line for the EU. Britain would only be in a customs union, which was consistent with the UK's June backstop proposal. The EU was hostile to an all-UK backstop, but had not *a priori* ruled out the possibility that the future relationship might incorporate a customs union between the EU and the UK as a whole. And the plan would be sufficient to avoid a hard border in Ireland, thus satisfying Dublin's major red line. Finally, while there would still need to be checks to ensure that goods entering Northern Ireland from Britain conformed with EU regulations, there would be no need for checks to make sure that rules of origin were being complied with, or that tariffs were being paid – since the entire UK would be in a customs union with the EU. Proponents of this plan pointed to the fact that the amendment passed by the House of Commons in July 2018, referred to earlier, ruled out the possibility of Northern Ireland and Britain being in separate customs territories; it did not rule out the possibility of purely regulatory checks in Northern Irish ports.[58]

This option would however still involve regulatory checks between Britain and the EU. Border controls would mean the end of frictionless trade between the two, and all the disruption that this would entail. Large companies relying on pan-European supply chains would in some cases pull out of the UK, while others might try to set up supply chains solely within it. Small companies would be faced with customs-related expenses that would be difficult for them to bear. And there would be major delays at British and European ports implying higher costs and greater inconvenience, but also making it difficult for trade in perishable food items, to take an obvious example, to continue as before. The main attraction of the 'Jersey minus' option lay not in the nature of the future relationship that it promised, but in the number of negotiating red lines with which it was consistent.

With the Conservative party conference out of the way, the negotiations accelerated. On 5 October Sabine Weyand proposed that the two teams enter what became known as a 'tunnel': they would work intensively in a 'safe space' and keep briefings to EU member state diplomats to a minimum so as to avoid the possibility of leaks.[59] By the end of the following week negotiators had agreed a draft withdrawal text. The essence of the agreement can be inferred from newspaper reports and a statement made by Theresa May to the House of Commons on 15 October.[60] The EU was still insisting on an 'all weather' Northern Irish backstop – which Mrs May rather confusingly referred to as the 'backstop to the backstop'. But it was willing to make a commitment to establishing a customs union, including the UK as a whole, as part of the future relationship. The problem for the British was that whereas the Northern Irish backstop would be part of the legally binding Withdrawal Agreement, the commitment to a future customs union would only be made in the accompanying Political Declaration. And as the Attorney General Geoffrey Cox pointed out to the British Government on 11 October, while the Withdrawal Agreement was legally binding, the Political Declaration was merely aspirational.[61] On 14 October David Davis' replacement as Brexit Secretary, Dominic Raab, was dispatched to Brussels to inform Barnier that the UK could not accept the existing document. The plan all along had been to conclude a withdrawal agreement before the European Council due to be held on 17 and 18 October, but that was not to be.

Undaunted, the negotiators re-entered the tunnel, and on 13 November Tony Connelly broke the news that a deal had been reached, handing Mrs May an unexpected concession.[62] The EU now accepted that the backstop would involve a UK-wide customs union with the EU, just as the UK had demanded, although Northern Ireland would also have to remain in regulatory alignment with the Union; in other words the back-stop looked very much like the 'Jersey minus' option. The deal made several member states nervous, since it was not at all what had been envisaged at the start of the process. A potential element of the future relationship between the EU and UK as a whole was now included in the legally binding Withdrawal Agreement, rather than in the Political Declaration. As we have seen, the Union had always insisted that any future trade relationship, even a mere free trade deal, could only be negotiated after Brexit and would need guarantees of a level playing field. Now, even if such negotiations were to fail the UK would be guaranteed a customs union arrangement with the EU. Level playing field guarantees were indeed included in the Withdrawal Agreement but they had been negotiated in a hurry. And the existence of the backstop seemed to preclude the EU's making access to British fishing waters a condition for a free trade deal – though it could still link access to fishing waters to tariff-free trade in fish. Sabine Weyand had to reassure worried EU diplomats that the EU would retain its negotiating leverage in future trade talks, and that the UK would eventually have to 'swallow a link between access to products and fisheries'.[63]

Mrs May's Cabinet approved the Withdrawal Agreement on 14 November, and the Withdrawal Agreement and accompanying Political Declaration on the future relationship (agreed in principle on 22 November) were formally endorsed at an EU Summit on 25 November. A deal had finally been struck: a triumph for all the negotiators involved.

The backstop was contained in a protocol to the Withdrawal Agreement.[64] The preamble to the protocol recalled 'the commitment of the United Kingdom to protect North-South cooperation and its guarantee of avoiding a hard border, including any physical infrastructure or related checks and controls,' and noted that 'any future arrangements [in the plural] must be compatible with these overarching requirements.' It also recalled the December 2017 Joint Report and its three scenarios for avoiding a hard border: the purpose of the Protocol was to flesh out the third of these scenarios, which was 'to apply unless and until an alternative arrangement implementing another scenario' was agreed.

The two sides were to use their 'best endeavours' to agree by the end of 2020 a future relationship that would supersede the Protocol while avoiding a hard border (Article 2.1). Such an agreement would have to spell out which parts of the Protocol it superseded (Article 2.2). If extra time were needed, the decision could be taken before 1 July 2020 to extend the transition period (Article 3). Since the UK had initially sought a longer transition period than the EU had been willing to grant this was another important concession secured by Mrs May. If the transition period came to an end before such a future relationship had been agreed the provisions of the Protocol (i.e. the backstop) would come into effect. While the backstop was designed to be temporary, it would apply 'unless and until' it was superseded by a subsequent agreement (Article 1.4). It would involve the EU and UK establishing a customs union, described as a 'single customs territory' (Article 6.1). Fishery products would not be covered by the provisions of the customs union unless the two sides reached an agreement about mutual access to fishing waters. An Annex set out the level playing field rules that would apply were the customs union to come into effect: for example, the two sides agreed so-called 'non-regression' clauses guaranteeing that a wide range of environmental protections, and labour and social standards, would not be reduced below the level prevailing at the end of the transition period (Annex 4, Articles 2 and 4). There were also limits on the UK's freedom of action in areas such as state aid.

As part of the UK Northern Ireland would become part of the single customs territory, but it would also remain subject to the EU's Union Customs Code.[65] This is an EU-wide system harmonizing the way in which customs and regulatory controls at external borders are carried out. In addition, the 69-page-long Annex 5 spelled out the many Single Market regulations that would need to be applied in Northern Ireland for a hard border to be avoided. For instance, Directive 2009/48/EC concerning the safety of childrens' toys, limiting for example the amount of lead or mercury that these can contain, would continue to be enforced there.[66]

In the EU's view the Withdrawal Agreement was supposed to serve three functions: phasing out UK membership of the EU in a smooth manner; protecting arrangements such as the Good Friday Agreement; and acting as a bridge towards whatever future relationship the EU and UK would ultimately agree on. The Northern Ireland-only backstop was consistent with the second of these purposes, but a UK-wide customs arrangement went beyond what was required. It could therefore only be justified legally if it served as a 'bridge to the future.' The preamble to the Protocol therefore mentioned the common objective of both sides to establish a close future relationship which would 'build on the single customs territory', and this language was repeated in the Political Declaration which set out both sides' aspirations for that relationship.[67]

The Political Declaration spoke not only of an 'ambitious, broad, deep and flexible partnership' (paragraph 3), but also of the UK's desire to end the freedom of movement and develop an independent trade policy (paragraph 4). Since ending free movement would mean exiting the Single Market and the return of border formalities, and since the Withdrawal Agreement implied that in such circumstances the backstop would apply, it was unclear how both aspirations could be fulfilled. The UK would certainly not be able to conclude free trade agreements with third countries involving tariff concessions.[68]

The Political Declaration recognized that the nature of the future relationship 'might evolve over time' (paragraph 5), and involve areas of cooperation not considered in the document (paragraph 3). Together with the fact that the Declaration was non-binding, this implied that the November deal left open a host of possible future relationships. These ranged all the way from UK-wide membership of the Single Market and a new customs union to a British free trade deal with the EU, in which case a Northern Ireland-only backstop would kick in. But attention in Britain soon focussed on the backstop arrangement itself, despite the fact that it was only meant to be a temporary solution to the Irish border problem, and might never come into effect in the first place. And it became clear that the last minute concessions obtained by May were not helping her politically: on the contrary.

The remaining Northern Ireland-only aspects of the

backstop were too much for the DUP and many Tories to swallow, dashing earlier hopes that it was customs barriers between Northern Ireland and Britain that posed the primary political problem for unionists: regulatory barriers, it seemed, were unacceptable too. The Irish government pointed out that up to 60% of the trade between Northern Ireland and Britain passed through Dublin, but to no avail.[69] Proponents of the deal also emphasized that under the backstop there would be no regulatory barriers facing Northern Irish firms exporting into Britain, and that Northern Ireland would, uniquely, enjoy frictionless access to both EU and British markets. Northern Irish business and agricultural interests were delighted but the DUP remained hostile.[70] Even worse from Mrs May's point of view, some Brexiteers were just as exercised about the fact that the entire UK would be in the single customs territory, and would thus be prevented from doing trade deals with third countries (or at least trade deals involving tariff concessions). What if Britain ended up being 'trapped' in such a customs union forever?

Mrs May's Brexit Minister, Dominic Raab, was one of those most exercised by the notion of an 'all weather' backstop that would apply 'unless and until' other means had been found to avoid a hard border in Ireland.[71] Article 20 of the Irish Protocol allowed either side to notify the other party that in its view the Protocol was no longer required to 'maintain the necessary conditions for continued North-South cooperation, avoid a hard border and protect the 1998 Agreement in all its dimensions'. If the EU and UK decided 'jointly' that the Protocol was 'no longer necessary to achieve its objectives' then it would cease to apply. But that meant that the EU would have to agree, which made sense from its point of view: a backstop that could be unilaterally terminated by the other side would not be a backstop.

The day after the British Cabinet approved the Withdrawal Agreement Raab resigned. His resignation letter cited not only concerns about 'the integrity of the United Kingdom' but also the UK's inability to exit the backstop unilaterally.[72] Raab was followed by six other members of the government, including the Work and Pensions Secretary Esther McVey. It was announced that the House of Commons would vote on the withdrawal deal on 11 December. However, both Labour and an increasing number of Tories were opposed to it. Tory Brexiteers hated the deal for the same reasons as Raab; Tory Remainers hated it because it seemed so inferior, from their point of view, to continued membership of the EU. On 9 November, before the deal had even been agreed, the Transport minister, Jo Johnson, had resigned and called for a second referendum: the people should in his view be asked if they still wanted to leave, and if so, whether they wanted to leave on the basis of 'vassalage' (i.e. the Withdrawal Agreement) or 'chaos' (i.e. without any withdrawal agreement at all).[73] Calls for a 'People's Vote' became ever more insistent.

The government argued that the Withdrawal Agreement was the only way of leaving the EU while avoiding a chaotic 'no deal' Brexit. The only alternatives to the agreement were no deal or no Brexit. The European Union concurred with this assessment: there could be no question of revisiting a deal that had finally been struck after a long and difficult negotiation. But the DUP and several Tory MPs argued that renegotiation of the Withdrawal Agreement was precisely what was required. More realistically perhaps, another group of MPs argued that the non-binding Political Declaration should be renegotiated instead, signposting the way towards a 'Norway plus' future relationship.[74] Proponents of a second referendum wanted the House of Commons to vote down the Withdrawal Agreement as a necessary first step leading ultimately to their preferred outcome. They were heartened by the European Court of Justice's ruling that the UK could unilaterally revoke Article 50 and stay in the Union, so long as the decision had been taken according to the UK's 'constitutional requirements' and was 'unequivocal and unconditional', bringing the withdrawal process to an end.[75] And some hard-core Brexiteers argued that 'no deal' was nothing to be feared: after all, had Mrs May herself not made it clear at Lancaster House that no deal was better than a bad deal? It became increasingly clear that the agreement would not obtain the support of the House of Commons.

On 10 December Theresa May dramatically announced that the House of Commons would not, after all, be voting on the Withdrawal Agreement the following day. She strongly defended the need for arrangements that would avoid a hard border, since the people of Northern Ireland did not want one: 'if this House cares about preserving our Union, it must listen to those people, because our Union will only endure with their consent.' She also reminded the House of her success in ensuring that the customs element of the backstop was now UK-wide, and that the transition period could be extended: this would give more time to work out ways of avoiding the backstop. But she recognized that concerns about the backstop were such that if a vote were to be held, the deal would be rejected: she would therefore 'discuss' the House's concerns with European leaders, and also explore ways of ensuring that 'any provision for a backstop has democratic legitimacy and . . . enable the House to place its own obligations on the government to ensure that the backstop cannot be in place indefinitely.' How such arrangements might be consistent with the UK's obligations under the Withdrawal Agreement was not spelled out.[76]

The Prime Minister proceeded to meet with other European leaders as she had promised. Despite clear signals that the EU would not renegotiate the Withdrawal Agreement, that had after all been approved by 28 governments just two weeks previously, on 11 December she asked Donald Tusk if the Irish backstop could be limited to a year. Not surprisingly the request was rejected out of hand, but the fact that it had been made in the first place deeply angered the Irish government.[77] As Leo Varadkar put it, 'We can't have a situation whereby any negotiating party – and this is true for any treaty or agreement – comes back every couple of weeks following discussions with their parliament looking for something extra . . . You can't operate international relations on that basis'.[78]

Matters soon became even more complicated. The following day Mrs May faced a no-confidence vote by her own MPs which she won by 200 votes to 117. While making her pitch to her party she told MPs that she would seek a 'legally binding' solution to the backstop issue that the DUP would be able to support. But the DUP wanted to be able to unilaterally leave the backstop arrangement, which from an EU point of view would mean that the backstop was no longer a back-stop. Unless she were subsequently to row back on this commitment it was hard to see how the UK could leave the EU with a withdrawal deal in hand. And without a withdrawal deal there would be no transition period.[79]

After the vote the Prime Minister said that she would be 'seeking legal and political assurances' that could 'assuage' the concerns of MPs regarding the backstop.[80] But whereas the member states and Commission were happy to provide clarifications about what had been agreed they were unwilling to do anything that might unpick the withdrawal deal's compromises. Indeed, talk of 'legal' assurances just made them suspicious of British intentions: care had to be taken to ensure that any texts that might be agreed between the parties, even purely clarificatory ones, could not be used to undermine the backstop at a later date.[81]

At a European Council on 13 and 14 December, May therefore tried a different tack. Instead of agreeing an end date to the backstop, perhaps leaders could agree on a binding deadline by which the future relationship had to be agreed (which would effectively cap the time spent in the backstop)? The suggestion made little sense, given that trade negotiations are long and complex, and given that the UK still seemed unclear about what it wanted from the future relationship. As Leo Varadkar said, 'For us to make a legal commitment to have a done deal at a particular moment or time, that is not possible because it is not in our gift to deliver that, we cannot promise anything that is not in our power to deliver . . . We can commit to our best endeavours and say we will work towards a target date . . . It is not possible to say that we will definitely meet that date.'[82]

Mrs May met with her fellow leaders for an hour, arguing for 'legal guarantees' that the UK would not be 'trapped' in the backstop. But it was unclear to her colleagues what exactly she wanted. She accepted in theory that the Withdrawal Agreement could not be renegotiated, but it sounded to some as though that was exactly what she wanted to do. Furthermore, it was unclear that any further concessions made by the EU would suffice to get the House of Commons to accept the deal. After all, the concessions made to David Cameron in February 2016 had not prevented a vote to leave the EU, and the concessions made to Mrs May in November 2018 had apparently not been enough to gain the support of the UK parliament. In the end the EU agreed that it would start preparations for the future trade negotiations immediately after the Withdrawal Agreement had been signed so that no time would be wasted. It expressed its 'firm determination to work speedily on a subsequent agreement that establishes by 31 December 2020 alternative arrangements, so that the backstop will not need to be triggered', and reiterated that the backstop, if it were to be triggered, would only apply 'temporarily, unless and until it is superseded by a subsequent agreement that ensures that a hard border is avoided'. The EU would in such circumstances 'use its best endeavours to negotiate and conclude expeditiously a subsequent agreement that would replace the backstop, and would expect the same of the United Kingdom, so that the backstop would only be in place for as long as strictly necessary.'[83]

It was hard to see what more Mrs May could have brought back from the summit, but her previous talk of 'legal assurances' meant that the summit was seen in Britain as yet another failure.[84] Such talk probably also reinforced the impression that the deal which she herself had negotiated, and which she was trying to get the Commons to pass, was unsatisfactory. Just as David Cameron had conceded in 2016 that the free movement of EU citizens was a problem, by seeking reforms of free movement that were in fact unobtainable, so she seemed to be seeking the unobtainable (i.e. the renegotiation of the Withdrawal Agreement), in the process undermining her own political position domestically.

On 17 December Mrs May announced that the House of Commons would vote on the Withdrawal Agreement in the week beginning Monday 14 January. The following day the British government announced that it was ramping up its 'no deal' planning, much to the horror of the UK's major business organizations and many MPs.[85]

CHAPTER 12
Crisis

The Withdrawal Agreement offered Brexiteers the certainty that the UK would leave the EU on 29 March 2019, and Remainers the certainty that nothing would change for up to almost four years. But many Remainers were willing to risk a no-deal Brexit in the hope of getting a second referendum, while many hard-line Brexiteers were willing to risk a second referendum in the hope, either of obtaining a new Withdrawal Agreement, or of exiting the EU without a deal at all. Nor was Labour about to come to Theresa May's assistance: Jeremy Corbyn opposed what he called 'a bad deal for Britain.'[1] And so it was no surprise when on 15 January Parliament rejected the Withdrawal Agreement. The scale of the rejection was however remarkable: 432 to 202. It was the largest parliamentary defeat suffered by a British government in the democratic era, with 118 Tories and the DUP voting against the deal.[2]

With so many MPs opposed to the Withdrawal Agreement, and for so many reasons, Mrs May now had to decide whose votes she was going to try to sway in the future. Cross-party talks began but soon petered out: Jeremy Corbyn wanted the Prime Minister to rule out a no-deal Brexit before entering discussions, something that she argued the government did not have the power to do. And so on 20 January Mrs May informed her cabinet that she would continue to seek changes to the backstop. It was a clear signal that her priority was still to obtain the support of the DUP and hard-line Tory Brexiteers associated with the European Research Group (ERG). On 29 January the government went so far as to support an amendment proposed by Sir Graham Brady calling for the Withdrawal Agreement to be approved, but only on the condition that the backstop be replaced by 'alternative arrangements to avoid a hard border.' What those alternative arrangements might be was not spelled out by the amendment, which was passed by 16 votes. The spectacle of the government voting to change an agreement that it had itself negotiated, and abandoning the backstop that it had itself defended in parliament just a few weeks previously, did not go down well elsewhere. In Dublin the move was seen as a clear breach of trust highlighting exactly why a legally enforceable backstop was required.[3] Donald Tusk and Emmanuel Macron immediately rejected the possibility of changing the Withdrawal Agreement.

The British parliament was sending out mixed signals, however. On the one hand, by passing the Brady amendment it was advocating the rejection of the Withdrawal Agreement's compromises: a hard-line message that seemed to point towards an eventual no-deal Brexit. But on the other hand, on the very same day MPs voted by 318 votes to 310 to rule out precisely that outcome. Nevertheless the UK government believed it had shown that the Withdrawal Agreement could be passed once the backstop had been replaced, and it set about trying to convince the EU that this should now happen. The extent to which it ever really believed that it had a chance of doing so is unclear. An alternative interpretation of the talks that now took place is that they were simply an attempt by Mrs May to run down the clock, leaving Parliament with a simple choice: accept her deal or leave without a deal (a prospect that as we have seen MPs had already rejected). On 6 February Mrs May herself told an audience in Northern Ireland that she was not seeking to remove the backstop, merely to change it, and by mid to late February the UK government had further shifted from seeking changes to the Withdrawal Agreement itself, to once again seeking legal guarantees that the backstop would only be temporary.[4] How the UK could have legally binding guarantees that the backstop would only be temporary, while at the same time Dublin had legally binding guarantees that a hard border would never return, was not clear.

The Attorney General, Geoffrey Cox, now briefly took centre stage, for it was he who was supposed, not only to advise the government as to whether or not any guarantees it might obtain were legally binding or not, but to negotiate those guarantees in the first place. By all accounts his talks with EU negotiators did not go smoothly.[5] The outcome was an agreement in Strasbourg on 11 March that committed both sides to beginning talks on the future relationship as soon as possible following Brexit, and to starting negotiations on 'alternative arrangements' (including technological ones) to the backstop as soon as the Withdrawal Agreement had been ratified. In the event that either side acted with the intention of applying the backstop permanently – something ruled out by the Withdrawal Agreement – the other side could trigger the Agreement's dispute settlement mecha-nisms which included arbitration. If the EU (say) ignored the arbitration panel's findings, the UK would 'have the right to enact a unilateral, proportionate suspension of its obliga-tions under the Withdrawal Agreement'.[6] The UK also issued a unilateral declaration of its own, in which it stated that if the EU were not to act in good faith, and if it were not pos-sible to negotiate a future relationship under such circum-stances, then it might be possible for the UK to withdraw from the backstop. However, this would have to be done in accordance with the Withdrawal Agreement's dispute settle-ment mechanisms, and was subject to the 'proviso that the UK will uphold its obligations under the 1998 Agreement in all its dimensions and under all circumstances and...avoid a hard border on the island of Ireland.'[7] It was on this basis that the EU did not object to the UK declaration.

The Strasbourg agreement made explicit the safeguards against EU gamesmanship – such as attempting to perman-ently lock the UK into the backstop against its will – that had, as far as the EU was concerned, already been implicit in the Withdrawal Agreement and Political Declaration. As such it carried some additional legal weight. However, the following day Geoffrey Cox correctly informed the House of Commons that the agreement he had negotiated did not give the UK the right to exit the backstop unilaterally, and MPs voted against the deal for a second time by 391 votes to 242.

29 March was now less than three weeks away. MPs had overwhelmingly rejected the Withdrawal Agreement, but the alternatives to accepting the deal were to leave without one and not leaving at all. On 13 March MPs voted again against

a no deal Brexit, by 321 votes to 278. And so on the following day, having exhausted the available alternatives, they voted by 413 to 202 in favour of delaying Brexit.[8] However, they also voted by 334 to 85 against a second referendum, leaving open the question of what they wanted the extension for.[9]

On 20 March Mrs May wrote to Donald Tusk requesting that Brexit be delayed until 30 June. The following day the EU's 27 other leaders decided that if Parliament approved the Withdrawal Agreement the following week then Brexit could be delayed until 22 May so that the UK Parliament had time to pass the necessary legislation. The May deadline was designed to ensure that the UK would have left before the European Parliament elections, due to be held between 23 and 26 May. If Parliament failed to approve the deal the extension would be for just two weeks, until 12 April, and the UK would be expected 'to indicate a way forward' before that date.[10] Given internal British divisions on Brexit that was not an innocuous request. The possibility of a subsequent, longer, extension was left open, but then the UK would have to take part in European elections.[11]

The House of Commons was now under severe time pressure, since if a way forward was not found by 12 April the UK would crash out without a deal. On 25 March MPs, led by Sir Oliver Letwin, voted to seize control of the Parliament's agenda two days later to see if they could find a consensus on what should happen next. There followed a set of 'indicative votes' on 27 March in which MPs were encouraged to vote in favour of all Brexit outcomes they could live with, to see whether a route could be found through the impasse. But in the event MPs voted against no deal; against the Jersey option (rebranded as 'Common Market 2.0'); against membership of the European Economic Area; against a customs union with the EU; against a customs union combined with 'alignment' with the Single Market; against revocation of Article 50 in the event that this would be required to avoid no deal; and against a referendum to confirm any deal passed by Parliament.[12] Not one of the possible ways forward secured a majority. On the same day Mrs May, sacrificing herself, promised her party that she would resign if they backed her Withdrawal Agreement: the offer was enough to persuade Boris Johnson, Jacob Rees-Mogg, and Dominic Raab to vote for the deal on 29 March (backstop and all), but it was defeated again anyway, by 344 votes to 286. The following Monday MPs once again voted against a customs union (by just three votes), the Jersey option, a referendum, and revocation as a last resort against no deal, and (for the moment at least) the Commons insurgency came to an end.

A no-deal Brexit now seemed highly likely. Over the course of the previous months Leo Varadkar had become increasingly worried by the prospect, even going so far as to claim that in the event of no deal, arrangements could somehow be devised eliminating the need for border controls between Ireland and Northern Ireland. This opened up a potential breach between the Irish government and the European Commission, which made it clear that checks would indeed be required to preserve the integrity of the Single Market. Varadkar's comments were also seized upon by Brexiteers eager to claim that the backstop had never been necessary in the first place.[13] But fortunately for him Mrs May, who had previously claimed that no deal would be better than a bad deal for Britain, was by now determined to prevent this from happening. It seems that a key reason for this apparent shift in her thinking was the risk that a no deal Brexit could trigger the breakup of the United Kingdom.[14] And Parliament was, as we have seen, staunchly opposed to no deal also. But the terms of the Brexit delay still required the UK to find a way forward, and so on 2 April Mrs May invited Jeremy Corbyn to talks to see if they could find one. Corbyn accepted, and three days later the Prime Minister used these talks to argue for a further Brexit delay in yet another letter to Donald Tusk. The extension should not last beyond 30 June, and could be shorter if the Withdrawal Agreement was ratified in time. The 'way forward' was for Mrs May to reach out to MPs across the House; she recognized that it would not involve reopening the Withdrawal Agreement but would focus instead on agreeing changes to the Political Declaration.[15]

A second short extension was unacceptable to many European leaders, tired of last-minute summits. Such member states wanted the extension to last until the end of the year or beyond. Others worried about Brexit 'infecting' the workings of the EU, were sceptical about granting an extension, and wanted any extension to be short. According to newspaper reports Donald Tusk, Angela Merkel, and the majority of other member states were in the first camp, while Emmanuel Macron, the Belgian Prime Minister Charles Michel, and a handful of other leaders were in the second.[16] Both sides agreed that the priority was to avoid the possibility of the UK revoking Article 50 and remaining in the EU without having participated in European elections: this would mean that the

European Parliament was illegally constituted, with serious consequences for the work of the EU as a whole.

The result, predictably enough, was a compromise. On 10 April the leaders agreed to a further extension until 31 October. The UK would leave the EU on Halloween, or earlier if the Withdrawal Agreement was ratified. If it had not left by 23 May it would hold European elections; if no elections were held the extension would end on 31 May. The June Council would review progress. Both sides agreed that 'This extension excludes any re-opening of the Withdrawal Agreement. Any unilateral commitment, statement or other act by the United Kingdom should be compatible with the letter and the spirit of the Withdrawal Agreement, and must not hamper its implementation. Such an extension cannot be used to start negotiations on the future relationship.'[17] Donald Tusk urged the UK not to waste the extra time it had been granted.[18]

It had been a dramatic and emotionally exhausting few weeks for all concerned. On 11 April MPs returned home for the Easter recess. Although Nigel Farage formally launched his new Brexit Party the following day, Brexit briefly receded from the headlines, much to the relief of many in Britain. The following weeks saw talks between Mrs May and Jeremy Corbyn about whether they could together find a way forward that would command the support of Parliament, and growing anxiety on the part of many Conservative MPs that the Brexit Party, which immediately took off in opinion polls, was threatening their electoral futures. Local elections held on 2 May saw the Tories lose 1,333 seats, with the Liberal Democrats making the biggest gains. The Conservative Party now risked being squeezed between the Remain-supporting Liberal Democrats on the one hand and the Brexit Party on the other. Nor did it help the mood of Tory Brexiteers when it became clear that the May-Corbyn talks were considering the UK staying in a *de facto* customs union with the EU. Labour suspended the talks on 17 May citing Cabinet divisions on the issue, and doubts that May would be able to deliver any compromise that had been agreed with Corbyn.[19]

Despite that setback, on 21 May the Prime Minister unveiled a package of measures that she hoped would secure a majority in the House of Commons and allow the Withdrawal Agreement to be passed. There was something in it for everyone. Remainers got the familiar promise of trade with the EU that would be as frictionless as possible; alignment with 'EU rules for goods and agri-food products that are relevant to checks at the border;' and a requirement that a vote be held on whether or not there should be a second referendum. Leavers got promises that the UK would leave the Single Market; that free movement would be abandoned; and that the government would 'seek to conclude the alternative arrangements process by December 2020, avoiding any need for the Northern Ireland backstop coming into force.'[20] Parliament was promised that it would be able to decide on the nature of any future customs arrangements between the UK and EU, and that it would have to approve the UK's negotiating objectives when it came to talks about the future relationship more generally. The Labour Party was promised that British workers' rights would be no lower than those enjoyed by their EU counterparts in the future, and that Brexit would not mean a diminution of environmental protection. And the

DUP was promised that Britain and Northern Ireland would remain 'aligned' if the backstop came into force, in line with Paragraph 50 of the December 2017 Joint Report, and that the Northern Ireland Executive and Assembly would have to consent to any new EU regulations that were added to the backstop. The package was very overtly a compromise between different British factions and it was unclear whether it would be acceptable to the EU.

In the event that didn't matter. Just as there was something in the package to appeal to everyone, so there was something for everyone to object to. Brexiteers were particularly opposed to the promise of a vote on a second referendum. By 22 May it was clear that Mrs May was losing the support of her Cabinet, and on 24 May she announced that she would be resigning as Tory Party leader on 7 June. It was an inglorious end to an unsuccessful premiership. Two days later the results of the European election, held on 23 May, started coming in. The Brexit Party was the big winner: the combined share of its vote plus the UKIP vote was 34.9%, up 7.4 percentage points from 2014. The Liberal Democrats came second: at 20.3%, their vote share was up by 13.4 percentage points. The pro-Remain Greens also increased their share of the vote (by 4.2 percentage points), while both Labour and the Conservatives did badly. The Labour share was down 11.3 percentage points, while the Tories only came in fifth overall, with just 9.1% of the vote, a loss of 14.8 percentage points. Parties that had clear positions on Brexit did well in the election; those that were divided or ambiguous on the issue did badly. If David Cameron's objective in promising the 2016 referendum had been to neutralize Nigel

Farage's threat to the Conservative Party, that had evidently not yet been secured.

Tories' attention quickly turned to the question of which of the candidates lining up to replace Mrs May had the greatest chance of winning back disenchanted voters, especially from the Brexit Party. MPs and Conservative Party members regarded Boris Johnson as the person best suited to this task, and on 24 July he replaced Theresa May as Prime Minister. In a speech outside 10 Downing Street he claimed that he was convinced that the EU and UK could 'do a deal without checks at the Irish border . . . and yet without that anti-democratic backstop', but that it was vital that the UK prepare itself for 'the remote possibility that Brussels refuses any further to negotiate and we are forced to come out with no deal.'[21] The following day he told the Commons that a time limit on the backstop was insufficient, and that 'the way to the deal goes by way of the abolition of the backstop.' To make his no deal threat more credible Johnson appointed a hard-line Cabinet, including Dominic Raab as Foreign Secretary, Jacob Rees-Mogg as Leader of the House of Commons, and Michael Gove as head of the Cabinet Office with special responsibility for no deal preparations. All ministers, he informed the House, were committed to Brexit on 31 October 'whatever the circumstances.'[22] Dominic Cummings was drafted in as special advisor to the Prime Minister, suggesting that the new government was already on an election footing and preparing to see off any attempt by MPs to block a no deal Brexit.

On 29 July the Prime Minister's spokesman upped the stakes further, stating that the abolition of the backstop was a precondition, not just for a deal, but for talks about a deal. 'The EU has said up to now it is not willing to renegotiate [the backstop] . . . The prime minister would be happy to sit down with leaders when that position changes. But he is making it clear to everybody he speaks to that that needs to happen.'[23] Perhaps the new government's hard-line stance was an attempt to isolate Ireland from its European partners: if the UK walked away without a deal, imposing costs not only itself but on the EU as a whole, this would be because of Dublin's insistence on the backstop. As we have seen, Mrs May's government had tried the same tactic without success, but perhaps a sufficiently credible threat to leave without a deal would succeed where she had failed. And the new British Prime Minister waited six days before speaking with Leo Varadkar, much longer than normal, adding to the impression that he was trying to put the Irish Taoiseach under pressure.

But if the British government was trying to isolate Varadkar the attempt was short-lived. On 25 July Mark Francois, a leading hard-line Brexiteer, stated that ERG MPs would vote against the Withdrawal Agreement even if the backstop was removed.[24] The following day the new Foreign Secretary told *The Times* that the removal of the backstop was necessary but not sufficient to avoid no deal.[25] On 31 July and 1 August the UK's new 'sherpa' charged with preparing EU-UK summits, David Frost, held a series of meetings in Brussels in which he not only reiterated that unless the Irish backstop were removed the UK would leave on 31 October without a deal, but also questioned other fundamental aspects of the Withdrawal Agreement, notably the divorce bill and the role of the ECJ in post-Brexit Britain. The day before, the *Independent* newspaper had reported that Frost was also opposed to guaranteeing British workers' rights, something that the EU regarded as a prerequisite for any post-Brexit trade deal with the UK.[26] EU officials concluded that there was no basis for meaningful discussions, that the negotiations were back to where they had been three years previously, and that a no-deal Brexit was now likely. The UK government had no plan, and 'No intention to negotiate, which would require a plan. A no deal now appears to be the UK government's central scenario.'[27]

Many in Britain also believed that the Johnson government was actively pursuing a no deal Brexit and preparing to blame it on the EU. On 6 August Michael Gove stated that he was 'deeply saddened that the EU now seem(ed) to be refusing to negotiate with the UK', while making it clear that the UK's preconditions for negotiations remained.[28] There was a debate about whether or not MPs would be able to prevent no deal: backbenchers like Dominic Grieve were optimistic that they could, while government insiders believed that MPs had left it too late. Concerns were even expressed that the Queen might find herself involved in the constitutional manoeuvring that might ensue. Sterling fell, and Johnson faced protests on visits to Scotland, Wales and Northern Ireland. There were reports that the EU was preparing a large aid package for Ireland to cushion the impact of no deal.[29] With little hope that negotiations would resume before a G7 summit due to begin on 24 August Britain, Ireland and Europe braced themselves for whatever was going to happen next.

What next?

Finishing a book about Brexit in August 2019 has its plusses and minuses. On the one hand I don't know how the story will end, and the only safe prediction is that whatever I predict will be wrong. On the other hand there are pedagogical advantages to this. In ten years' time journalists and academics will be able to explain why it was that we ended up where we did, and they may succeed in making the final outcome seem inevitable. But today there is a thicket of possible futures branching out ahead of us and nothing is certain. This is what history feels like while it is being made.

The first area of uncertainty concerns whether, and to what extent, the EU will facilitate Boris Johnson in his stated desire to remove the backstop from the Withdrawal Agreement and keep the bits he likes. Perhaps the Union will provide more clarification, but it is difficult to see them being willing to accommodate him in this manner. That would mean abandoning a member state on an issue of fundamental national importance because of the intransigence and bad faith of a third country, and would hardly be a positive advertisement for the EU. On the other hand, if the Union holds firm it will show that EU solidarity means something, and that the EU is an umbrella that can protect the interests of all its members no matter how small. The backstop ensures the future integrity of the EU Single Market in a way that no other currently available solution does, while caving in to Mr Johnson would destroy the EU's reputation as a tough negotiator on the world stage. Perhaps the EU will be prepared to return to the original Northern Ireland-only backstop, which is its preferred option anyway, but that possibility aside it seems highly likely that the British political system will still be faced in September with a choice between the existing Withdrawal Agreement, backstop and all; no deal; and no Brexit.

There is far more uncertainty regarding the Johnson government's true intentions. Does it have a thought-out strategy or is it improvising, and if it does have a strategy then what is it? Perhaps Johnson really does believe that the EU will reopen the Withdrawal Agreement, abandoning the backstop when faced with an imminent no-deal Brexit. If he does then it will be interesting to see how he responds when this does not happen. But it is hard to imagine that Johnson could be so naïve, and it thus seems more likely that he is indeed aiming for a no deal Brexit on 31 October, perhaps with the intention of holding a snap election and neutralizing the Brexit Party, and with any concessions made by the EU being regarded as an unexpected bonus.

If that is the case then the next question is whether the House of Commons will be able to prevent no deal, which is of course the legal default. As already noted there is considerable disagreement on this point, but at the time of writing (7 August) there are good reasons to doubt that it will. It could pass a vote of no confidence in the Johnson government, but even if that happens and an election is subsequently called there may be nothing to prevent the Prime Minister from holding it on or after 31 October, thus ensuring that the UK leaves without a deal. An alternative might be to form a temporary national government whose sole purpose would be to seek another extension with the aim of, say, holding a second referendum, but it is far from clear that the opposition parties will be able to agree on such a course of action. Some argue that Parliament could directly legislate to prevent no deal, while others deride such claims as pipe dreams. It seems extremely unlikely that MPs would pass an act revoking Article 50, but might they do so when faced with the certain alternative of no deal? Only time will tell.

If the UK leaves without a deal, what will happen then, not only in the UK but in Ireland, whose economy will face severe disruption, and where controls will have to be re-established to protect the integrity of the European Single Market?[30] On 9 July the Irish government finally accepted the obvious, namely that no deal would require 'tariffs and . . . customs and SPS requirements and associated checks necessary to preserve Ireland's full participation in the Single Market and Customs Union': discussions were on-going with the Commission regarding how to minimize the costs associated with these.[31] Exactly how will border controls work, and what will their political and economic implications be? How will the UK discharge its responsibilities, which are not only economic but also political, to manage this border in the interests of the people of Northern Ireland? And what will the reaction be, not only in Ireland but in Northern Ireland, Scotland and Wales as well? What will the impact of a no deal Brexit be on the British economy?[32] Will UK citizens blame the EU, accepting the disruption as the necessary cost of a clean break from an unreasonable partner? Or will they blame the Conservative Party in general, and Boris Johnson in particular? The only safe prediction about a no deal scenario is that it would be a hugely informative, if costly, civics lesson for the people of Britain, Ireland and the rest of Europe.

Negotiations between the EU and UK may well break down in the event of a no deal Brexit, but they will presumably resume at some point. The nature of those negotiations will probably depend greatly on the identity of the government in power in London: given the likelihood of a British general election in the next few months that identity is uncertain. The assumption on the EU side is that the UK will seek to resume negotiations and will do so from a position of weakness: it is bound to decide sooner or later that a free trade deal with its closest and most important trading partner is in its best interests. And before getting to that point the three divorce issues will still have to be dealt with. As Leo Varadkar said on 6 August, 'If we have no deal, we're going to have to talk. The first things on the agenda are going to be citizens' rights, the financial settlement and the solution to the Irish border – before we even start to talk about a free trade agreement.'[33] If this is what ends up happening, then the UK may ultimately end up in a scenario identical to the one it would have found itself in had the Withdrawal Agreement been passed, but with one crucial difference: during the free trade negotiations it will not benefit from a transition period. And it is hard to see how that could be to its advantage.

But is the assumption that the UK will soon come back to the negotiating table warranted, or will a wave of English nationalism lead to the UK government rejecting any talks with Brussels, no matter the cost? How long might such a stance last? And will the EU be able to maintain its present degree of cohesion after a no-deal Brexit, as well as the determination not to allow London to use the three divorce issues as leverage in an eventual free trade negotiation? Or will the desire to diminish the costs of a no-deal Brexit lead to a series of bilateral side deals with the UK, and to EU unity splintering?

Alternatively, might a Johnson government try to quickly negotiate a trade deal with the US in an attempt to 'lock Brexit in'? Will it succeed in doing so, or will the Irish-American lobby block any deal, as it has threatened to do in the event that Brexit leads to a hard border in Ireland?[34] Will London be willing to make the necessary concessions to the US on agriculture, healthcare and other sensitive issues in order to get an agreement quickly over the line, and how will the House of Commons and British public opinion respond to those? And will such a move lead to the EU being more accommodating towards the UK, fearing that it might otherwise permanently drift out of its orbit? Or will the EU further tighten border controls so as to keep out undesired products and protect itself against what it regards as unfair competition?

From the vantage point of August 2019 it seems extremely improbable that the House of Commons will ratify the Withdrawal Agreement at the fourth time of asking. However the possibility cannot be entirely ruled out. For example Johnson could decide that a post-no-deal election was not in his interests, go to the country before Halloween, be returned to government with a majority sufficient large that he could abandon the DUP, and force through a Withdrawal

Agreement with a Northern-Ireland only backstop, thus eliminating the risk that Britain could be 'trapped' in it. But even in the highly unlikely event of such an outcome this will not be the end of the uncertainty, for the future trade relationship with the EU will still have to be negotiated.[35] That will require the UK government to decide how close it wants the relationship between Britain and the EU to be, and as we have seen that could take a while. It will also take time to negotiate such a future relationship, and so – barring unforeseen technological breakthroughs – it is entirely possible that the backstop will have to come into effect, at least temporarily. Who knows what the political ramifications of that might be?

These are just some of the possible outcomes ahead of us. More likely is one I haven't thought of yet. Could the UK leave and then decide it had made a mistake, and if so how long might this learning process take? Will the Conservative and Unionist Party, whose Liberal Unionist component was born because of Ireland, split up largely because of Ireland? And there are wider questions that arise too, such as: will Brexit and Russian-backed populism in other countries weaken Europe at a dangerous time? Or will the departure of a recalcitrant member make it easier for the European Union to deepen economic, political and security cooperation among its remaining members? Conversely, if Remainers somehow succeed in winning a second referendum will this strengthen or weaken the European project?

As Halloween draws nearer we don't yet know how this story will end. But Brexit has always been about borders. The British decided in 2016 to take back control of theirs; the

Europeans have insisted on retaining control of theirs; and the Irish are determined to avoid one on their island. And so it is perhaps not surprising that wherever Brexit is ultimately headed, the Irish border issue will have been central to the process of getting there.

Bibliography

Autor, David H., David Dorn and Gordon H. Hanson. 'The China Syndrome: Local Labor Market Effects of Import Competition in the United States.' *American Economic Review* 103, no. 6 (2013): 2121–68.

— and Kaveh Majlesi. 'Importing Political Polarization? The Electoral Consequences of Rising Trade Exposure.' *National Bureau of Economic Research Working Paper Series*, no. 22637 (2016).

Barry, Frank and John Bradley. 'FDI and Trade: The Irish Host-Country Experience.' *Economic Journal* 107, no. 445 (1997): 1798–811.

Barry, Frank and Clare O'Mahony. 'Costello, Lemass and the Politics of the New Foreign Investment Regime of the 1950s.' Mimeo, Trinity College Dublin (2016).

Becker, Sascha O., Thiemo Fetzer and Dennis Novy. 'Who Voted for Brexit? A Comprehensive District Level Analysis.' *Economic Policy* 32, no. 92 (2017): 601–50.

Bolt, Jutta, Robert Inklaar, Herman de Jong and Jan Luiten van Zanden. 'Maddison Project Database, Version 2018.' https://www.rug.nl/ggdc/historicaldevelopment/maddison/releases/maddison-project-database-2018 (2018a).

— 'Rebasing "Maddison": New Income Comparisons and the Shape of Long-Run Economic Development.' *Maddison Project Working Paper* 10 (2018b).

Bonfatti, Roberto and Kevin Hjortshøj O'Rourke. 'Growth, Import Dependence, and War.' *Economic Journal* 128, no. 614 (2018): 2222–57.

Boxer, C. R. *The Portuguese Seaborne Empire, 1415–1825*. New York: Alfred A. Knopf, 1975.

Broadberry, Stephen and Mark Harrison. 'The Economics of World War I: An Overview.' In *The Economics of World War I*, edited by Stephen Broadberry and Mark Harrison, 3–40. Cambridge, UK: Cambridge University Press, 2005.

Broadberry, Stephen and Alexander Klein. 'Aggregate and Per Capita GDP in Europe, 1870–2000: Continental, Regional and National Data with Changing Boundaries.' *Scandinavian Economic History Review* 60, no. 1 (2012): 79–107.

de Bromhead, Alan, Alan Fernihough, Markus Lampe and Kevin Hjortshøj O'Rourke. 'When Britain Turned Inward: The Impact of Interwar British Protection.' *American Economic Review* 109, no. 2 (2019): 325–52.

Bromund, T. 'Whitehall, the National Farmers' Union, and Plan G, 1956–57.' *Contemporary British History* 15, no. 2 (2001): 76–97.

Brouard, Sylvain and Vincent Tiberj. 'The French Referendum: The Not So Simple Act of Saying Nay.' *PS: Political Science & Politics* 39, no. 2 (2006): 261–8.

Bruno, Michael and Jeffrey Sachs. *Economics of Worldwide Stagflation*. Oxford: Basil Blackwell, 1985.

Campos, Nauro F., Fabrizio Coricelli and Luigi Moretti. 'Economic Growth and Political Integration: Estimating the Benefits from Membership in the European Union Using the Synthetic Counterfactuals Method.' *Centre for Economic Policy Research Discussion Paper* 9968 (2014).

Camps, Miriam. *Britain and the European Community, 1955–1963*. London: Oxford University Press, 1964.

Catterall, Peter, ed. *The Macmillan Diaries, Vol II: Prime Minister and After (1957–66)*. Basingstoke: Macmillan, 2011.

Chamberlain, Joseph. *The Radical Programme*. London: Chapman and Hall Ltd, 1885. Available at https://archive.org/details/radicalprogramme00chamiala

—. *Imperial Union and Tariff Reform: Speeches Delivered from May 15 to Nov. 4, 1903: With an Introduction*. London: G. Richards, 1903. Available at https://archive.org/details/cu31924030186658

Clark, Gregory, Kevin Hjortshøj O'Rourke and Alan M. Taylor. 'The Growing Dependence of Britain on Trade during the Industrial Revolution.' *Scandinavian Economic History Review* 62, no. 2 (2014): 109–36.

Clemens, Michael A., and Jeffrey G. Williamson. 'Why Did the Tariff–Growth Correction Change after 1950?' *Journal of Economic Growth* 9, no. 1 (2004): 5–46.

Coats, A. W. 'Political Economy and the Tariff Reform Campaign of 1903.' *Journal of Law & Economics* 11, no. 1 (1968): 181–229.

Colantone, Italo and Piero Stanig. 'Global Competition and Brexit.' *American Political Science Review* 112, no. 2 (2018): 201–18.

Condliffe, J. B. *The Reconstruction of World Trade: A Survey of International Economic Relations*. London: George Allen & Unwin, 1941.

Connelly, Tony. *Brexit and Ireland: The Dangers, the Opportunities, and the Inside Story of the Irish Response*. Dublin: Penguin Ireland, 2018.

Cook, Chris. *Defeated by Brexit*. London: Tortoise Media, 2019.

Costa, Leonor Freire, Pedro Lains and Susana Münch Miranda. *An Economic History of Portugal, 1143–2010*. Cambridge: Cambridge University Press, 2016.

Crafts, Nicholas and Kevin Hjortshøj O'Rourke. 'Twentieth Century Growth.' In *Handbook of Economic Growth*, edited by Philippe Aghion and Steven N. Durlauf, 263–346. Amsterdam: Elsevier, 2014.

Crawford, Ian, Michael Keen and Stephen Smith. 'Value Added Tax and Excises.' In *Dimensions of Tax Design: The Mirrlees Review*, edited by James Mirrlees et al., 275–362. Oxford: Oxford University Press, 2010.

Dangerfield, George. *The Strange Death of Liberal England*. London: MacGibbon & Kee, 1966. First published 1935.

das Neves, João L. César. 'Portuguese Postwar Growth: A Global Approach.' In *Economic Growth in Europe since 1945*, edited by Nicholas Crafts and Gianni Toniolo, 329–54. Cambridge: Cambridge University Press, 1996.

Dorsett, Richard. 'The Effect of the Troubles on GDP in Northern Ireland.' *European Journal of Political Economy* 29 (2013): 119–33.

Ebrill, Liam P., Michael Keen, Jean-Paul Bodin and Victoria Summers. *The Modern VAT*. Washington, D.C.: International Monetary Fund, 2001.

Eichengreen, Barry J. *Reconstructing Europe's Trade and Payments: The European Payments Union*. Manchester: Manchester University Press, 1993.

—. *The European Economy since 1945: Coordinated Capitalism and Beyond*. Princeton, N.J.; Oxford: Princeton University Press, 2007.

— and Andrea Boltho. 'The Economic Impact of European Integration.' In *The Cambridge Economic History of Modern Europe: Volume 2: 1870 to the Present*, edited by Kevin H. O'Rourke and Stephen Broadberry, 267–95. Cambridge: Cambridge University Press, 2010.

— and Kevin Hjortshøj O'Rourke. 'A Tale of Two Depressions.' *VoxEU. org* (2009).

Ellison, James. *Threatening Europe: Britain and the Creation of the European Community, 1955–58*. Basingstoke: Macmillan Press in association with Institute of Contemporary British History, 2000.

Emerson, Michael. *The Economics of 1992: The E.C. Commission's Assessment of the Economic Effects of Completing the Internal Market*. Oxford: Oxford University Press, 1988.

de la Escosura, Leandro Prados and Jorge C. Sanz. 'Growth and Macroeconomic Performance in Spain, 1939–93.' In *Economic Growth in Europe since*

1945, edited by Nicholas Crafts and Gianni Toniolo, 355–87. Cambridge: Cambridge University Press, 1996.

Evans, Richard J. *The Pursuit of Power: Europe, 1815–1914*. London: Penguin Books, 2017.

Ferreira da Silva, Álvaro. 'Multinationals and Foreign Direct Investment: The Portuguese Experience (1900–2010).' *Journal of Evolutionary Studies in Business* 2, no. 1 (2016): 40–68.

Fetzer, Thiemo. 'Did Austerity Cause Brexit?' *Warwick Economics Research Papers* 1170 (2018).

Findlay, Ronald and Kevin H. O'Rourke. *Power and Plenty: Trade, War, and the World Economy in the Second Millennium*. Princeton, N.J.: Princeton University Press, 2007.

Freris, Andrew. *The Greek Economy in the Twentieth Century*. London: Croom Helm, 1986.

Gillingham, John. 'The European Coal and Steel Community: An Object Lesson?' In *Europe's Post-War Recovery*, edited by Barry J. Eichengreen, 151–68. Cambridge: Cambridge University Press, 1995.

Grob-Fitzgibbon, Benjamin John. *Continental Drift: Britain and Europe from the End of Empire to the Rise of Euroscepticism*. Cambridge: Cambridge University Press, 2016.

Gstöhl, Sieglinde. 'EFTA and the European Economic Area or the Politics of Frustration.' *Cooperation and Conflict* 29, no. 4 (1994): 333–66.

Headrick, Daniel R. *The Tools of Empire: Technology and European Imperialism in the Nineteenth Century*. New York; Oxford: Oxford University Press, 1981.

Hennessy, Peter. *Having It So Good: Britain in the Fifties*. London: Allen Lane, 2006.

Hoffman, Philip T. *Why Did Europe Conquer the World?* Princeton; Oxford: Princeton University Press, 2015.

Huberman, Michael. *Odd Couple: International Trade and Labor Standards in History*. New Haven, Conn.: Yale University Press, 2012.

Irwin, Douglas A. 'Political Economy and Peel's Repeal of the Corn Laws.' *Economics & Politics* 1, no. 1 (1989): 41–59.

—. 'Free Trade and Protection in Nineteenth-Century Britain and France Revisited: A Comment on Nye.' *Journal of Economic History* 53, no. 1 (1993): 146–52.

Jackson, Julian. *A Certain Idea of France: The Life of Charles de Gaulle*. London: Allen Lane, 2018.

Jones, E. L. *The European Miracle: Environments, Economies and Geopolitics in the History of Europe and Asia*. Cambridge: Cambridge University Press, 2003.

Kaiser, Wolfram. *Using Europe, Abusing the Europeans: Britain and European Integration, 1945–63*. Basingstoke: Macmillan, 1996.

— *Christian Democracy and the Origins of European Union*. Cambridge: Cambridge University Press, 2007.

Katzenstein, Peter J. *Small States in World Markets: Industrial Policy in Europe*. Ithaca: Cornell University Press, 1985.

Keen, Michael and Stephen Smith. 'The Future of Value Added Tax in the European Union.' *Economic Policy* 11, no. 23 (1996): 373–420.

Kenny, Mike and Nick Pearce. *Shadows of Empire: The Anglosphere in British Politics*. Cambridge: Polity Press, 2018.

Kopsidis, Michael, and Martin Ivanov. 'Industrialization and De-industrialization in Southeast Europe, 1870–2010.' In *The Spread of Modern Industry to the Periphery since 1871*, edited by Kevin Hjortshøj O'Rourke and Jeffrey Gale Williamson, 91–114. Oxford: Oxford University Press, 2017.

Krugman, Paul R. *End This Depression Now!* New York; London: W.W. Norton & Company, 2013.

Laffan, Brigid and Jane O'Mahony. *Ireland and the European Union*. Basingstoke: Palgrave Macmillan, 2008.

Lambert, Nicholas A. *Planning Armageddon: British Economic Warfare and the First World War*. Cambridge, Mass.; London: Harvard University Press, 2012.

Leary, Peter. *Unapproved Routes: Histories of the Irish Border, 1922–1972*. Oxford: Oxford University Press, 2016.

Loughlin, James. 'Joseph Chamberlain, English Nationalism and the Ulster Question.' *History* 77, no. 250 (1992): 202–19.

Lynch, Frances M. B. 'De Gaulle's First Veto: France, the Rueff Plan and the Free Trade Area.' *Contemporary European History* 9, no. 1 (2000): 111–35.

Maher, D. J. *The Tortuous Path: The Course of Ireland's Entry into the EEC, 1948–73*. Dublin: Institute of Public Administration, 1986.

Milward, Alan S. *The European Rescue of the Nation-State*. London: Routledge, 2000.

Mitchell, B. R. *International Historical Statistics: Europe, 1750–2000*. 5th ed. Basingstoke: Palgrave Macmillan, 2003.

Mody, Ashoka. *Eurotragedy: A Drama in Nine Acts*. New York: Oxford University Press, 2018.

Moravcsik, Andrew. *The Choice for Europe: Social Purpose and State Power from Messina to Maastricht*. Ithaca, N.Y.: Cornell University Press, 1998.

—. 'De Gaulle between Grain and Grandeur: The Political Economy of French EC Policy, 1958–1970 (Part 1).' *Journal of Cold War Studies* 2, no. 2 (2000a): 3–43.

—. 'De Gaulle between Grain and Grandeur: The Political Economy of French EC Policy, 1958–1970 (Part 2).' *Journal of Cold War Studies* 2, no. 3 (2000b): 4–68.

Neary, J. Peter and Cormac Ó Gráda. 'Protection, Economic War and Structural Change: The 1930s in Ireland.' *Irish Historical Studies* 27, no. 107 (1991): 250–66.

Nye, John Vincent. 'The Myth of Free-Trade Britain and Fortress France: Tariffs and Trade in the Nineteenth Century.' *Journal of Economic History* 51, no. 1 (1991): 23–46.

—. 'Reply to Irwin on Free Trade.' *Journal of Economic History* 53, no. 1 (1993): 153–8.

Offer, Avner. *The First World War: An Agrarian Interpretation.* Oxford: Clarendon Press, 1989.

Ó Gráda, Cormac. *A Rocky Road: The Irish Economy since the 1920s.* Manchester New York: Manchester University Press, 1997.

—. *Black '47 and Beyond: The Great Irish Famine in History, Economy and Memory.* Princeton, N.J.; Chichester: Princeton University Press, 1999.

—and Kevin O'Rourke. 'Irish Economic Growth, 1945–88.' In *Economic Growth in Europe since 1945*, edited by Nicholas Crafts and Gianni Toniolo, 388–426. Cambridge: Cambridge University Press, 1996.

— and Kevin H. O'Rourke, 'Living Standards and Growth.' In *The Economy of Ireland: Policy and Performance of a European Region*, edited by John O'Hagan, 178–204. Dublin: Gill and Macmillan, 2000.

O'Rourke, Kevin. 'Burn Everything British but Their Coal: The Anglo-Irish Economic War of the 1930s.' *Journal of Economic History* 51, no. 2 (1991): 357–66.

—. 'The European Grain Invasion, 1870–1913.' *Journal of Economic History* 57, no. 4 (1997): 775–801.

—. 'Economists and the European Democratic Deficit.' *Critical Quarterly* 57, no. 2 (2015): 121–6.

—. 'Independent Ireland in Comparative Perspective.' *Irish Economic and Social History* 44, no. 1 (2017): 19–45.

— and Alan M. Taylor. 'Cross of Euros.' *Journal of Economic Perspectives* 27, no. 3 (2013): 167–92.

— and Jeffrey G. Williamson. *Globalization and History: The Evolution of a Nineteenth-Century Atlantic Economy.* Cambridge, Mass.: MIT Press, 1999.

— and Jeffrey Gale Williamson, eds. *The Spread of Modern Industry to the Periphery since 1871*. Oxford: Oxford University Press, 2017.

O'Toole, Fintan. *Heroic Failure: Brexit and the Politics of Pain*. London: Head of Zeus, 2018.

Paavonen, Tapani. 'Finland and the Question of West European Economic Integration, 1947–1961.' *Scandinavian Economic History Review* 52, no. 2–3 (2004): 85–109.

Pašeta, Senia. *Modern Ireland: A Very Short Introduction*. Oxford: Oxford University Press, 2003.

Piketty, Thomas. *Le Capital au XXIe Siècle*. Paris: Seuil, 2013.

—, Emmanuel Saez and Gabriel Zucman. 'Distributional National Accounts: Methods and Estimates for the United States.' *Quarterly Journal of Economics* 133, no. 2 (2018): 553–66.

Piris, Jean-Claude. *The Lisbon Treaty: A Legal and Political Analysis*. Cambridge: Cambridge University Press, 2010

Rae, Allan N, Anna Strutt and Andrew Mead. *New Zealand's Agricultural Exports to Quota Markets*: Centre for Applied Economics and Policy Studies, Massey University, 2006

Ring, Raymond J. 'The Proportion of Consumers' and Producers' Goods in the General Sales Tax.' *National Tax Journal* 42, no. 2 (1989): 167–79.

Roberts, Andrew. *Churchill: Walking with Destiny*. London: Penguin Books, 2018.

Saunders, Robert. *Yes to Europe!: The 1975 Referendum and Seventies Britain*. Cambridge: Cambridge University Press, 2018.

Schaad, Martin. 'Plan G – a "Counterblast"? British Policy towards the Messina Countries, 1956.' *Contemporary European History* 7, no. 1 (1998): 39–60.

Schonhardt-Bailey, Cheryl. *From the Corn Laws to Free Trade: Interests, Ideas, and Institutions in Historical Perspective*. Cambridge, Mass.; London: MIT Press, 2006.

Seldon, Anthony, and Daniel Collings. *Britain under Thatcher*. London: Longman, 2000.

Shipman, Tim. *All Out War: The Full Story of Brexit*. Revised and updated edition. London: William Collins, 2017.

—, *Fall Out: A Year of Political Mayhem*. London: William Collins, 2018

Simms, Brendan. *Britain's Europe: A Thousand Years of Conflict and Cooperation*. London: Penguin Books, 2017.

Sinnott, Richard, Johan A. Elkink, Kevin O'Rourke and James McBride. 'Attitudes and Behaviour in the Referendum on the Treaty of Lisbon.' *Report prepared for the Irish Department of Foreign Affairs* (2009).

Södersten, Jan E. 'Why Europe Chose the VAT.' Mimeo, Uppsala University (2000).

Stiglitz, Joseph E. The Euro: *And Its Threat to the Future of Europe*. London: Allen Lane, 2016.

Sykes, Alan. *Tariff Reform in British Politics: 1903–1913*. Oxford: Clarendon Press, 1979.

Timothy, Nick. *Our Joe: Joseph Chamberlain's Conservative Legacy*: Conservative History Group, 2012.

Tooze, J. Adam. *Crashed: How a Decade of Financial Crises Changed the World*. London: Allen Lane, 2018.

Tracy, Michael. *Government and Agriculture in Western Europe, 1880–1988*. New York: London: Harvester Wheatsheaf, 1989.

Trentmann, Frank. *Free Trade Nation: Commerce, Consumption, and Civil Society in Modern Britain*. Oxford: Oxford University Press, 2008.

Urlanis, B. *Wars and Population*. Moscow: Progress Publishers, 1971.

Urwin, Derek W. *The Community of Europe: A History of European Integration since 1945*. 2nd ed. London: Longman, 1995.

Warlouzet, Laurent. 'Négocier au pied du mur: la France et le projet britannique de zone de libre-échange (1956–1958).' *Relations internationales* 136, no. 4 (2008): 33–50.

—. 'De Gaulle as a Father of Europe: The Unpredictability of the FTA's Failure and the EEC's Success (1956–58).' *Contemporary European History* 20, no. 4 (2011): 419–34.

Williamson, Jeffrey G. 'The Impact of the Corn Laws Just Prior to Repeal.' *Explorations in Economic History* 27, no. 2 (1990): 123–56.

—. *Trade and Poverty: When the Third World Fell Behind*. Cambridge, Mass.: MIT Press, 2011.

Young, Hugo. *This Blessed Plot: Britain and Europe from Churchill to Blair*. Updated edition. London: Papermac, 1999.

Young, John W. *Britain and European Unity, 1945–1992*. Basingstoke: Macmillan, 1993.

Zebel, Sydney H. 'Fair Trade: An English Reaction to the Breakdown of the Cobden Treaty System.' *Journal of Modern History* 12, no. 2 (1940): 161–85.

Notes

INTRODUCTION

1. Grob-Fitzgibbon (2016), p. 271.
2. On EMU, see O'Rourke and Taylor (2013), freely available at https://www.aeaweb.org/articles?id=10.1257/jep.27.3.167, as well as numerous blog posts and opinion columns available at http://www.irisheconomy.ie/index.php/author/korourke/. On the democratic deficit, see O'Rourke (2015), freely available at https://onlinelibrary.wiley.com/doi/full/10.1111/criq.12197.

CHAPTER 1: THE ORIGINS OF SUPRANATIONAL EUROPE

1. https://www.gov.uk/government/speeches/pms-florence-speech-a-new-era-of-cooperation-and-partnership-between-the-uk-and-the-eu.
2. NAFTA is due to be replaced by a new United States–Mexico–Canada Agreement, similar to the old agreement, but with a much less easily pronounceable name (USMCA).
3. The text of the treaty is available at https://www.nafta-sec-alena.org/Home/Texts-of-the-Agreement/North-American-Free-Trade-Agreement.
4. A classic reference remains Jones (2003). For a more recent treatment, see Hoffman (2015).
5. Boxer (1975), pp. 52–3.
6. Broadberry and Harrison (2005), p. 27; Urlanis (1971), p. 295.
7. The Americans lost more than 100,000 soldiers in the First World War, and around 300,000 in the Second (see the previous note for sources).
8. '*L'armée française n'est pas la seule à se sacrifier. Au prix de lourdes pertes, les Canadiens mènent l'offensive à Vimy, les Britanniques à Passchendaele, les Italiens sont vaincus à Caporetto. Les États-Unis rompent avec*

l'isolationnisme et s'engagent aux côtés de l'Entente. L'arrivée progressive des soldats américains change le rapport de forces et va contribuer à forger la victoire . . . Traversée par les deux révolutions, la Russie connaît de profonds bouleversements et signe, le 15 décembre, un armistice avec l'Allemagne.' http://discours.vie-publique.fr/notices/173002294.html. Author's translation.

9. *'Quand on vit à Compiègne, ou plus loin, là-bas en Belgique, aux Pays-Bas, en Allemagne, aimer la paix, c'est aimer l'Europe. Ses peuples, ses cultures, sa diversité, bien sûr. C'est aimer s'y promener, y étudier, en découvrir les beautés et l'histoire. Mais c'est aussi aimer l'Europe politique, celle des libertés, de la citoyenneté commune. C'est l'aimer avec ses imperfections, ses insuffisances. Malgré sa complexité ou ses lenteurs. Oui, aimer la paix quand on est Européen, c'est aimer l'Europe. Une Europe qui nous rappelle à la fois les valeurs éternelles qui nous unissent et les désastres qui nous ont endeuillés.'* http://www.gouvernement.fr/partage/9722-commemoration-de-l-armistice-clairiere-de-rethondes. Author's translation.

10. 'My Tory colleagues have actively whitewashed Remembrance Sunday to fuel their dreams of a hard Brexit', *Independent*, Friday 3 November 2017.

11. Headrick (1981), p. 3. See also Findlay and O'Rourke (2007).

12. In some parts of the world the process started surprisingly early: for a recent overview of the phenomenon, see O'Rourke and Williamson (2017).

13. Cited, for example, in Roberts (2018), p. 897.

14. *'Sans l'empire, la France ne serait qu'un pays libéré. Grâce à son empire, la France est un pays vainqueur.'*

15. It was to some, as we will see in the next chapter.

16. *'Voyez-vous, mes chers amis, nous vivons encore aujourd'hui sur une fiction qui consiste à dire: il y a quatre «Grands» dans le monde. Eh bien, il n'y a pas quatre Grands, il y en a deux: l'Amérique et la Russie. Il y en aura un troisième à la fin du siècle: la Chine. Il dépend de vous qu'il y en ait un quatrième: l'Europe.'* *Journal Officiel de la République française*, 6 July 1957, p. 3305. Author's translation.

17. Huberman (2012).

18. Simms (2017), p. 164.

19. Milward (2000).

20. According to Eichengreen (2007), the bargains involved workers moderating wage growth, which increased profits, but required capitalists to use those profits to invest in new and better jobs, rather than paying them out to shareholders as dividends.

21. Milward (2000), p. 18.

22. The argument of the following paragraphs is based on Milward (2000, pp. 186–90).
23. Articles 119 and 120. The text of the treaty may be consulted at https://eur-lex.europa.eu/legal-content/FR/TXT/PDF/?uri=CELEX:11957E/TXT&from=EN; an English translation is available at https://ec.europa.eu/romania/sites/romania/files/tratatul_de_la_roma.pdf.
24. Milward (2000), p. 190.
25. Milward (2000).
26. O'Rourke (1997), O'Rourke and Williamson (1999).
27. Tracy (1989), chap. 11.
28. Ibid., p. 219.
29. Mitchell (2003), Tables B1 and J2.

CHAPTER 2: NINETEENTH-CENTURY LEGACIES

1. Simms (2017), p. xiv.
2. Williamson (2011).
3. O'Rourke (1997), p. 791.
4. The figures are taken from the Bank of England's excellent dataset, a millennium of macroeconomic data, available at https://www.bankofengland.co.uk/statistics/research-datasets.
5. Clark et al. (2014) find, using computable general equilibrium techniques, that the impact of trade on British economic welfare was an order of magnitude higher in the 1850s than in the 1760s.
6. Offer (1989), Lambert (2012). For a recent theoretical exploration of some of the issues involved, see Bonfatti and O'Rourke (2018).
7. Williamson (1990).
8. Irwin (1989). The standard reference on the Repeal of the Corn Laws is the excellent book on the subject by Schonhardt-Bailey (2006).
9. Zebel (1940), pp. 169, 171.
10. Chamberlain (1885).
11. Loughlin (1992), p. 212.
12. Ibid., p. 214.
13. Cited in Evans (2017).
14. 'The true conception of Empire', 1897, in which Chamberlain further stated:'No doubt, in the first instance, when these conquests have been made, there has been bloodshed, there has been loss of life among the

native populations, loss of still more precious lives among those who have been sent out to bring these countries into some kind of disciplined order, but it must be remembered that that is the condition of the mission we have to fulfil . . . You cannot have omelettes without breaking eggs, you cannot destroy the practices of barbarism, of slavery, of superstition, which for centuries have desolated the interior of Africa, without the use of force.'

15. Chamberlain (1903), p. 7.

16. Ibid., p. 18.

17. Ibid., p. ix.

18. Offer (1989), p. 402. The speech on 15 May was cautiously worded, merely asking for public debate on the issue; but it was clear where Chamberlain's preferences lay.

19. The latter statement is not quite true. Even after the switch to free trade, the UK retained tariffs for revenue-raising purposes on goods that were subject to domestic excise duties (notably alcoholic drinks) or that were not produced at all domestically (e.g, tea and tobacco). French wine imported into Britain was thus subject to tariffs. However, there was no great British wine industry benefiting from this protection, and British beer, whisky and whiskey manufacturers were subject to equivalent excise duties. Douglas Irwin describes British tariffs during the period as 'the natural extension of domestic excise taxes to foreign goods' (Irwin, 1993, p. 147). It seems only fair to mention that John Nye (1991, 1993) strongly disagrees with this assessment.

20. Dangerfield (1966), p. 22.

21. Sykes (1979), p. 40.

22. Sykes (1979), p. 35.

23. Coats (1968), p. 184.

24. As the historian Frank Trentmann (2008, p. 185) puts it, 'Joseph Chamberlain was the best thing that could have happened to Free Trade.'

25. Sykes (1979), p. 285.

26. Offer (1989), Broadberry and Harrison (2005). The argument that Allied victory in the First World War was largely due to economic factors is usefully summarized in https://voxeu.org/article/world-war-i-why-allies-won.

27. http://opac.oireachtas.ie/AWData/Library3/Library2/DL067254.pdf, p. 13.

28. The conference also called for common product standards throughout the Empire because of the advantages these would confer on both consumers and producers, and the increases in trade that would result: shades of the European Single Market of the 1990s. Ibid., pp. 45–6, 54–5.

29. Hansard, Commons Sitting of Thursday, 4 February, 1932.
30. de Bromhead et al. (2019).
31. Condliffe (1941), p. 287.
32. https://www.wto.org/english/thewto_e/history_e/tradewardarkhour41_e.htm.
33. https://www.wto.org/english/docs_e/legal_e/gatt47_01_e.htm.
34. Ibid.

CHAPTER 3: THE PATH TO ROME

1. Grob-Fitzgibbon (2016), p. 8.
2. Ibid., p. 18.
3. https://winstonchurchill.org/publications/finest-hour/finest-hour-160/articles-wsc-s-three-majestic-circles/.
4. Grob-Fitzgibbon (2016), pp. 51–2.
5. Ibid., p. 39.
6. Roberts (2018), pp. 900, 917.
7. Ibid., p. 71.
8. I enjoy pointing this out to multinational groups of students since it irritates both the British and the French, albeit for different reasons.
9. The OEEC became the OECD of our own day in 1961, with Canada and the United States joining in that year.
10. Initially, Germany was represented at the OEEC by two delegations acting on behalf of the Anglo-American Bizone and the French occupied zone. There were thus eighteen participants, rather than seventeen, in the original OEEC. In 1949 the British, French and American occupation zones were merged to form the Federal Republic of Germany, henceforth referred to for simplicity as 'Germany'. In addition, that portion of the Free Territory of Trieste which was under Anglo-American control also participated in the organization, until it was handed back to Italy in 1954.
11. Urwin (1995), p. 20.
12. Grob-Fitzgibbon (2016), p. 68.
13. Dollars were convertible, but no one had enough of them.
14. The classic reference on the EPU is Eichengreen (1993).
15. The text of the treaty is available on the site of the now-defunct Western European Union, www.weu.int. Unlike the Treaty of Dunkirk, which had been signed by the UK and France a mere six months earlier, the Treaty

of Brussels did not single out Germany as the only potential aggressor, although it was named as a potential aggressor.

16. I recognize that the title of this chapter and the present subsection has become a cliché, but I am using it in part in memory of my godfather Joe, whose first present to his future wife Pauline was a copy of Belloc's book.

17. 'Cette proposition réalisera les premières assises concrètes d'une Fédération européenne indispensable à la préservation de la paix.'

18. Grob-Fitzgibbon (2016), pp. 125–9.

19. Ibid., p. 129.

20. Ibid., p. 144.

21. See notably Gillingham (1995).

22. Eichengreen and Boltho (2010).

23. Gillingham (1995).

24. Grob-Fitzgibbon (2016), pp. 169–72.

25. Milward (2000), pp. 151–71.

26. Camps (1964), chap. II.

27. Ibid., p. 39.

28. Ibid., p. 41.

29. Kaiser (1996), pp. 48–9; Schaad (1998), pp. 44–5.

30. Kaiser (1996), pp. 91–2.

31. https://eur-lex.europa.eu/legal-content/FR/TXT/PDF/?uri=CELEX:11957E/TXT&from=EN. An English translation is available at https://ec.europa.eu/romania/sites/romania/files/tratatul_de_la_roma.pdf.

CHAPTER 4: BRENTRY

1. Bromund (2001), p. 77.

2. Grob-Fitzgibbon (2016), pp. 210–12.

3. Ibid.

4. Cited in Bromund (2001), p. 81.

5. See Kaiser (1996), Moravcsik (1998), Schaad (1998), Ellison (2000).

6. Camps (1964), p. 102.

7. Lynch (2000), Warlouzet (2008).

8. Kaiser (1996), Ellison (2000), Camps (1964), Warlouzet (2011).

9. As we saw in the previous chapter the European *Communities* had since 1967 brought together the ECSC, the EEC and EURATOM. The European

Community, on the other hand, is the name given to the EEC under the Treaty of Maastricht from 1993 onwards (see Chapter 8).

10. Finland was also involved in the discussions. However, the latter state was not even a member of the OEEC, and given its relationship with the Soviet Union would have to content itself with associate membership of EFTA, beginning in 1961.

11. Kaiser (1996), pp. 101–7.

12. Young (1993), p. 67.

13. Urwin (1995), pp. 117–20.

14. Hennessy (2006), p. 615.

15. Camps (1964), Kaiser (1996).

16. Camps (1964), p. 336.

17. Catterall (ed.) (2011), p. 313.

18. Grob-Fitzgibbon (2016), pp. 271, 278, 285.

19. Grob-Fitzgibbon (2016), p. 290.

20. For a recent discussion see Jackson (2018), pp. 584–94.

21. Grob-Fitzgibbon (2016), p. 288; the citation is my translation. The original reads: *'un autre marché commun . . . celui qu'on bâtirait à onze. Et puis à treize. Et puis peut-être à dix-huit . . . Il est à prévoir que la cohésion de tous ses membres qui seraient très nombreux, très divers n'y résisterait pas longtemps. Et qu'en définitive il apparaîtrait une Communauté atlantique colossale sous dépendance et direction américaine.'* The text of the 14 January 1963 press conference is available, *inter alia*, at https://www.les-crises.fr/les-deux-veto-du-general-de-gaulle-a-langleterre/.

22. Moravcsik (1998, 2000a, 2000b).

23. The four countries had submitted membership applications in 1967, and had again been vetoed by de Gaulle. On this occasion, however, their applications had remained dormant, rather than being withdrawn.

24. Rae et al. (2006).

25. As a result, aged ten, I and my family moved, not to Oslo, where an Irish embassy would have been opened had the vote gone the other way, but to Brussels, arriving there on April Fool's Day 1973.

26. The words are those of the Labour Party's National Executive Committee, from 1962: see Grob-Fitzgibbon (2016), p. 293. Not only was Europe less multiracial than the Commonwealth, it was also largely Catholic, and British socialists could be just as susceptible to the ambient anti-Catholicism of the period as their conservative compatriots. Ernest Bevin, whom we have already met, shared the prejudice, as did his deputy at the Foreign Office, Kenneth Younger. While sympathetic to the Schuman

Plan, Younger worried that it might 'be just a step in the consolidation of the Catholic "black international", which I have always thought to be a big driving force behind the Council of Europe' (Young 1999, pp. 50–51). In fairness to Younger, it was surely significant that Christian Democrats were in government in all six founding member states during 1950–52. This transnational network 'fulfilled multiple functions, not least creating political trust, deliberating policy, especially on European integration, marginalising internal dissent within the national parties, socialising new members into an existing policy consensus, coordinating government policy-making and facilitating Parliamentary ratification of integration treaties. These and other functions together provided crucial guarantees for the exercise of what political scientists have called entrepreneurial leadership by politicians like Robert Schuman and Konrad Adenauer, for example, by limiting their domestic political risks in a decisive way to facilitate bold and at times extremely controversial policy choices.' In turn, these choices reflected a common project of middle-class Catholic elites 'for creating an integrated Europe based on a curious mélange of traditional confessional notions of occidental culture and anti-communism and broadly liberal economic ideas' (Kaiser 2007, pp. 9–10).

27. His speech is available online at https://www.cvce.eu/content/ publication/1999/1/1/05f2996b-000b-4576-8b42-8069033a16f9/ publishable_en.pdf.

28. Young (1999), p. 292.

29. Young (1999), p. 240.

30. Saunders (2018), p. 306.

31. Saunders (2018), pp. 123–4.

CHAPTER 5: THE SINGLE MARKET PROGRAMME

1. Eichengreen (2007).

2. The standard reference on stagflation is probably still Bruno and Sachs (1985).

3. Eichengreen (2007), Crafts and O'Rourke (2014).

4. The figures are calculated based on the data on GDP deflator inflation given in the World Bank's World Development Indicators.

5. Young (1999), pp. 307–8.

6. The share has declined to around 40 per cent today: see https://ec.europa. eu/agriculture/sites/agriculture/files/cap-post-2013/graphs/graph1_en.pdf.

7. In fact Mrs Thatcher didn't quite say 'I want my money back' at the press conference following the Council, but she very nearly did: see https://www.margaretthatcher.org/document/104180.

8. The White Paper is available online at http://aei.pitt.edu/1113/1/internal_market_wp_COM_85_310.pdf.

9. Emerson (1988).

10. There were ten member states when the White Paper was published in 1985. On 1 January 1986 Portugal and Spain joined the European Communities, bringing the number of member states to twelve.

11. https://eur-lex.europa.eu/legal-content/EN/TXT/HTML/?isOldUri=true&uri=CELEX:61978CJ0120.

12. The text of the Single European Act is available at http://eur-lex.europa.eu/legal-content/EN/TXT/?uri=CELEX:11986U/TXT.

13. '*L'art de l'imposition consiste à plumer l'oie pour obtenir le plus possible de plumes avec le moins possible de cris.*' The initial (tax-inclusive) rate was 16.75 per cent. The German in question was Wilhelm von Siemens, the American Thomas Adams, but it is the Frenchman Maurice Lauré who is called 'le père de la TVA'. According to some definitions, the first VAT appeared in France in 1948. See Södersten (2000) and Ebrill et al. (2001), on whom much of what follows is based.

14. Although at the time of writing the European Commission is proposing a turnover tax to be levied on digital services companies above a certain size.

15. This is how the retail sales tax works in theory. In practice many retail sales taxes end up being paid by businesses, as noted in the text below.

16. I am assuming here, for the sake of simplicity, that the consumer does not respond to the higher price of beer in the pub by drinking less. If she did, that would obviously hit all three businesses' sales; or more systematically, thinking about adjustments in the economy as a whole, it might lower the prices they each receive for their output.

17. Ring (1989).

18. Article III.

19. Article XVI.

20. The discussion that follows is based on Keen and Smith (1996), Crawford et al. (2010), and Cnossen's comment on Crawford et al. in the same volume.

21. Unfortunately, the delay between the times when the export VAT is refunded and import VAT is paid gives rise to profitable opportunities for fraud. In 2017 the European Commission claimed that so-called 'carousel fraud' costs taxpayers €50 billion annually. This involves fictitious companies setting up with the sole purpose of importing goods from an

accomplice in the exporting country (that recoups export VAT from
the government); when the time comes for them to pay their import VAT
they have vanished. Eventually the goods can be re-exported back to the
original country (and perhaps the original firm), with export VAT being
reclaimed, and then the carousel can recommence. See for example
Crawford et al. (2010).

22. See https://www.consilium.europa.eu/en/council-eu/voting-system/
qualified-majority/.

23. Article 18.2.

24. Young (1999), p. 338.

CHAPTER 6: IRELAND, EUROPE AND THE GOOD FRIDAY AGREEMENT

1. Unless you consider the abbreviation 'UK' to be an adjective.

2. 'Politics and the English Language', 1946. Widely available online, for
example at https://archive.org/details/PoliticsAndTheEnglishLanguage.

3. Shipman (2017).

4. Which helps to explain the presence of Irish colleges in many European
cities, including Paris, whose function was to educate Irish Catholics. The
Parisian college, on the rue des Irlandais, is now an Irish cultural centre.

5. See note 26 in Chapter 4.

6. Wales and England had previously been united in 1536.

7. In 1913 the militias were organized into the Ulster Volunteer Force (UVF).

8. A rebranding of the Irish Volunteers.

9. A facsimile of the treaty is available at http://treaty.nationalarchives.ie/
the-treaty/.

10. The Northern Ireland Census 1991, Religion Report, available at http://
www.nisra.gov.uk/archive/census/1991/religion-report.pdf. Another option
would have been to choose only the four Ulster counties with Protestant
majorities, while yet another would have been to choose all of Ulster. The
actual solution led to a substantial Catholic minority in Northern Ireland,
and a small Protestant minority in the Irish Free State.

11. Leary (2016), p. 125.

12. The declaration came unexpectedly when the Irish Taoiseach, John
A. Costello, was on an official visit to Canada, and there has been
speculation over the years about why it happened. When I was a graduate
student at Harvard in the 1980s the distinguished Irish Studies Professor

John Kelleher, who had been there at the time, gave me the Cambridge Massachusetts explanation. Costello apparently visited Harvard before going to Canada, and was shown the Irish book collection in Widener Library. Unfortunately, the idiosyncratic cataloguing system used there shelved (and for all I know still shelves) Irish-related history books under the bookmark 'Br': Br for Britain. The librarians realized that this might be provocative, and got a workman to do up a sign with an 'Ir' bookmark for the occasion. Unfortunately, he only arrived to nail it up on the shelves while the Taoiseach was being shown around, and offence was duly taken. And the rest, according to Kelleher, was history.

13. The legislation is available at http://www.legislation.gov.uk/ukpga/Geo6/12-13-14/41/enacted.

14. For a fascinating account of these 'word wars' see Mary Daly's 'Ireland: The Politics of Nomenclature', available at http://www.these-islands.co.uk/publications/i279/ireland_the_politics_of_nomenclature.aspx.

15. There is good evidence for occupational segmentation, which was one important driver of inequality: as late as 1992 only 5 per cent of the workforce at Harland and Wolff, the famous shipbuilding company, was Catholic (http://news.bbc.co.uk/1/hi/northern_ireland/2861269.stm). While there are few good empirical studies of discrimination per se, there is anecdotal evidence of discrimination when it came to hiring and promotions.

16. Based on Table 8 in the 1971 Northern Irish Census's Religion Tables, available at https://www.nisra.gov.uk/sites/nisra.gov.uk/files/publications/1971-census-religion-tables.PDF.

17. Pašeta (2003), p. 110.

18. All figures are calculated based on the Sutton Index of Deaths; the cross-tabulations are available at http://cain.ulst.ac.uk/sutton/crosstabs.html.

19. https://www.insee.fr/fr/statistiques/serie/000067671.

20. The text of the agreement is available at http://cain.ulst.ac.uk/events/sunningdale/agreement.htm.

21. The quotations are taken from the said committee's report, available at https://publications.parliament.uk/pa/ld201617/ldselect/ldeucom/76/7607.htm.

22. The minister in question being Paddy Hillery.

23. The text of the Anglo-Irish Agreement is available at https://www.dfa.ie/media/dfa/alldfawebsitemedia/treatyseries/uploads/documents/treaties/docs/198502.pdf.

24. The text of the Declaration is available at https://www.dfa.ie/media/dfa/alldfawebsitemedia/ourrolesandpolicies/northernireland/peace-process--joint-declaration-1993.pdf.

25. You will recall that Sinn Féin was also the name of the party that swept to victory in the 1918 general election and achieved independence subsequently. The Sinn Féin politicians who accepted the treaty founded Cumann na nGaedhal, which subsequently merged with other smaller groupings to form Fine Gael, the party currently (September 2018) in power in Dublin. Those who did not, but who eventually entered Dáil Éireann in the 1920s under Éamon de Valera, formed the Fianna Fáil party as we have already seen.

26. The text of the Good Friday Agreement is available at http://cain.ulst.ac.uk/events/peace/docs/agreement.htm.

27. I am using the Census's 'Classification 1', and excluding respondents who identified themselves as having in whole or in part another EU identity (i.e. an EU identity other than British or Irish). The data are available at http://www.ninis2.nisra.gov.uk/Download/Census%202011_Winzip/2011/DC2238NI%20(a).ZIP.

28. In contrast, only 2 per cent of Protestants defined themselves as 'Irish only', and 16 per cent as 'Northern Irish only'. The percentage of Protestants defining themselves as Irish declined during the Troubles: as might have been expected, violence led to a hardening of attitudes making a political settlement harder to find. 55% of Catholics defined themselves as 'Irish only'.

29. http://data.parliament.uk/writtenevidence/committeeevidence.svc/evidencedocument/european-union-committee/brexit-ukirish-relations/oral/42544.html.

30. https://publications.parliament.uk/pa/ld201617/ldselect/ldeucom/76/7607.htm#_idTextAnchor069.

31. https://www.bbc.co.uk/news/uk-northern-ireland-42412972.

CHAPTER 7: EUROPE AND THE IRISH ECONOMIC MIRACLE

1. This chapter is in large part an abbreviated version of O'Rourke (2017), which was itself a revised version of a lecture delivered on 11 November 2016 at the NUIG National Conference entitled '1916–2016: The Promise and Challenge of National Sovereignty'.

2. The data are available at www.cso.ie, Key Table E2001.

3. For a similar discussion, see Ó Gráda (1997), pp. 2–4.

4. I document this at great length in O'Rourke (2017).

5. Neary and Ó Gráda (1991); O'Rourke (1991).

6. Ó Gráda (1997), pp. 21–5.

7. O'Rourke (2017) also discusses the recurrent balance of payments crises of the period, a problem that Ireland shared with the UK and other former British colonies.

8. Clemens and Williamson (2004).

9. In light of recent controversies it is interesting to note that this soon figured as a potential concern on the radar screens of foreign governments, appearing to be potentially in breach of the OEEC ban on artificial aids to exporters. The OEEC approved the initiative, however, since it seemed to signal a growing outward orientation on the part of the Irish government (Barry and O'Mahony, 2016).

10. de la Escosura and Sanz (1996), pp. 369–70.

11. Costa et al. (2016), pp. 308–9.

12. Paavonen (2004).

13. Freris (1986), pp. 201–2.

14. The classic reference remains Maher (1986). On the history of Ireland's subsequent membership of the EU, see for example Laffan and O'Mahony (2008).

15. Freris (1986), pp. 171–2.

16. Kopsidis and Ivanov (2017), p. 108.

17. Ferreira da Silva (2016). According to the same author, the inflow in 1961 was as high as the total inflow experienced during the entire 1950s.

18. Barry and Bradley (1997), p. 1809.

19. Recall that EFTA aimed not only to dismantle industrial tariffs between its own member states, but eventually to negotiate tariff reductions vis-à-vis the EEC as well.

20. Which is when reliable GDP estimates for Wales and Northern Ireland become available.

21. See Chapter 5 and Ó Gráda and O'Rourke (1996).

22. Campos et al. (2014).

23. Katzenstein (1985).

24. Ó Gráda and O'Rourke (2000).

CHAPTER 8: BREXIT

1. Young (1999), p. 483.

2. The speech is available at https://www.margaretthatcher.org/ document/113686.

3. Young (1999), p. 479.

4. Grob-Fitzgibbon (2016), pp. 438–9.

5. The speech itself, as well as a superbly useful range of accompanying documents, is available at https://www.margaretthatcher.org/archive/Bruges.asp.

6. Young (1999), p. 423.

7. Grob-Fitzgibbon (2016), p. 451.

8. Grob-Fitzgibbon (2016), p. 453; https://www.nybooks.com/articles/1990/09/27/the-chequers-affair/.

9. A reference presumably to the European Commission's Commissioners.

10. Cited in Seldon and Collings (2000).

11. Young (1999), p. 362.

12. https://www.margaretthatcher.org/document/108234.

13. http://www.britpolitics.co.uk/speeches-sir-geoffrey-howe-resignation.

14. http://news.bbc.co.uk/2/hi/uk_news/politics/1701003.stm.

15. Young (1999), p. 433.

16. I have put the word 'victory' in inverted commas to highlight the way in which much of the British political class and media have traditionally portrayed EU negotiations in terms of victory and defeat, rather than compromise and mutual benefit.

17. The origins of these numbers, which seem arbitrary, are murky. On one account the 3 per cent figure is, like VAT, a gift from France to the world: see https://www.latribune.fr/opinions/tribunes/20101001trib000554871/a-l-origine-du-deficit-a-3-du-pib-une-invention-100-francaise.html.

18. Which is why I and 38 other Irish citizens were able to stand for election in the French municipal elections of 2014. And it should be noted that there were also 389 British candidates; see http://www.lefigaro.fr/politique/le-scan/decryptages/2014/03/19/25003-20140319ARTFIG00358-d-o-viennent-les-candidats-etrangers-aux-municipales.php.

19. See Eichengreen and Wyplosz (1993) for a detailed account of the EMS crisis of 1992–3. Like all the Brookings Papers it is freely available online at https://www.brookings.edu/project/brookings-papers-on-economic-activity/.

20. Young (1999), p. 369.

21. Both statements are equally true of the Clinton years.

22. https://www.bbc.co.uk/news/uk-politics-37550629.

23. Shipman (2017), p. 6.

24. Kenny and Pearce (2018).

25. Ibid., pp. 131, 145.

26. Shipman (2017), p. 7.

27. Ibid., p. 8.
28. Delors's statement is available at https://core.ac.uk/display/76794060; the quotations in the text are taken from pp. 17–18.
29. Gstöhl (1994).
30. Shipman (2017), p. 15.
31. Available at http://www.consilium.europa.eu/media/21787/0216-euco-conclusions.pdf.
32. Shipman (2017), pp. 588–9.
33. See O'Toole (2018).
34. See for example https://www.cbc.ca/news/world/boris-johnson-european-union-hitler-1.3583108.
35. Although I was a member of the Centre for European Reform's Commission on the UK and the Single Market, I declined to sign a resultant letter to the newspapers on what the UK ought to do, as well as similar subsequent efforts, for two reasons. First, I'm not British, and I know from the Irish experience how irritating it is to have foreigners telling you what to do at times like this. And second, it wasn't at all clear to me that economists' letters were particularly helpful. On that score at least, I think I was (unfortunately) right.
36. The statement led to a sharp rise in the British pound and a bigger subsequent collapse, all of which helped certain lucky investors to make a lot of money (Shipman 2017, pp. 432–4).

CHAPTER 9: EXPLAINING BREXIT

1. For a notable recent example of an Anglocentric and cultural explanation of Brexit, see O'Toole (2018).
2. See the European Commission's 2016 'Vade mecum' on the Stability and Growth Pact available at https://ec.europa.eu/info/sites/info/files/file_import/ip021_en_2.pdf, or Protocol 15 of the Treaty on the Functioning of the European Union (TFEU), available at https://eur-lex.europa.eu/legal-content/EN/TXT/PDF/?uri=CELEX:12012E/TXT&from=EN. The Commission does monitor UK public finances and, if it deems it necessary, issues recommendations. But there is not the same legal obligation on the UK to comply as there is on other member states: it only has to 'endeavour' to avoid excessive deficits whereas others 'shall' avoid them (Article 26.1).

3. Eichengreen and O'Rourke (2009).
4. The original bank guarantee in 2008 was as far as we know the fault of the Irish government alone, but by 2010 it had been convinced of the error of its ways. It resolved to 'burn the bondholders', or at least those who remained to be burned, but this was vetoed by Jean-Claude Trichet, the President of the European Central Bank, and Tim Geithner, the US Treasury Secretary (Mody 2018, pp. 279–80).
5. For an authoritative account of the Eurozone crisis written by a former IMF staffer, see Mody (2018). See also Krugman (2013), Stiglitz (2016) and Tooze (2018).
6. https://dealbook.nytimes.com/2007/01/27/lies-fallacies-and-truths/.
7. The European integration that has been the focus of this book was a regional, not a global, phenomenon, and even the liberalization efforts of the GATT were for many years an affair mainly of the rich countries. The 1960s saw newly independent countries in many cases turning inwards, erecting trade barriers and trying to develop domestic industry. From the 1980s onwards, however, an ever-increasing number of developing countries turned their backs on this strategy and began liberalizing trade.
8. O'Rourke and Williamson (1999), pp. 286–7.
9. Alternatively, median wages were only 6.3 per cent higher in 2016 than in 1973, the first year for which they are available: see the Economic Policy Institute's *State of Working America Data Library* available at https://www.epi.org/data/#?subject=wage-avg.
10. It would be wrong not to cite Thomas Piketty (2013) in this context.
11. Piketty et al. (2016).
12. See http://blogs.lse.ac.uk/politicsandpolicy/real-wages-and-living-standards-the-latest-uk-evidence/.
13. Notably Autor et al. (2013).
14. Brouard and Tiberj (2006).
15. Piris (2010) argues that the Lisbon treaty marked a clear defeat for federalists.
16. Sinnott et al. (2009). The report is available at http://www.joselkink.net/research.php.
17. Autor et al. (2016).
18. Ibid.
19. Colantone and Stanig (2018), p. 201.
20. Becker et al. (2017).
21. Ibid.
22. Fetzer (2018).

23. https://dominiccummings.com/2017/01/09/on-the-referendum-21-branching-histories-of-the-2016-referendum-and-the-frogs-before-the-storm-2/.

24. That last point is mine, not Cummings's or Shipman's. Shipman entertains seriously the possibility that Cameron could have obtained a more serious reduction of the rights of European citizens. I regard that as fanciful in the extreme.

25. The Gisela in question being Gisela Stuart, a German-born Labour Party politician and leading Brexiteer.

26. Shipman (2017), p. 9.

CHAPTER 10: THE AFTERMATH

1. See https://www.theguardian.com/politics/2016/sep/25/that-didnt-go-to-plan-cameron-spin-doctor-brexit-vote-craig-oliver and https://www.theguardian.com/politics/2016/apr/16/cameron-wouldnt-last-30-seconds-if-he-lost-eu-vote-says-ken-clarke.

2. The speech is available at https://www.independent.co.uk/news/uk/politics/theresa-may-s-speech-to-the-conservative-party-conference-in-full-a6681901.html.

3. https://www.thetimes.co.uk/article/a-borderless-eu-harms-everyone-but-the-gangs-that-sell-false-dreams-nrqqz3hdzbb.

4. Shipman (2017), p. 21.

5. *'Victoire de la liberté! Comme je le demande depuis des années, il faut maintenant le même référendum en France et dans les pays de l'UE.'*

6. https://franceintheus.org/spip.php?article7630#4.

7. A brief introduction to this unpleasant subject can be found in http://www.liberation.fr/planete/2016/07/14/boris-johnson-le-boulet-diplomatique_1466219.

8. *'Dans la campagne, il a beaucoup menti aux Britanniques.'*

9. To Davis's credit he keeps such tweets available online: https://twitter.com/DavidDavisMP/status/735770073822961664.

10. I am being a little bit pedantic here. In common parlance people talk of the UK wanting to leave *the* customs union, but by definition it has to do so once it leaves the EU. The question then becomes whether or not it wants to join *a* new one.

11. 'Leaders must make the case for globalization', *Financial Times*, 17 July 2016.

12. See https://www.project-syndicate.org/commentary/british-anti-imigrant-sentiment-by-kevin-hjortshoj-o-rourke-2016-07.

13. Timothy (2012). In fairness, it is Chamberlain's radicalism that appealed to Timothy, not his protectionism or imperialism; but on the other hand, Timothy also notes (p. 56) that among the radical measures which Chamberlain advocated was the control of immigration.

14. https://www.politicshome.com/news/uk/political-parties/conservative-party/news/79517/read-full-theresa-mays-conservative. I was not the only one who was shocked. 'It was a surprise,' Mrs May's Chancellor Philip Hammond later said of the speech, 'to see that the Prime Minister had chosen to define Brexit in the hardest possible terms.' According to Hammond he had not been aware of the decision to pursue what he described as 'quite an extreme version of Brexit' beforehand. See 'Panorama: Britain's Brexit Crisis', BBC1, 18 July 2019.

15. According to Tim Shipman (2018) the decisions to leave the jurisdiction of the ECJ, and the EU Single Market and customs union, were taken by May and Timothy: he comments (p. 12) that 'it is extraordinary that these, the foundational decisions of Britain's withdrawal strategy, which would shape the next two years of negotiations, were taken, in essence, by two people. The cabinet certainly had no chance to debate them.' The implications of the speech were immediately understood in EU capitals but not, apparently, by everyone in the UK: 'Nick Timothy had defined British policy on Brexit. Now Theresa May had to guide her cabinet to the same place without admitting the policy was already set in stone' (p. 19).

16. The speech is available at https://www.gov.uk/government/speeches/the-governments-negotiating-objectives-for-exiting-the-eu-pm-speech.

17. The citations in the text are taken from a very helpful briefing prepared by the European Parliament, available at http://www.europarl.europa.eu/RegData/etudes/BRIE/2017/599267/EPRS_BRI(2017)599267_EN.pdf; for a list of financial services covered by passporting, see https://www.ceps.eu/system/files/IEForum52016_3.pdf.

18. The speech is reproduced at https://www.gov.uk/government/speeches/chancellors-hsbc-speech-financial-services.

19. Alex Barker and Peter Campbell, 'Honda faces the real cost of Brexit in a former Spitfire plant', 26 June 2018, available at https://www.ft.com/content/8f46b0d4-77b6-11e8-8e67-1e1a0846c475.

20. The letter was published in February 2019, following Nissan's decision to move X-Trail production back to Japan. It is available at https://assets.publishing.service.gov.uk/government/uploads/system/uploads/attachment_data/file/776095/Letter-from-BEIS-Secretary-of-State-to-Carlos-Ghosn-October_2016.pdf.

21. https://www.nytimes.com/2016/11/29/world/europe/uk-brexit-european-union.html.

22. The letter is available at http://data.consilium.europa.eu/doc/document/XT-20001-2017-INIT/en/pdf.

23. The statement is available on the European Council's fabulously helpful website, http://www.consilium.europa.eu/en/policies/eu-uk-after-referendum/.

24. http://jackofkent.com/2016/06/why-the-article-50-notification-is-important/.

25. Cecilia Malmström broke the bad news in an interview on *Newsnight*: see https://www.bbc.com/news/uk-politics-eu-referendum-36678222.

26. Connelly (2018), p. 34.

27. https://www.welt.de/english-news/article161182946/Philip-Hammond-issues-threat-to-EU-partners.html. To be fair, he said that it might do this if it were shut out of European markets after Brexit.

28. An exception is Chris Giles of the *Financial Times*: see for example https://www.ft.com/content/7ff44a0c-59e2-11e8-b8b2-d6ceb45fa9d0.

29. First, the name of the state is not 'southern Ireland', and second the frontier is not internal to the United Kingdom.

30. The anecdote about the email is contained in Connelly (2018), p. 56, while Davis's remark about the frontier can be found here: https://www.bbc.com/news/amp/uk-scotland-scotland-politics-36819182.

31. Connelly (2018), p. 53.

32. The Guiers was set as the frontier between the Dauphiné and Savoie under the terms of the 1355 Treaty of Paris. Unfortunately, that treaty did not specify whether the Guiers in question was the Vif or the Mort, a question which was only clarified in 1760 under the terms of the Treaty of Turin. Until that time the region between the two Guiers was disputed, much to the benefit of local smugglers.

33. https://www.bbc.co.uk/news/uk-politics-40949424.

34. According to the British government there were seventeen of these approved crossings in 1972: see its August 2017 position paper on 'Northern Ireland and Ireland', available at https://assets.publishing.service.gov.uk/government/uploads/system/uploads/attachment_data/file/638135/6.3703_DEXEU_Northern_Ireland_and_Ireland_INTERACTIVE.pdf.

35. https://www.lrb.co.uk/v39/n07/susan-mckay/diary.

36. The quotation is taken from the wonderful Irish Borderlands project website, available at http://www.irishborderlands.com/index.html.

37. Connelly (2018), p. 252.

38. See https://www.thetimes.co.uk/article/police-chief-hard-border-threatens-to-blow-holes-in-our-fragile-peace-29wzcklq9.

39. Connelly (2018), chs 4, 9 and 14 provides an excellent account of the negotiations, upon which I draw in the following paragraphs.

40. My article in the *Irish Times* on the subject is available at https://www.irishtimes.com/business/economy/no-special-deal-possible-to-stop-the-return-of-border-controls-1.2981088.

41. As I pointed out here at the time: http://www.irisheconomy.ie/index.php/2016/10/04/what-should-ireland-be-looking-for/.

42. Like other documents referred to subsequently, they are available on the Council's website (see note 22 above).

43. As pointed out by Donald Tusk in the post-summit press conference: see http://www.consilium.europa.eu/en/press/press-releases/2017/04/29/tusk-remarks-special-european-council-art50/.

44. Connelly (2018), p. 298.

CHAPTER 11: THE NEGOTIATIONS

1. https://www.express.co.uk/news/uk/793561/general-election-2017-theresa-may-strengthen-britain-negotiating-hand-brexit-eu.

2. Position paper on 'Essential Principles on Citizens' Rights', 12 June 2017, available at https://ec.europa.eu/commission/sites/beta-political/files/essential-principles-citizens-rights_en_3.pdf.

3. 'The United Kingdom's exit from the European Union: safeguarding the position of EU citizens living in the UK and UK nationals living in the EU', 26 June 2017, available at https://www.gov.uk/government/publications/safeguarding-the-position-of-eu-citizens-in-the-uk-and-uk-nationals-in-the-eu.

4. This fear proved unfounded.

5. https://eur-lex.europa.eu/LexUriServ/LexUriServ.do?uri=OJ:L:2004:158:0077:0123:EN:PDF.

6. The speech is available at https://www.gov.uk/government/speeches/pms-florence-speech-a-new-era-of-cooperation-and-partnership-between-the-uk-and-the-eu.

7. 'Joint technical note on citizens' rights', 8 December 2017, available at https://ec.europa.eu/commission/publications/joint-technical-note-expressing-detailed-consensus-uk-and-eu-positions-respect-citizens-rights_fr. It is important to note that although it proved relatively easy to reach an agreement on the issue of citizens' rights, this does not mean that

the citizens concerned will conserve all of their existing rights under the agreement.

8. Communication from the Commission to the European Council (Article 50), 8 December 2017, available at https://ec.europa.eu/commission/sites/beta-political/files/1_en_act_communication.pdf.

9. 'Heading into troubled waters', *Financial Times*, 13 October 2017, available at https://www.ft.com/content/c3f464ac-b006-11e7-beba-5521c713abf4.

10. '"Now they have to pay": Juncker says UK stance on Brexit bill untenable', Guardian, 13 October 2017, available at https://www.theguardian.com/politics/2017/oct/13/brexit-wrangle-over-citizens-rights-is-nonsense-says-juncker.

11. 'UK bows to EU demands with breakthrough offer on Brexit bill', *Financial Times*, 29 November 2017, available at https://www.ft.com/content/cabf22e2-d462-11e7-8c9a-d9c0a5c8d5c9.

12. This was certainly how I saw it in July 2017: see http://www.irisheconomy.ie/index.php/2017/07/30/using-ireland/. And Tony Connelly (2018, p. 74) reports that European Commission officials feared precisely the same thing.

13. 'Business leaders feel the heat during Chevening Brexit talks', *Financial Times*, 7 July 2017, available at https://www.ft.com/content/7def4e2a-6314-11e7-91a7-502f7ee26895.

14. 'Conservative–DUP agreement due "next week"', 15 June, 2017, available at https://news.sky.com/story/conservative-dup-agreement-due-next-week-10916703.

15. See https://www.bbc.co.uk/news/uk-northern-ireland-41232991. Chris Cook (2019, p. 70) even reports being asked by an official whether anyone had yet told him about facial recognition for pigs. The relevant chapter is available online at https://members.tortoisemedia.com/2019/05/25/brexit-part-6/content.html?sig=qQNRyVUD13SL3GHE3PZP_BaQKSZTKVTShKe5nQslqFU.

16. Shipman (2018), p. 524.

17. https://www.politico.eu/article/uk-faces-e2-billion-eu-payment-for-china-fraud-trade.

18. https://www.gov.uk/government/publications/future-customs-arrangements-a-future-partnership-paper.

19. https://www.irishtimes.com/news/politics/coveney-ireland-will-not-be-used-as-pawn-in-eu-uk-talks-1.3188523. The UK's Northern Ireland position paper is available at https://www.gov.uk/government/publications/northern-ireland-and-ireland-a-position-paper.

20. https://www.dw.com/en/eu-worries-that-uk-wants-to-use-ireland-as-customs-test-case/a-40412996.

21. https://ec.europa.eu/commission/publications/guiding-principles-dialogue-ireland-northern-ireland_en.

22. See https://www.standard.co.uk/news/politics/ireland-warns-theresa-may-increased-40-billion-brexit-deal-cant-buy-you-trade-talks-a3697201.html.

23. Connelly (2018), p. 359.

24. https://www.theguardian.com/politics/2017/nov/17/irish-pm-brexit-backing-politicians-did-not-think-things-through.

25. On 8 November 2017 a working paper circulated by Commission officials contained the following bullet point: 'It consequently seems essential for the UK to commit to ensuring that a hard border on the island of Ireland is avoided, including by ensuring no emergence of regulatory divergence from those rules of the internal market and the Customs Union which are (or may be in the future) necessary for meaningful North-South cooperation, the all-island economy and the protection of the Good Friday Agreement.' According to both Tony Connelly and Tim Shipman this was the backstop's first appearance in written form: Connelly's account of how it was born is available at https://www.rte.ie/news/brexit/2018/1019/1005373-backstop-tony-connelly/. Apparently Ollie Robbins was not pleased (Shipman 2018, p. 524).

26. https://www.dfa.ie/news-and-media/speeches/speeches-archive/2017/november/eurofound-foundation-forum-2017/.

27. Connelly (2018), ch. 17.

28. The mapping exercise was deemed to be too sensitive to publish while the negotiations were ongoing. The British government published the list of areas where there was ongoing North-South cooperation in December 2018, once the negotiations had concluded. It is available at https://assets.publishing.service.gov.uk/government/uploads/system/uploads/attachment_data/file/762820/Technical_note-_North-South_cooperation_mapping_exercise__2_.pdf.

29. http://www.consilium.europa.eu/en/press/press-releases/2017/12/01/remarks-by-president-donald-tusk-after-his-meeting-with-taoiseach-leo-varadkar/.

30. The Joint Report is available at https://ec.europa.eu/commission/sites/beta-political/files/joint_report.pdf.

31. A potential complicating factor was that the Northern Ireland Executive had been dissolved in January 2017 following a scandal involving renewable heat incentives. As of December 2018 there was still no Executive in Northern Ireland.

32. http://www.irisheconomy.ie/index.php/2017/12/09/who-is-fudging-answer-not-the-eu/.

33. Both documents are available on the European Council's website, https://www.consilium.europa.eu/en/policies/eu-uk-after-referendum/.

34. In this manner they implicitly recognized that the UK had not been a vassal state when it was an EU member.
35. https://www.bbc.co.uk/news/uk-politics-42298971.
36. http://www.europarl.europa.eu/sides/getDoc.do?pubRef=-//EP//TEXT+TA+P8-TA-2017-0490+0+DOC+XML+V0//EN.
37. https://ec.europa.eu/commission/publications/draft-agreement-withdrawal-united-kingdom-great-britain-and-northern-ireland-european-union-and-european-atomic-energy-community-0_en.
38. https://www.bbc.co.uk/news/uk-politics-43224785.
39. https://www.daera-ni.gov.uk/articles/introduction-importing-animals-and-animal-products.
40. http://www.consilium.europa.eu/media/33458/23-euco-art50-guidelines.pdf.
41. See the superb article by Tony Connelly available at https://www.rte.ie/news/analysis-and-comment/2018/1207/1015924-brexit-backstop-uk/.
42. The proposal is available here: https://assets.publishing.service.gov.uk/government/uploads/system/uploads/attachment_data/file/714656/Technical_note_temporary_customs_arrangement.pdf.
43. And VAT area, I should have added: http://www.irisheconomy.ie/index.php/2017/10/07/what-if-it-was-the-europeans-picking-the-cherries/. See also https://www.cer.eu/node/6563, and https://www.ft.com/content/5f6fedcc-db3e-11e7-a039-c64b1c09b482.
44. https://assets.publishing.service.gov.uk/government/uploads/system/uploads/attachment_data/file/723460/CHEQUERS_STATEMENT_-_FINAL.PDF. Mind you, the statement doesn't tell us what form of backstop the government had in mind.
45. In a nod to those opposed to following EU regulations, the statement said that the UK would do so voluntarily, realizing that if it chose not to do so 'this would have consequences'. In other words there was no legal obligation on it to do so!
46. Tony Connelly's analysis of the events is outstanding: see https://www.rte.ie/news/analysis-and-comment/2018/0721/980069-brexit-tony-connelly/.
47. https://www.theguardian.com/politics/2018/sep/02/michel-barnier-strongly-opposes-may-brexit-trade-proposals.
48. The evidence of both Weyand and Barnier is available at https://t.co/65yAG3VKmt.
49. https://www.dailymail.co.uk/news/article-6146853/BORIS-JOHNSON-JEREMY-HUNT-debate-Chequers-deal.html.
50. The article is available at https://www.welt.de/debatte/kommentare/article181579426/Theresa-May-May-warns-EU-not-to-treat-UK-unfairly-in-Brexit-talks.html.

51. The report in question is available at http://uk.businessinsider.com/
liam-fox-trade-deal-scrap-european-union-food-standards-after-brexit-
2018-9. Good analyses of the Salzburg summit can be found inter alia
at https://www.theguardian.com/politics/2018/sep/20/macron-puts-
the-boot-in-after-mays-brexit-breakfast-blunder, https://www.nytimes.
com/2018/09/21/world/europe/eu-theresa-may-brexit-salzburg.html,
https://www.reuters.com/article/us-britain-eu-salzburg/may-has-only-
self-to-blame-for-salzburg-sandbagging-europeans-say-idUSKCN1M129D,
and https://www.rte.ie/news/analysis-and-comment/2018/0921/
995292-salzburg-chronic-misreading/.

52. https://www.consilium.europa.eu/en/press/press-releases/2018/09/
20/remarks-by-president-donald-tusk-after-the-salzburg-informal-
summit/.

53. https://news.sky.com/story/pm-attacks-disrespectful-eu-the-angriest-
quotes-from-her-brexit-speech-11504324.

54. https://www.consilium.europa.eu/en/press/press-releases/2018/09/21/
statement-by-president-donald-tusk-on-the-brexit-negotiations/.

55. https://www.theguardian.com/politics/2018/sep/21/humiliation-and-
disaster-how-uk-press-covered-theresa-may-salzburg-ordeal; https://www.
express.co.uk/news/uk/1021145/brexit-news-dup-leader-arlene-foster-
theresa-may-eu-chequers-salzburg-summit. Hunt's speech is available at
https://www.conservativehome.com/parliament/2018/09/never-mistake-
british-politeness-for-british-weakness-hunts-conference-speech-full-
text.html.

56. See however note 68 and the associated discussion in the text.

57. Future historians with access to more information may end up disputing
the use of the definite pronoun here, but from the vantage point of 2018
it seems merited. According to a May adviser speaking in 2016, 'The vote
for Brexit was about controlling immigration. Everything else flows from
there' (Shipman (2018, p. 14). And it also seems that Mrs May intervened
personally to ensure that the words 'ending of free movement of people'
be added to the first page of the Political Declaration agreed by both
sides in November 2018: see https://www.buzzfeed.com/albertonardelli/
theresa-may-ending-free-movement-first-page-brexit.

58. For an early discussion of this option, see for example https://www.ft.com/
content/350519e2-8a91-11e8-b18d-0181731a0340.

59. See https://www.lemonde.fr/referendum-sur-le-brexit/article/2018/10/13/
brexit-dernier-tunnel-de-negociations-avant-un-accord-ou-pas_5368982
_4872498.html, and https://www.theguardian.com/politics/2018/nov/14/
how-the-draft-brexit-agreement-emerged-from-the-tunnel.

60. The statement is available at https://www.gov.uk/government/speeches/
pm-statement-on-brexit-15-october-2018. See also, inter alia,
https://www.irishtimes.com/news/politics/brexit-deal-within-theresa-may-
s-grasp-but-party-backing-elusive-1.3664561.

61. Ibid.

62. See https://twitter.com/tconnellyRTE/status/1062373393046167552. For an
account of how the deal came about, see https://www.rte.ie/news/analysis-
and-comment/2018/1117/1011485-brexit/.

63. https://www.thetimes.co.uk/edition/news/may-accused-of-betrayal-as-
she-unveils-brexit-deal-ks9frvbwz; Emmanuel Macron later offered similar
reassurances to French fishermen (see https://www.theguardian.com/
politics/2018/nov/25/eu-leaders-back-theresa-mays-brexit-deal-in-
brussels).

64. The Withdrawal Agreement is available at https://www.consilium.
europa.eu/media/37099/draft_withdrawal_agreement_incl_art132.pdf.
A summary of the backstop is available at http://europa.eu/rapid/
press-release_MEMO-18-6423_en.htm.

65. The code is set out here: https://eur-lex.europa.eu/legal-content/EN/
TXT/?uri=CELEX%3A32013R0952.

66. The Directive is available at https://eur-lex.europa.eu/legal-content/EN/
TXT/?uri=celex%3A32009L0048.

67. See https://www.rte.ie/news/analysis-and-comment/2018/1207/
1015924-brexit-backstop-uk/.

68. However, as Sam Lowe of the Centre for European Reform pointed
out, 'Being in such a customs union would place no constraints on the
UK's ability to negotiate in the areas of services, intellectual property,
public procurement, data and regulatory barriers to trade in goods'.
See https://www.cer.eu/publications/archive/bulletin-article/2018/
effective-uk-trade-policy-and-customs-union-are.

69. https://www.rte.ie/news/brexit/2018/1010/1002349-brexit-border/.

70. See for example https://www.rte.ie/news/analysis-and-
comment/2018/1123/1012997-brexit-and-dup/.

71. The British government had in fact drawn up plans for a termination
clause to be inserted into the Withdrawal Agreement, that would have
allowed the UK to unilaterally exit the backstop even in the absence of
a mutually agreed-upon alternative for achieving that objective. This
had not been made a formal demand, since the Irish government had
made it clear that such an approach would never fly. See Times Brexit
Briefing, November 29, 2018; https://www.thetimes.co.uk/my-articles/
irish-leader-lays-down-red-lines-on-brexit-border-deal-5c89bqrg2.

72. The resignation letter is available, inter alia, at https://www.metro.news/
    seven-members-of-government-who-said-they-could-not-support-the-pms-
    brexit-deal/1312216/. It emerged later that Raab had also been unhappy
    about the backstop being used as the basis for the future relationship.
    See https://www.thetimes.co.uk/article/dominic-raab-exclusive-brexit-
    interview-i-was-hoodwinked-x02m350kx. The British Attorney General,
    Geoffrey Cox, later confirmed that the backstop had indeed been solidly
    constructed by the EU negotiators: his advice to the UK government is
    available at https://static.rasset.ie/documents/news/2018/12/05-december-
    eu-exit-attorney-general-s-legal-advice-to-cabinet-on-the-withdrawal-
    agreement-and-the-protocol-on-ireland-northern-ireland.pdf.
73. See https://medium.com/@JoJohnsonUK/why-i-cannot-support-the-
    governments-proposed-brexit-deal-3d289f95f2bc.
74. The proposal was primarily associated with the Conservative MP Nick
    Boles, and the case for it can be found at http://betterbrexit.org.uk.
75. The judgement is available at http://curia.europa.eu/juris/document/
    document.jsf?text=&docid=208636&pageIndex=0&doclang=en&mode=req
    &dir=&occ=first&part=1&cid=1087903.
76. Mrs May's statement is available at https://www.gov.uk/government/
    speeches/pms-statement-on-exiting-the-european-union-10-december-
    2018.
77. See https://www.rte.ie/news/brexit/2018/1214/1017288-tony-connelly-
    brexit/, on which much of what follows draws.
78. https://www.bloomberg.com/news/articles/2018-12-14/
    eu-leaders-just-aren-t-sure-they-can-trust-theresa-may-anymore.
79. https://www.irishtimes.com/news/world/uk/
    may-s-promise-to-dup-could-make-brexit-deal-impossible-1.3729389.
80. https://www.rte.ie/news/brexit/2018/1212/1016666-brexit-uk/.
81. EU suspicion of British intentions emerges strongly from the afore-
    mentioned report by Tony Connelly available at https://www.rte.ie/news/
    brexit/2018/1214/1017288-tony-connelly-brexit/.
82. https://www.irishexaminer.com/breakingnews/ireland/theresa-mays-post-
    brexit-trade-deal-suggestion-dismissed-by-taoiseach-892179.html.
83. The European Council's conclusions on Brexit are available at https://
    www.consilium.europa.eu/en/press/press-releases/2018/12/13/
    european-council-art-50-conclusions-13-december-2018/.
84. Taking the draft conclusions of the summit as the basis of the outcome,
    before these had been discussed either by COREPER or at the summit
    itself, and spinning accordingly, was an unforced error on the part of the

British government, heightening the impression back in the UK that the summit had been a 'failure'.

85. On 9 January the Commons voted to deprive the Treasury of the right to make certain tax changes in the event of a no deal Brexit that Parliament had not approved. Twenty Tory MPs broke a three-line whip to vote against the amendment: it was the first defeat for a government finance bill since 1978. While largely symbolic the vote was a sign of things to come.

CHAPTER 12: CRISIS

1. https://labour.org.uk/press/jeremy-corbyn-mp-leader-labour-party-closing-speech-eu-withdrawal-agreement-debate-house-commons/.

2. Not counting instances such as the vote in March 1977 on IMF-related public spending cuts, when the Labour government instructed its MPs not to vote: see https://www.bbc.com/news/uk-46879887.

3. See https://www.rte.ie/news/brexit/2019/0201/1027016-brexit/.

4. https://www.theguardian.com/politics/live/2019/feb/05/brexit-latest-news-developments-theresa-may-speech-northern-ireland-eu-will-be-to-blame-if-theres-no-deal-says-transport-secretary-chris-grayling-politics-live; https://www.reuters.com/article/us-britain-eu-barclay/uk-says-focus-in-brexit-talks-is-now-backstop-guarantees-idUSKCN1QA2FU.

5. See Tony Connelly's report of the events here: https://www.rte.ie/news/analysis-and-comment/2019/0315/1036688-backstop-deal-cox/.

6. See the 'Instrument relating to the Withdrawal Agreement', available at https://data.consilium.europa.eu/doc/document/XT-21014-2019-INIT/en/pdf.

7. The Unilateral Declaration is available at https://assets.publishing.service.gov.uk/government/uploads/system/uploads/attachment_data/file/785124/2019-03-11_Unilateral_Declaration.pdf.

8. However Tory MPs voted 188 to 112 against a delay: see https://www.bbc.com/news/uk-politics-47576813.

9. https://www.theguardian.com/politics/2019/mar/14/mps-amendments-for-the-brexit-article-50-extension-vote.

10. Mrs May's letter is available at https://data.consilium.europa.eu/doc/document/XT-20005-2019-INIT/en/pdf; the Council's decision at https://www.consilium.europa.eu/en/meetings/european-council/2019/03/21/art50/.

11. Which in turn explains the 12 April date: this was the deadline by which the UK would have to give notice of forthcoming European elections.

12. https://www.theguardian.com/politics/live/2019/mar/27/brexit-latest-news-live-debate-indicative-votes--to-vote-on-alternative-votes-as-speculation-mounts-may-could-announce-plans-to-quit-live-news?page=with:block-5c9be548e4b0347f70e74e28#block-5c9be548e4b0347f70e74e28.

13. See for example https://www.ft.com/content/05114d7e-1e42-11e9-b126-46fc3ad87c65, https://twitter.com/KateHoeyMP/status/1158470926398369792?s=20.

14. See for example https://www.dailymail.co.uk/debate/article-6892599/PETER-OBORNE-backed-soft-Brexiters-patriotic-duty-Britain-together.html, who dates the shift in thinking to February 2019; and Cook (2019, p. 34) who dates it to 2017 (available online at https://members.tortoisemedia.com/2019/05/19/brexit-day-part-3/content.html?sig=E3d47ah7KaTSOK4dQuuWIwRjFBYSIOT7WcPX78sOWyc).

15. The letter can be found at https://assets.publishing.service.gov.uk/government/uploads/system/uploads/attachment_data/file/793058/PM_letter_to_His_Excellency_Mr_Donald_Tusk__1_.pdf.

16. https://www.liberation.fr/planete/2019/04/11/brexit-les-europeens-accordent-un-nouveau-report-jusqu-au-31-octobre_1720646.

17. https://data.consilium.europa.eu/doc/document/XT-20013-2019-INIT/en/pdf.

18. https://www.consilium.europa.eu/en/press/press-releases/2019/04/10/remarks-by-president-donald-tusk-after-the-special-meeting-of-the-european-council-art-50-on-10-april-2019/.

19. https://twitter.com/jeremycorbyn/status/1129332731748528131?s=20.

20. However, in a nod to reality the Prime Minister also acknowledged that 'it is not possible to use alternative arrangements to replace the backstop in the withdrawal agreement.' The ten-point plan is set out in her 22 May statement to the House of Commons, available at https://hansard.parliament.uk/commons/2019-05-22/debates/3A0B2FC5-86DF-484B-B8BE-9B28DF8F5ED7/LeavingTheEuropeanUnion.

21. https://www.gov.uk/government/speeches/boris-johnsons-first-speech-as-prime-minister-24-july-2019.

22. https://hansard.parliament.uk/commons/2019-07-25/debates/D0290128-96D8-4AF9-ACFD-21D5D9CF328E/PrioritiesForGovernment.

23. https://www.theguardian.com/politics/live/2019/jul/29/brexit-boris-johnson-prime-minister-news-latest-dominic-raab-suggests-boris-johnson-wont-reopen-talks-with-eu-this-summer-until-it-agrees-to-abandon-

backstop?page=with:block-5d3ed7568f0845f89e316601#block-5d3ed7568
f0845f89e316601.

24. https://inews.co.uk/news/politics/brexit-no-deal-mark-francois-boris-
johnson-erg-video/. The threat was repeated a few days later: see https:
//www.telegraph.co.uk/politics/2019/08/01/sixty-backbench-tories-will-
vote-withdrawal-agreement-even-irish/.

25. https://www.thetimes.co.uk/article/dominic-raab-interview-no-more-
weakness-the-eu-must-know-we-re-serious-zcxtbq2lm?shareToken=eac34fa
b549b7fcea468ffd5a1731197.

26. https://www.ft.com/content/29dc5fac-b44e-11e9-8cb2-799a3a8cf37b; https://
www.bbc.com/news/uk-politics-49240809; https://www.independent.
co.uk/news/uk/politics/brexit-boris-johnson-eu-workers-rights-david-
frost-theresa-may-barnier-a9025596.html.

27. https://www.theguardian.com/politics/2019/aug/05/no-deal-brexit-is-boris-
johnsons-central-scenario-eu-told.

28. https://www.bbc.com/news/uk-politics-49251257.

29. https://www.thetimes.co.uk/article/eu-prepares-huge-aid-package-for-
ireland-dnckkgp5t?shareToken=faab7433fc9ba4d562a664af01a23562.

30. The Irish have long been aware that insisting on a backstop might lead to
a no-deal Brexit. For an argument as to why, from an Irish point of view,
it might nevertheless be rational to insist on the backstop, see http://www.
irisheconomy.ie/index.php/2017/09/24/is-no-deal-better-than-a-bad-deal-
irish-edition/.

31. https://www.dfa.ie/media/dfa/eu/brexit/keydocuments/Contingency-
Action-Plan-Update.-July-2019.pdf.

32. In 2019 Honda announced that it would close its plant in Swindon, Nissan
announced that the X-Trail would, after all, be produced in Japan, and
Ford announced the closure of its Bridgend plant. All three companies
strongly denied that their decisions had anything to do with Brexit. On the
other hand PSA made it clear that its decision about whether to continue
producing Vauxhall and Opel Astra cars at Ellesmere Port would be
'conditional on the final terms of the UK's exit from the European Union.'
See https://www.ft.com/content/64917b84-98e5-11e9-9573-ee5cbb98ed36.

33. https://www.rte.ie/news/ireland/2019/0806/1067131-brexit/.

34. https://www.theguardian.com/politics/2019/jul/31/brexit-mess-with-good-
friday-and-well-block-uk-trade-deal-us-politicians-warn.

35. I am assuming that a Parliament that had approved the Withdrawal
Agreement would also be willing to ask for an extension so that it could
pass the necessary legislation, and that the request would be granted.

Index

Page references in *italic* indicate figures.

C

PELICAN BOOKS

PELICAN BOOKS

PELICAN BOOKS